Bayern

New Highlight
6

für M-Klassen

**New Highlight
Band 6 für M-Klassen**

Im Auftrage des Verlages erarbeitet von
Sydney Thorne, York

Auf Grundlage der ursprünglichen Ausgabe ENGLISH H · Highlight, Band 6
(herausgegeben von Roderick Cox und Raymond Williams · erarbeitet von Roderick Cox und Frank Donoghue)

Verlagsredaktion
Susanne Döpper (Projektleitung) • Karin Jung (verantwortliche Redakteurin)
Eva Baumgart • Stefanie Dalhoff • Natasha Doerrie • Christine Maxwell • Jutta Seuren • Bastian Wiesemann

Anhang
Ingrid Raspe, Düsseldorf

Beratende Mitwirkung
Matthias Fischer, Aschaffenburg • Barbara Gehlhaar, München
Joy Pringsheim, Erlangen • Christoph Vatter, Großkarolinenfeld

Grafik
John Batten, London • Carlos Borrell, Berlin • Jeongsook Lee, Köln • Andy Peters, Norfolk

Umschlaggestaltung
Klein & Halm Grafikdesign, Berlin

Layoutkonzept
Christoph Schall

Layout und technische Umsetzung
Heike Freund, Hameln

Begleitende Tonträger zu diesem Band
Text-CDs zum Schülerbuch
ISBN 978-3-06-330001-0

www.cornelsen.de

Die Links zu externen Webseiten Dritter, die in diesem Lehrwerk angegeben sind, wurden vor Drucklegung sorgfältig auf ihre Aktualität geprüft. Der Verlag übernimmt keine Gewähr für die Aktualität und den Inhalt dieser Seiten oder solcher, die mit ihnen verlinkt sind.

1. Auflage, 5. Druck 2015

Alle Drucke dieser Auflage sind inhaltlich unverändert und können im Unterricht nebeneinander verwendet werden.

© 2009 Cornelsen Verlag, Berlin
© 2013 Cornelsen Schulverlage GmbH, Berlin

Das Werk und seine Teile sind urheberrechtlich geschützt.
Jede Nutzung in anderen als den gesetzlich zugelassenen Fällen bedarf
der vorherigen schriftlichen Einwilligung des Verlages.
Hinweis zu den §§ 46, 52 a UrhG: Weder das Werk noch seine Teile dürfen ohne eine
solche Einwilligung eingescannt und in ein Netzwerk eingestellt oder sonst öffentlich
zugänglich gemacht werden.
Dies gilt auch für Intranets von Schulen und sonstigen Bildungseinrichtungen.

Druck: Mohn Media Mohndruck, Gütersloh

ISBN 978-3-06-330000-3

PEFC zertifiziert
Dieses Produkt stammt aus nachhaltig
bewirtschafteten Wäldern und kontrollierten
Quellen.
www.pefc.de

INHALT

6 **A world language**

	SPRECHABSICHTEN	REDEMITTEL	LERNTECHNIKEN

Unit 1   Ireland

8 **LEAD-IN**
LISTENING   An info box
  for Ireland
12 **SKILLS**
SPEAKING   Picture-based
  conversation
READING   What do celebrities
  do with their money?
LISTENING   Ireland and Dublin
MEDIATION   Why are ghosts so
  popular in Ireland?
WRITING   Two open-ended
  stories
20 **LOOK AT LANGUAGE**
STRUCTURES • WORDPOWER •
  • REVISION

SPRECHABSICHTEN	REDEMITTEL	LERNTECHNIKEN
Geografische, historische, politische und kulturelle Aspekte Irlands kennenlernen und diskutieren Bilder beschreiben und vergleichen Über Ereignisse sprechen, die weiter in der Vergangenheit zurückliegen als andere	*I had never been in Ireland before I went there last year.* *After I had washed, I ate my dinner.* *on the right/left* *in the centre* *at the top/bottom* *in front of/behind* *in the background* *I think that the first picture ... while on the other hand the second picture ...* *[the largest English-speaking population, the ruined houses]*	Internettexten Kerninformationen entnehmen Gehörtes und Gelesenes mit Hilfe von Stichwörtern wiedergeben *(note taking)* Schlüsselstellen eines Lesetexts auf Deutsch wiedergeben Umgang mit Nachschlagewerken Wortbildung durch Ableitung, Zusammensetzung *note making*

Unit 2   South Africa

24 **LEAD-IN**
LISTENING   The "rainbow
  nation"
28 **SKILLS**
SPEAKING   A visit • A topic-
  based talk about South Africa
READING   From Soweto to the
  Kruger Park
LISTENING   Two radio diaries
MEDIATION   The 2010 World Cup
WRITING   When you have
  to complain
36 **LOOK AT LANGUAGE**
STRUCTURES • WORDPOWER •
  • REVISION

SPRECHABSICHTEN	REDEMITTEL	LERNTECHNIKEN
Über die Lebensumstände in Südafrika sprechen Über Ereignisse sprechen, die durch einen Zeitplan festgelegt sind Über Pläne und Absichten sprechen Informationen erfragen	*Our boat leaves tomorrow at 10.30 p.m.* *When are you leaving tomorrow? – I'm leaving after lunch.* *How long does the visit take?* *When does the next boat leave?* *[no running water, badly-paid jobs, a guided tour]* *[If I had stayed there, I would have had a boring life.]*	Internettexten Kerninformationen entnehmen Gehörtes und Gelesenes mit Hilfe von Stichwörtern wiedergeben *(note taking)* ein Kurzreferat präsentieren Schlüsselstellen eines Lesetexts auf Deutsch wiedergeben Synonyme und Antonyme nutzen Wortbildung durch Ableitung, Präfixe *by-passing strategies* (Umschreibungen)

3

three

	SPRECHABSICHTEN	REDEMITTEL	LERNTECHNIKEN
Unit 3 India			

40 **LEAD-IN**
LISTENING   Introduction to
  India: Which five topics
  are discussed?
44 **SKILLS**
SPEAKING   Interpreting:
  In India • A topic-based talk
  about India
READING   Why India matters –
  to you!
LISTENING   Indian culture
  in Britain
MEDIATION   Information about
  Mohandas Gandhi
52 WRITING   A keyword story
LOOK AT LANGUAGE
STRUCTURES • WORDPOWER •
REVISION
	Über religiöse, kulturelle
	und wirtschaftliche
	Lebensgewohnheiten
	in Indien sprechen
	und sie mit den
	eigenen vergleichen
	Berichten, was jemand
	gesagt hat
		*Uttam said that he
		visited his relatives in
		Britain once a year.*
			Dolmetschen
			ein Kurzreferat
			  präsentieren
			Gehörtes und Gelesenes
			  mit Hilfe von Stich-
			  wörtern wiedergeben
			  (note taking)
			by-passing strategies
			  (Umschreibungen)
			Umgang mit Nach-
			  schlagewerken

56 *****EXTRA PAGES** A short story: Nightmare			
Unit 4 Young adults			

60 **LEAD-IN**
LISTENING   An interview:
  Teenage mothers
62 **SKILLS**
SPEAKING   Talking about
  driving lessons • Picture-
  based conversation
READING   About a boy
LISTENING   Two audio
  messages
MEDIATION   An online
  book review
WRITING   Formal letters and
  emails
70 **LOOK AT LANGUAGE**
STRUCTURES • WORDPOWER •
REVISION
	Die Belange junger
	  Erwachsener disku-
	  tieren
	Über Fahrstunden
	  sprechen
	Sagen, was unter
	  bestimmten Bedin-
	  gungen passieren
	  wird/würde
		*If parents listened more
		  to their children, life
		  would be much easier.*
		*You can drive a car in
		  Britain if you're 17.*
		*I'm taking my driving
		  test next week.*
		*How are you feeling
		  about the test?*
		*Are you looking forward
		  to learning to drive?*
		*[driving test, a best-
		  selling book]*
			Gehörtes und Gelesenes
			  mit Hilfe von Stich-
			  wörtern wiedergeben
			  (note taking)
			Schlüsselstellen eines
			  Lesetexts auf
			  Deutsch wiedergeben
			Wortbildung durch
			  Ableitung
			by-passing strategies
			  (Umschreibungen)
			Umgang mit Nach-
			  schlagewerken

		SPRECHABSICHTEN	REDEMITTEL	LERNTECHNIKEN
	Unit 5 One world			
74	**LEAD-IN**	Umweltprobleme und deren Auswirkungen diskutieren	*Fortunately some progress has been made.*	Internettexten Kerninformationen entnehmen
	LISTENING A TV programme about environmental problems			
76	**SKILLS**	Sagen, was gemacht worden ist und was gemacht werden wird	*Polar bears will be threatened with extinction.*	Dolmetschen ein Kurzreferat präsentieren
	SPEAKING Talking about the environment			
	READING Life after the end of the world		*[No new buildings are being built.]*	Schlüsselstellen eines Lesetextes auf Deutsch wiedergeben
	LISTENING Big yellow taxi			
	MEDIATION A news story			Umgang mit Nachschlagewerken
	WRITING A picture-based story			
84	**LOOK AT LANGUAGE**			
	STRUCTURES • WORDPOWER • REVISION			

88	**PARTNER PAGES**
	Units 3, 4, 5
92	**SUMMARY**
102	***REVISION AND PRACTICE**
	Unit 1
	Unit 2
	Unit 3
	Unit 4
	Unit 5
112	***EXAM PRACTICE**

	ANHANG
122	**VOCABULARY**
141	In English
142	**DICTIONARY**
178	Names
180	Irregular verbs
182	Classroom phrases
184	Wichtige Wörter zur Grammatik
186	Bildquellen
187	Text- und Liedquellen

  Als Hörtext oder Song auf der Audio-CD vorhanden

1⊙2 = CD 1, Track 2

W1 Workbook, Übung 1 der Unit

* wahlfreie Bestandteile

[ ] 1. Vorkommen von Strukturen, die nur verstanden werden sollen (rezeptive Strukturen)

  Wiederholungsübungen

A world language

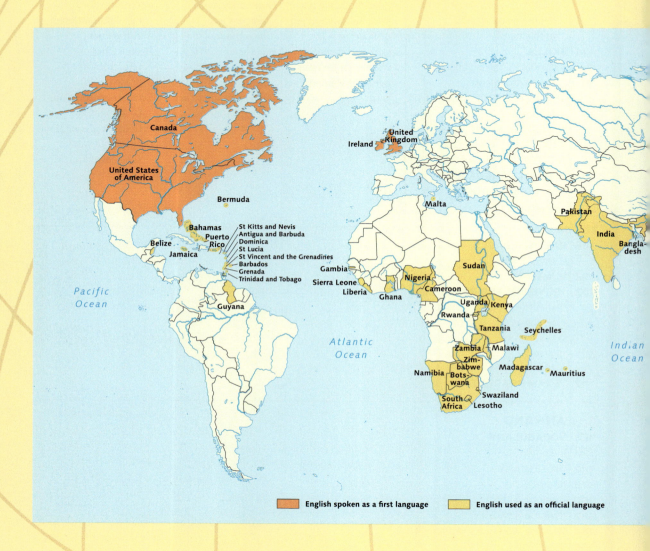

English is spoken as a first language   English used as an official language

English is spoken as a first language by well over 309 million people in the world. It's also spoken by 1500 million people as a second language. So it's a widely-spoken language – all in all almost two billion people can speak English, a third of the world's population. And did you know that …
• all over the world pilots and airports talk to each other in English?
• over 50% of home pages on the Web are in English?

1 The map shows countries where English is spoken as a first or an official language. Where do people speak English as a first language? Make a list.

In some English-speaking countries English isn't the only language, e.g. in Ireland, in South Africa and in India. In *New Highlight 6* you'll learn more about these countries.

Ireland
Both English and Irish (a Celtic language which is different from English) are official languages, but a large majority of people speak English as a first language.

South Africa
Only 8.2 % of South Africans speak English at home. But while other languages are spoken in some regions only, English is spoken and understood in every part of the country. English is also the language of government, banks and big companies.

India
A minority of Indians speak English – but as the Indian population is so large, India has the second largest English-speaking population in the world – only the USA has more.

2 Languages and countries
1 Why is English important in South Africa?
2 Which two countries have the most English speakers?
3 Which language is spoken by most people in Ireland?

 3 Irish, Indian and South African English

a) Listen to three people. Who do you think is from Ireland, India and South Africa?

b) Now listen to the three people again and write the towns where they live.

Unit 1

Ireland

1 What do you already know about Ireland? Perhaps the photos can help you.

2 Choose one of the photos and describe it to your partner.

In the picture there is/are / I can see / …
On the right/left …
In the middle …
At the top/bottom I can see …
In front of / Behind the …
In the background …

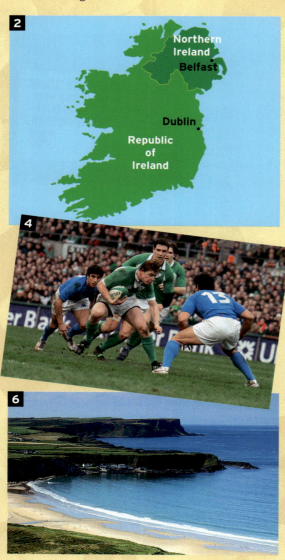

▶W1

3 Read the following paragraphs and match each one with one of the photos on the left.

A The Republic of Ireland (population: a little over four million) is an independent country and uses euros. Northern Ireland is a province of the United Kingdom and uses British pounds.

B The Republic of Ireland and Northern Ireland each have a national football team. But in rugby the two countries play together in one Irish team.

C Dublin (city population: 506,000) is the capital and the largest city of the Republic of Ireland. One of its tourist sights is the Spire – a very tall, narrow tower.

D Many multinational computer companies have factories in Ireland. The tourist industry is also enormously important.

F Did you know that the *Titanic* was built in Belfast, the largest city in Northern Ireland? Now modern offices, shops, houses and flats stand where the *Titanic* was built.

E The west coast of Ireland is rocky and very beautiful. Some parts have high cliffs, other parts have wide sandy beaches. There are few large towns in the west.

G The Republic of Ireland has two official languages: English and Irish. So road signs are in both languages.

4 An info box for Ireland

a) With the information from this page make notes for an info box for the Republic of Ireland and another one for Northern Ireland (e.g. official name, population, capital, money, official languages, sports, industry).

 b) Now listen and add one piece of information to each category in your info box.

c) Now with all your notes write the info boxes for the Republic of Ireland and Northern Ireland.

5 Questions for discussion in class
1. Why was the *Titanic* so special and what happened to it?
2. What other countries use euros?
3. What three things (e.g. cinemas, large parks, …) do *you* think a great city should have?
4. What other countries play rugby?
5. What industries are important in Bavaria?
6. What's the climate like where you live?
7. What other countries have two or more languages?

9

nine

LEAD-IN

🎧 Ireland – past and ...

1 ◉ 7, 8

Dingle, County Kerry
The peaceful village of Dingle, where Irish is still spoken, is a favourite place for tourists in the southwest of Ireland, but like so many villages in Ireland, it hides a terrible past.
150 years ago the people here and in most parts of Ireland were very poor and apart from some fish their only food was potatoes. In 1846, however, a terrible disease destroyed the potatoes and the people then had nothing to eat. People were so hungry that they sold their fishing equipment.
All over Ireland, men, women and children starved. Here in Dingle five thousand people died, while many others emigrated to Britain or the USA. Their sad monuments are the ruined houses which they left behind. One of them, a few miles west of Dingle, is now a little museum. It's still a sad place.

Enniskillen, Northern Ireland
In 1921 most of the island of Ireland became an independent republic, but the Protestants of Northern Ireland, who were the majority in the province, voted to stay in the United Kingdom. From then on extreme Catholic and Protestant groups fought each other in Northern Ireland and 3500 people were killed.
In Enniskillen both Catholics and Protestants were killed. The worst day was when eleven people died on November 8th, 1987. Fortunately there is peace in Northern Ireland now – and Enniskillen is famous again: not for its bombs, but for some of the best fishing rivers in Ireland.

1 **True or false? Correct the false sentences.**
1. Tourists don't like Dingle because it has a terrible past.
2. In the nineteenth century the poor people of Dingle only ate potatoes and a little fish.
3. All the people of Dingle died in 1846.
4. In 1921 the Protestants of Northern Ireland didn't want to be part of the Republic of Ireland.
5. Enniskillen is still a dangerous place today.

▶ W 2

Unit 1

... present: Why not work in Ireland?

Meet some young people who have come from abroad and now work in Ireland.

> Hi, I'm Olek. I'm Polish and I came to Ireland three years ago. I'm a nurse in a large hospital in Dublin city centre. I really like it here because Dublin is so multicultural: there are people here from Poland, from Germany or from China. Somebody told me that 8 % of the people who work in Ireland come from abroad, more than in any other country in Europe. And the Irish people are very friendly. My only problem is that I don't like flying – but if I want to go back to Poland, I have to fly. It takes too long by boat and train and it's too expensive!

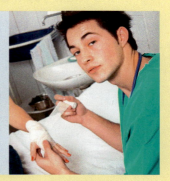

> Hi! I'm Teresa and I come from Detroit in the USA. I've always been interested in computers and I got my first job with a company which makes computers. Two years ago the company sent me to their factory here in Ireland. It's the company's largest factory in the European Union and we're not the only computer company here: did you know that 40 % of all European software is made in Ireland? So many things are new and exciting here – like rugby matches! On the other hand I miss baseball – and doughnuts for breakfast.

2 Olek and Teresa

a) Answer the questions in full sentences.
1 Why does Olek like Dublin? What's his problem in Ireland?
2 Why is Teresa in Ireland? What does she miss about America?

b) Explain these numbers in German:
1 8 % *(Olek)*   2 40 % *(Teresa)*

3 Jakob and Olivia also work in Ireland.
Listen and take notes.
What ...
1 do they do?
2 do they like in Ireland?
3 don't they like there?

4 Project: Use the Internet and learn more about Ireland.
1 Go to **www.new-highlight.de** and put in **NHL-BY-6-11**.
2 Choose one of the following topics:
  a) Immigrants in Ireland   **b)** Episodes in Irish history   **c)** Dublin   **d)** Sport in Ireland
3 Then give a short talk about your topic.

▶ W 3, 4

SKILLS

SPEAKING – Picture-based conversation

1 In the exam you'll perhaps have to talk about two pictures.

a) First look at the two pictures below.

Belfast, 1979

Belfast, 2009

b) Read the tips and examples.

Beschreibe zunächst, was auf dem Bild zu sehen ist.	▶ The first picture shows violence in Belfast in 1979.
Orientiere dich im Bild mit Hilfe von *on the left/right, in the centre, at the top/bottom, in front of/behind, in the background, …*	▶ On the left …
Beschreibe, was gerade passiert und benutze dafür die *present progressive*-Form.	▶ Some people are sitting outside.
Verwende Adjektive und Adverbien.	▶ A young family is walking happily down the street.
Manchmal kann es auch wichtig sein zu beschreiben, was im Bild **nicht** zu sehen ist.	▶ There's no violence in the second picture.
Beschreibe auch, was die Personen denken oder fühlen könnten.	▶ I think the people on the left are very angry.
Zum Schluss sagst du deine Meinung und versuchst die beiden Bilder zu vergleichen.	▶ I think that in the first picture … while on the other hand the second picture …

c) Now prepare what you're going to say about each picture.
You can make notes – but don't write complete sentences.

d) A student is talking about the two pictures.
1⊙12 Listen carefully – perhaps you can copy some ideas for your own talk.

e) Now talk to your partner about the two pictures.
You can look at your notes while you speak. Can you talk for two minutes?

▶ W 5

2 An old house

a) Look at the scene and read the text.

"In the picture there's a house. Some people are talking. Some people are holding farming equipment. It's an old picture."

**b) The text is too short, isn't it?
Try to make it longer and more interesting.
Make notes for your talk.**
- Where's the house? What does it look like?
- Where are the people? Who's talking to who?
- Why are they carrying equipment?
- Why do you think the picture is old?

"In the background of the picture there's a house which looks very small. ..."

3 Holiday in Ireland

**a) Now it's your turn.
Look at the posters below and plan what you can say about them. Make notes.**

**b) Then talk to your partner about the two tourist posters.
Describe the pictures briefly, compare them and give your opinion.**

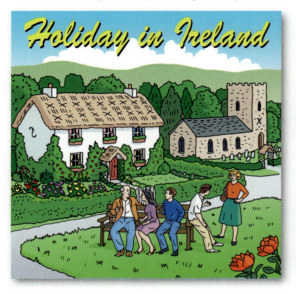
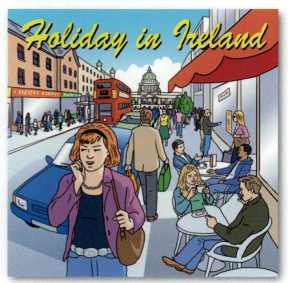

SKILLS

READING – A blog

» Words with * are not in the *Dictionary* at the back of this book.

What do celebrities do with their money?
Posted by Stephen Harper, 30th June 2009, 8.28 p.m.

I really don't agree that all celebrities are selfish and only spend their money on mansions*, luxury yachts and fast cars. Many stars give some of their money to good causes and work hard in order to help poor people all over the world.

1 Have you heard of Bono, for example? If not you've probably heard of U2. Bono and some friends formed the band U2 in the 1970s while he was still at school in Dublin. Bono wrote the lyrics of many of the band's songs. His lyrics often have a social message and he won the *Golden Globe Award* for the most original song in 2003. U2 became one of the most successful bands that Ireland has ever produced and they're still one of the richest bands in the world: in the list of the Irish people who have a fortune* of more than £22 million, the members of U2 are sixth out of 200.

2 (Oh, if you're wondering about the name: Bono's real name is Paul Hewson. But when he was a boy in Dublin he was in a gang and all the members gave each other nicknames. Paul could sing well and was called Bona Vox – which means "good voice" in Latin – and soon the name became Bono. The nickname is used not only by his fans, but also by his friends and family.)

3 Anyway, my point is that Bono has given a lot of his money to organisations which fight against poverty, famine* and disease in poorer countries. In 1984, for example, he took part in the Band Aid project (which was organised by another Irish singer, Bob Geldof). Bono and some other famous singers produced the single "Do they know it's Christmas?" together. It was the number one single in Britain for five weeks and all the money it earned (over £8 million) went not to the stars themselves, but to organisations which were helping hungry children in Ethiopia. The year after that, Bono was one of many singers at the Live Aid concert at Wembley stadium in London. This concert, together with one on the same day in Philadelphia, USA, raised about £150 million for the fight against famine in the world.

4   But that's not all. Bono is still working against poverty, injustice and HIV/AIDS. He talks with presidents and prime ministers – and they listen to him because they know he's popular. He has given talks at international conferences* and he often takes bankers* and politicians to Africa so that they can see some of the problems for themselves. And he has been successful: because of Bono's work, governments in some richer countries now give more money to poorer countries.

5   Now, celebrities like Bono aren't perfect, of course. I know people criticise him (and U2) because in 2006 the band moved their business from Ireland to the Netherlands where taxes are lower. They also complain that Bono bought a large hotel in the centre of Dublin in 1993 and that U2 now have plans to build Ireland's tallest building next to the river in Dublin. Why, they ask, doesn't Bono give all his money to poor people?

6   Well, I don't know if the plans for the hotel and the tower are good or not. But I know that if Bono earns lots of money with his new buildings, he will use it for good causes* and that will help poor people too. People believe what he says – that's why they said in a poll in Britain in 2002 that Bono was one of the 100 greatest British people who have ever lived (although actually of course he's Irish!).

Your comments

7   I think you're idealistic and naive, Stephen! Singers get a lot of good publicity when they do work for good causes, so their work often helps them more than it helps poor or hungry people. And remember that they often have to pay less tax if they have paid money to good causes. I think that many stars earn a lot too much and could do a lot more for poor people in the world!
Goodwin Sands

8   You're right that lots of stars support good causes. Shakira once paid for 10,000 pairs of tennis shoes for the poor children in her hometown in Colombia. Elton John gave almost $43 million to good causes in 2004. Madonna helped to found *Raising Malawi,* an organisation which helps children in that country, while Angelina Jolie, Brad Pitt, George Michael and many others give money to people who suffer from HIV/AIDS or who live in countries where there is war.
Sedna III

SKILLS

1 Find a title for each paragraph (1–8). You won't need two titles.
A Stars are selfish even when they support good causes.
B Working with politicians
C Bono's family life
D Bono, the musician
E Bono's first visit to a poor country
F It's good for poor people if Bono is rich.
G Examples of how stars support good causes
H Singing in order to help hungry people
I Three projects which many fans don't like
J Why is this man called Bono?

1 D   2 …   3 …   4 …   5 …   6 …   7 …   8 …

2 True or false? Correct the sentences that are wrong.
1 Stephen Harper doesn't believe that all celebrities are selfish.
2 Bono wrote the words for many of U2's songs.
3 The members of U2 are the richest people in Ireland.
4 U2 has already built Ireland's tallest building.
5 Goodwin Sands thinks that many celebrities have too much money.
6 Sedna III says that Elton John gave more than $43 million to good causes in 2004.

3 Stephen Harper likes Bono because he helps people in poorer countries. Give three examples of how Bono has done this.

4 Explain in German …
1 how Bono got his name.
2 what U2 did in 2006 which many fans didn't like.

5 Explain the following words in complete sentences. You can use a dictionary.
1 mansion   (line 3)
2 fortune   (line 19)
3 famine   (line 28)
4 conference (line 42)
5 banker   (line 43)
6 good cause (line 57)

Example: 1   A mansion is a large, luxury house.

6 And you?
Do you think rich celebrities should give time and money to good causes? Why (not)? Write a few sentences.

| I think | rich celebrities should … | because … |
| I don't think | | |

▶ W 6–10

Unit 1

🎧 LISTENING – Ireland and Dublin

1 🔊 20, 21

1 Two tourist sights in Ireland: Skellig Michael and the Giant's Causeway

a) Look at the photos: Would you like to visit these two places? Why (not)?

b) Listen and take notes:
• Where are the sights?
• How can you get there?
• What can you see there?

c) Now look at your notes and tell your partner about one of the places.

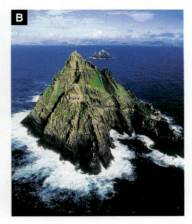

2 A tour of Dublin

a) Look at the photos. Then listen and write the right order of the photos.

b) Listen again and answer the questions.
1 When was the Book of Kells written?
2 What's near O'Neill's?
3 When did people stop paying to cross the Ha'penny Bridge?
4 What's the name of Dublin's river?
5 How high is the Spire and when was it built?
6 What animals can you see in Phoenix Park? Give three examples.

▶ W 11–13

SKILLS

MEDIATION – Why are ghosts so popular in Ireland?

Tipps

1 In diesem Prüfungsteil darfst du ein Wörterbuch verwenden, aber aufgepasst:
Viele Wörter haben mehr als eine Bedeutung. Der Kontext hilft dir, die richtige auszuwählen.
Beispiel:

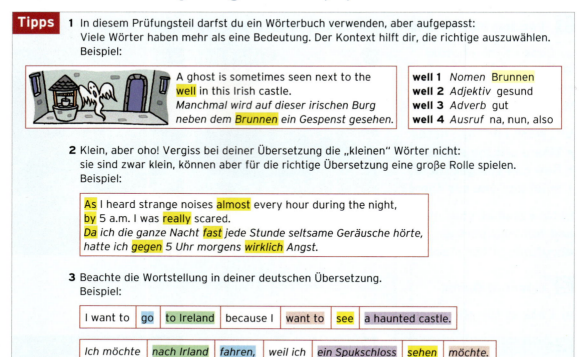

A ghost is sometimes seen next to the well in this Irish castle.
Manchmal wird auf dieser irischen Burg neben dem Brunnen ein Gespenst gesehen.

well 1	Nomen	Brunnen
well 2	Adjektiv	gesund
well 3	Adverb	gut
well 4	Ausruf	na, nun, also

2 Klein, aber oho! Vergiss bei deiner Übersetzung die „kleinen" Wörter nicht:
sie sind zwar klein, können aber für die richtige Übersetzung eine große Rolle spielen.
Beispiel:

As I heard strange noises almost every hour during the night,
by 5 a.m. I was really scared.
Da ich die ganze Nacht fast jede Stunde seltsame Geräusche hörte,
hatte ich gegen 5 Uhr morgens wirklich Angst.

3 Beachte die Wortstellung in deiner deutschen Übersetzung.
Beispiel:

| I want to | go | to Ireland | because I | want to | see | a haunted castle. |

| Ich möchte | nach Irland | fahren, | weil ich | ein Spukschloss | sehen | möchte. |

1 Why are ghosts so popular in Ireland?
Translate this text into German.

» You can use a dictionary to find the meaning of new words.

In Carlow people have seen ghosts in a pub[1]. In Ballymena people say that they have seen a headless rider[2] on a white horse. In Kinsale the voice of a woman is sometimes heard[3] at night (some people say that she is putting earrings into her ears). But when people look for her she has always disappeared. Every village in Ireland, it seems, has its own ghost.

Why are ghosts so[4] popular in Ireland? Well, Irish people love telling stories – and ghost stories are always popular. Also[5] there are many ruined houses which can look spooky, especially on wet and windy nights. The result? Ghosts (whether they exist or not!)[6] have become enormously important for Ireland's tourist industry: tourists can go on ghost tours[7] and spend whole weekends in ruined castles.

[1] *In ... people have seen ...:* Achtung, deutsche Wortstellung!
[2] *rider:* Fahrer/in oder Reiter/in?
[3] *is heard:* Passiv (siehe Seite 101)!
[4] *so:* Vergiss nicht das (kleine) Wort „so" zu übersetzen.
[5] *also:* Achtung, *false friend!*
[6] *whether they exist or not:* ob sie nun existieren oder nicht
[7] *go on ghost tours:* Gespenstertouren machen

▶ W 14

Unit 1

WRITING – Two open-ended stories

1 A ghost story
Finish the ghost story. Look at the ideas below and write at least 120 words.

Tom was hiking in Ireland. On the third evening it was raining and he couldn't find a campsite, so he asked at a farm. The farmer said he could put up his tent in a ruined house, where the wind was less strong.
At first Tom slept well. But when he woke up at two o'clock in the morning, he was scared …

Ideas

1. What was the night and the weather like?
   - It was raining: what was wet in the tent?
   - It was dark: what couldn't Tom see? What could he almost see?
   - The wind sounded like …?

2. What happened?
   - What did Tom see/hear?
   - What did the ghost look like? What did it do?
   - How did Tom feel? What did he do?
   - Did he try to touch/talk to the ghost?

3. What happened next?
   - What did the ghost do?
   - Could Tom sleep again?
   - What did he do?

4. What did Tom do the next morning?
   - Did he run away?
   - Or did he tell the farmer what he had seen?

2 The first race
Finish the story. Write at least 120 words.

Olivia worked on a special farm in Ireland: she looked after racehorses. Olivia loved her work because she loved horses and her favourite one was called Star; it was young and white. One day the owner of the farm said to Olivia, "Star is going to Dublin tomorrow. She's going to run in her first race. Would you like to go too? You could look after Star and watch the race."
Of course, Olivia said, "Yes".
The next day …

▶ W 15, 16

LOOK AT LANGUAGE

STRUCTURES

Pat's Irish ancestors

In this blog Pat Curran, an American, describes why his family came from Ireland to the USA in 1850.

My Irish ancestors

My ancestors, the Currans, came to the USA in 1850. Before that they had lived in a village in Ireland. They had not owned their land, but they had rented it from an English landowner. They had always worked hard and they had always been poor and often hungry.
The worst year had been 1846. The men had planted potatoes and the plants had begun to grow. But when the men had wanted to pick them, they had found that the potatoes had a disease: they were black and had an awful smell.
In that terrible year, four years before my ancestors emigrated to the United States, hundreds of people in the area had starved. My family had not been able to pay the rent and they had had to go to the workhouse: a terrible place where the men were separated from the women and weak and hungry people had to work all day in order to earn some food for the evening meal.
It's not surprising that my family decided to emigrate.

1 Pat's Irish ancestors came to the USA in 1850.
Look at the text again and find ten actions that had happened before 1850.

1 They *had lived* in a village.   2 They *had rented* ...   3 They ...

In another blog Pat Curran describes a strange experience that he had on his first visit to Ireland.

A ghost in modern Ireland

Although I had never visited Ireland before I went there in February 2009, I knew that the country was famous for its ghosts. But I wasn't thinking about ghosts when I arrived at the *Irish Joker* hotel.
After I had washed and had put on some new clothes, I ate my dinner in the dining room. But when I went back to my room, I saw at once that my money had disappeared. I had put it on the table next to my bed before I left the room. I phoned the reception.
"Room 243," I said. "My money has disappeared from my room. It disappeared while I was in the dining room."
The receptionist wasn't surprised because this had happened before.
"It's the ghost of room 243," he said.
"Ghost?" I answered. "I don't believe in ghosts that steal money!"

Unit 1

2 What happened before? Look at the text and complete the sentences.
1 Before I went there in February 2009, *I had never visited Ireland.*
2 Before I ate my dinner, *I had ...*
3 When I came back to my room, I saw that ...
4 Before I left my room, I ...
5 The receptionist said that this ...

3 Read the checkpoint and complete the example.

CHECKPOINT

Mit der *past perfect*-Form kannst du anzeigen, welches von mehreren Ereignissen weiter in der Vergangenheit zurücklag als die anderen. Die *past perfect*-Form bildest du mit **had** und dem **Partizip Perfekt**.
Beispiel: I **had** never **been** to Ireland before I went there last year.
After I ... some new clothes, I ate my dinner.

4 Later the chambermaid tells Pat what really happened. Use the *past perfect*.

1 I went into your room, Sir, after you (begin) your meal.
2 I saw the money on the table where you (put) it.
3 I put it under the clothes which you (take) off.
4 I (already/tell) the receptionist what I (do) before you phoned.

So it was only a joke, Sir. You're not angry with me, are you?

5 Now write about an immigrant family from Bosnia. Use the *simple past* and the *past perfect* in each sentence.
1 Zoran's parents (marry) after they (meet) at a friend's party.
2 When Zoran (begin) school in Sarajevo, his parents (already/buy) a house there.
3 But after the family (live) in Sarajevo for a few years, the war (begin).
4 They (decide) to emigrate after some bombs (explode) near their house.
5 Before they (move) to Bavaria, they (spend) six weeks with friends in Austria.

AND YOU?

Write your family's story. Use the *past perfect*.
My parents / grandparents / mother and I / We came to ... in 1961 / in ... / ... years ago.
Before that we/they had lived • had worked • had been to school in ...
We/They had ...

▶ W 17–19

LOOK AT LANGUAGE

WORDPOWER

> **Tipp** In der Prüfung darfst du im Teil *Language Test* kein Wörterbuch benutzen. Versuche deshalb die folgenden Übungen ohne Wörterbuch zu lösen. Danach kannst du mit Hilfe des Wörterbuchs deine Antworten überprüfen.

1 Smaller things: What are the missing words?

  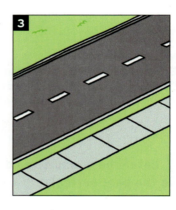

A mountain – a ...   The sea – a ...   A road – a ...

2 Word families: Write the missing words.

verbs	nouns
1 live	*life*
2 ...	flight
3 build	...
4 invite	...
5 ...	service

nouns	adjectives
6 peace	*peaceful*
7 rock	...
8 death	...
9 ...	criminal
10 poverty	...

3 Match the sounds with the words.

→ wide • loud • child • grey • power • raise • peace • sheep

1 [eɪ] ...   2 [aɪ] ...   3 [iː] ...   4 [aʊ] ...

4 Head, hair, ears and fingers: Write what the words mean.
1 What are headphones and when do you wear them?
2 What does a hairdresser do?
3 What are earrings?
4 What does a friend mean if she/he says "Fingers crossed!" to you?

Example: Headphones are things that you put over your head and ears, e.g. when listening to an MP3 player.

Unit 1

REVISION
» If you need help on this page, look at the *Summary Pages* (92–101).

1 Tourists in Ireland

a) Look at the text below and copy the time phrases in red. What tense is needed with each one?

Example: every year → simple present

b) Now write the text with the right form of the verbs.

About six and a half million foreign tourists (visit) Ireland every year. The largest number of foreign tourists (come) from Great Britain, but Ireland is popular with Germans too: about 300,000 Germans (visit) Ireland last year. In the past British tourists usually (travel) by ferry, but since 1990 more and more of them (fly) instead. More visitors (arrive) in Northern Ireland after 1998, although very few tourists (visit) Northern Ireland before that. The number of tourists (grow) fast at the moment and in the next few years the province (need) many more hotels and bed and breakfasts.

2 Irish – Ireland's own language
Write the information in passive sentences.
1. The British banned the Irish language before 1916.   *The Irish language ... by ...*
2. But all students in Irish schools learn the Irish language today.
   But today the Irish language ... by ...
3. About 1% of Ireland's population regularly speak Irish.   *Irish is ...*
4. And TG4 shows TV programmes in Irish.   *And TV programmes in Irish ...*

3 Quick check

a) Questions about Ireland
1. What does   a) the Irish country and   b) the Irish coast look like?
2. Why did many Irish people starve in 1846?
3. Where in Ireland is Dublin? Is the city bigger or smaller than Munich?
4. How is Northern Ireland different from the Republic of Ireland? Give three examples.

b) Poor Phil: Look at the pictures and finish the sentence.
Phil (can not) play football last Saturday because (break) his leg on Wednesday.

Wednesday ...   Saturday ...

c) Complete the sentence in German.
Die *past perfect*-Form wird gebraucht, wenn ein Ereignis in der Vergangenheit ...

► W 20–22

23
twenty-three

Unit 2

South Africa

South Africa (population: 48 million) has large cities with good railways, roads and airports. The cities have modern centres and some suburbs are very wealthy. The largest city is Johannesburg.

Cities also have very poor suburbs where many houses have no electricity or running water. There are few schools and hospitals and many people suffer from HIV/AIDS and unemployment.

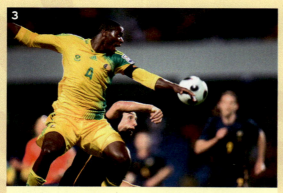

Cricket and rugby are very popular, but football has the most fans, especially with the World Cup in South Africa in 2010.

The Kruger National Park in the northeast is famous for its "Big Five": rhinoceroses, leopards, elephants, buffaloes and lions.

1 Read the texts and look at the photos.
1. Does the city centre of Johannesburg look like a German one? Why (not)?
2. How are the poor suburbs of South African cities different from the rich city centres?
3. What are three popular sports in South Africa? And what's the World Cup?
4. What are the "Big Five"? Describe each animal (e.g. colour, dangerous or not, what they eat, etc.).

2 Picture-based conversation: Compare photos 1 and 2. » The tips on page 12 can help you.
Talk about the buildings, people, jobs, activities, problems, etc.

► W 1

3 The "rainbow nation"

a) When do you usually see a rainbow?

b) Now read the text: Why is South Africa called the rainbow nation?

Black South Africans, who form the large majority of the population, belong to nine different groups, each with its own language and culture. The Whites speak Afrikaans (a language like Dutch) or English. The Asians are mostly Indian and Chinese and the Coloureds are people with black and white ancestors. With so many colours, languages and cultures, no wonder that South Africa is called the "rainbow nation"!

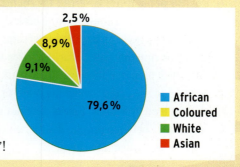

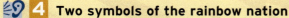 **4 Two symbols of the rainbow nation**

a) The South African flag: Listen and choose the right option.
1 It has been South Africa's flag since   a) 1954.   b) 1994.
2 The government had chosen it   a) seven days   b) seven weeks   before it was first used.
3 The old flag had   a) an elephant   b) the British flag   on it.

b) The South African national anthem: Listen and answer the questions.
1 How many verses does it have?
2 How many languages does it have?
3 When did the first verse become part of the national anthem?

c) Listen again to the last verse: What are the four missing words in the English verse?
Sounds the call to come ♪♪♪,
And united we shall ♪♪♪.
Let us ♪♪♪ and strive for freedom,
In South Africa our ♪♪♪.

5 Going up and going down: Make four sentences.

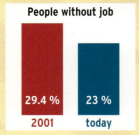 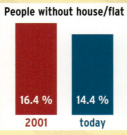 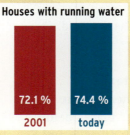 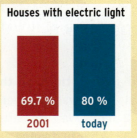

| The number of | people / houses | with / without | ... | has been | going up. / going down. |

6 Do you agree or disagree with the sentences below? Say why.
1 The black people of South Africa share one culture.
   I agree/disagree with the first sentence because the black people of South Africa …
2 Unemployment is still a big problem in South Africa.   *I agree/disagree …*
3 Life is getting better for the poorer people in South Africa.   *I agree/disagree …*

▶ W 2, 3

twenty-five

LEAD-IN

"Apartheid" and after

Although 80% of South Africa's people are Blacks, only Whites (9% of the population) governed the country before 1994. Black people weren't allowed to vote back then. They had to live outside city centres in areas called townships which often had no electricity or running water. Black children went to different schools which prepared them for badly-paid jobs. Blacks were not allowed to use parks, swimming pools or public toilets which were used by Whites. Blacks were not allowed to marry Whites and sex between people of different colours was a crime. This system was called "apartheid".

In Sharpeville, after the police had fired ...

Of course, the Blacks protested. During a peaceful protest in Sharpeville in 1960, the (white) police fired at the unarmed Blacks: 69 people were killed and 180 were injured. During 1976 pupils and students in Soweto protested because the white government wanted them to speak Afrikaans in some of their lessons at school. Again the police fired at unarmed people and 566 people died. Students and pupils had become the symbol of the fight against apartheid.

By the end of the 1980s there was more and more violence in the streets. In the end the government decided to free the black leader, Nelson Mandela, from prison on Robben Island. They hoped he could stop the violence. In 1994, when Blacks were able to vote for the first time, Mandela became president.

Since 1994 South Africa has tried to be a country which fights against injustice. However, black South Africans still suffer from many disadvantages. They're usually much poorer than the Whites, they get a worse education and suffer more from crime, violence and unemployment. They also have one of the highest rates of HIV/AIDS in the world.

1 Questions on the text
1. Who was in government before 1994?
2. How was life hard for Blacks before 1994?
3. What happened at Sharpeville and Soweto?
4. Where was Nelson Mandela in the 1980s?
5. Why did the white government free Mandela?
6. What disadvantages do Blacks still have today?

2 You're a reporter in 1960: Look at photo 2 and make a report for TV news.
"I'm standing in ... In front of me I can see ...
The black people are angry because ... Oh no! Now the police have fired at ...
And now I can see ... People are shouting and ... This is the worst violence I've ever seen!"

▶ W 4

Unit 2

Young South Africans

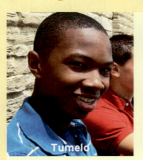

Tumelo
Lots of cool things happen in Joburg. This is where kwaito music started, for example. It's a sort of black South African hip-hop with lyrics in one of our African languages – not in English. My friends and I love it. We listen to kwaito on *YFM* radio and we go to kwaito concerts with thousands of other kids. But kwaito is more than just music – it's how we dance, how we dress and even how we walk. Kwaito makes us feel good!

Gavin
We're having a *braai* (that's an Afrikaans word for barbecue) in the garden. We're cooking ostrich steaks – boy, they taste great!
However, dad isn't with us because he's working today. Dad puts up security fences: lots of people here are buying them in our area because they're afraid of thieves. I often help dad – but not today: this December is hot in Joburg and I prefer to chill out in the pool!

Makobo
I like Joburg, but life isn't easy: drugs, street violence and unemployment are huge problems in the suburb we live in. My mum, my sisters and I came to Joburg from a quiet village two years ago. Mum had hoped to find a job here, but it was impossible. Then she died of AIDS last February, so I had to leave school and look after my younger sisters. I'm worried about them because lots of young people here suffer from AIDS too.

Mafuane
I love sport (especially rugby and cricket) and I'm really proud that South Africa was chosen for the 2010 World Cup.
I live in Sandton, a rich suburb of Joburg. Only Whites lived here during apartheid, but now black, coloured and Asian people live here too. My mum is a lawyer and my dad has a company that sells expensive German cars. People call rich Blacks like us *Black Diamonds*.

3 Young people in South Africa

a) Who talks about what? Find at least one topic per person.

| 1 family | 2 language | 3 sport | 4 food |
| 5 (no) work | 6 music | 7 a disease | 8 crime |

b) Compare Makobo and Gavin's lifestyles (e.g. family, house, money, disease, future). Use information from the texts and your own ideas.
Example: Makobo has a small house with no running water, while Gavin …   ▶ W 5, 6

4 Mafuane invites Tumelo to a kwaito concert.

a) Listen and take notes.
1 Who got the tickets?   2 When is the concert?
3 Where and when will the friends meet?

b) Now listen to Bouga Luv's kwaito music. Do you like it?

SKILLS

SPEAKING – A visit

During apartheid Nelson Mandela spent 18 years in prison on Robben Island. Now you can visit the island which is 12 km away from Cape Town.

 How much will the Kemas pay?

1●36
- **MR KEMA** Hi, I'd like tickets for the Robben Island tour, please. Two adults and two children.
- **ASSISTANT** No problem, that's 150 rand for each adult and 75 rand for each child.
- **MR KEMA** Does the ticket include the boat trip?
- **ASSISTANT** Yes, it does. And it also includes the visit to the prison and a bus tour on the island.
- **MR KEMA** That sounds good! How long does the visit take?
- **ASSISTANT** It's about three and a half hours altogether.
- **MR KEMA** And when does the next boat leave?
- **ASSISTANT** It leaves at 11 o'clock – over there, in front of that tower.
- **MR KEMA** Thanks very much.
- **ASSISTANT** No problem.

What's 150 rand in euros? Find out on the Internet!

1 Partner work: Make dialogues for the two places below. Then practise the dialogues with your partner.

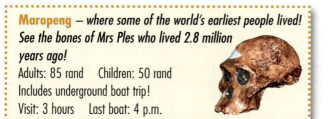

 What did the Kemas like on Robben Island?

1●37
- **MRS KEMA** Well, what did you think of the tour?
- **KOSAN** Visiting the prison was a bit scary, but on the other hand the guide was great.
- **GANIA** Yes, and the tour of the island was brilliant too – especially the penguins! I had never seen penguins before outside a zoo.
- **MR KEMA** But it's a pity that we couldn't get out of the bus. I wanted to take more photos.
- **KOSAN** I think the shop was very good, but they should have a café too.
- **GANIA** I don't agree. I think they should leave the island like it was. It's a special place.

2 Have you ever been to a famous place? Tell your partner about your visit.

Ideas
- Visiting … was …
- I had never … before.
- The … was great – especially the …
- But it's a pity that …
- I think they should …

Tipp Sage, wie dir der Besuch oder die Besichtigung gefallen hat, z. B.: *The guide was incredibly boring.* Du darfst deinen Bericht auch ausschmücken und Dinge „erfinden", z. B.: *If I have more time, I'll go there again next summer.*

Unit 2

SPEAKING – A topic-based talk about South Africa

1 Choose one of these two topics for a topic-based talk.

Nelson Mandela

The Kruger National Park

2 Find information about your topic.
1. Use information in this unit and on the Internet, e.g. at **www.new-highlight.de**. Put in **NHL-BY-6-29**.
2. Divide your topic into three or four parts. Here are two examples – but you can use your own ideas, of course.
   - **Nelson Mandela**
     early life, prison, president
   - **The Kruger National Park**
     location, size, the animals, work for the environment, the future
3. Find information for each part, e.g. early life: date/place of birth, school, interests.
4. What do *you* think about your topic? *Your* opinion is important!

3 A card for your topic

> **Tipp** In der Prüfung bekommst du passend zu einem deiner vorbereiteten Themen eine Karte mit einer These und Fragen zu deinem Thema. Du stellst das Thema vor und beantwortest dann die Fragen auf der Karte möglichst ausführlich. Dabei bringst du all dein Wissen zu diesem Thema ein. Abgerundet wird dein Vortrag, der ca. 3–4 Minuten dauern sollte, mit einer persönlichen Stellungnahme.

1 "Free Nelson Mandela!"
(poster, 1980)
- Why was Mandela in prison?
- Who wanted Mandela out of prison? Why?
- What do you admire most about Nelson Mandela? Why?

2 "Spend a week in Kruger National Park!"
(tourist brochure, 2008)
- Why does South Africa need national parks?
- Why is the Kruger Park important for jobs in South Africa?
- Would you like to visit the park? Why (not)?

4 Listen to two students, Sarah and Karl. Who uses the card better? Why?

5 Now give your talk.
1. Introduce the topic on your card.
   My topic is … • I'm going to talk about …
2. Then give detailed answers to the questions.
   You can say everything that you know about your topic.
3. Give your opinion about the topic.
   I think it's wrong/right to … • All in all I think … • In my opinion …
   From my point of view … • On the one hand …, but on the other hand …

> **Tipp** Gib an, woher du deine Informationen hast, z.B.: "I got my information from the Internet / a guidebook / a book in the library / …".

29 twenty-nine

SKILLS

READING – A life story

From Soweto to the Kruger Park
Written by Dominique Mathebula

I was born in Soweto and I was a child in the first few years after the end of apartheid. Life still wasn't easy. Our house had electricity, but we only got running water when I was six. Before that I often had to fetch water for my mother in a big heavy bucket. I didn't like that at all!

When people think of Soweto, they always think of crime, violence, drugs and unemployment. Well, these problems certainly existed, but there were a lot of good things too. I had great friends when I was small and we had good fun. We played outside and often got into trouble. Nothing serious, I mean, just kids stuff. Then there were lots of bands in Soweto – kwaito bands, rock bands, traditional bands – and when we were older some of my friends played in them. We often listened to music in the evenings – and in Soweto, listening meant dancing, singing and taking part! There was a special atmosphere in Soweto because people still felt proud of the role which they had played in the fight against apartheid. We felt that we belonged together.

I left school as soon as I could and then I had to find a job. That was really difficult, but after a few months I got a job in a fast-food restaurant in Johannesburg. It wasn't very well paid and it was quite a long way from home, so I walked or cycled every day because I didn't want to spend my money on the bus. The work itself was boring and if I had stayed there, I would have had a very boring life. But I didn't really think that I could do anything else.

But then I was lucky! A teacher from my school, who lived quite near us, told me about a course in Johannesburg which trained young people in different skills – computer skills, language skills, maths, etc. – in order to get a better job. Well, I applied for a place and I got one. The course was in the evenings after work, so I usually came home quite late – but I really enjoyed it. The teachers were so positive and I began to feel much more confident. I was a different person.

Then one day I saw an advert for a job in a big hotel – not just washing up and making the beds, but working in reception, really meeting the guests. It sounded good and I applied for it – and I was really disappointed when I didn't get it. I felt completely and absolutely useless. Luckily, my friends and family helped me through that awful time. And soon after that I saw an advert for a job in a hotel in the Kruger Park – and this time I was successful! So I packed my bags …

The Kruger Park is in the northeast of the country, on the borders with Mozambique and Zimbabwe – 19,000 square kilometres of wilderness. What a change from Soweto!

At first I missed my friends and the buzz of the township, but I enjoyed my work here from the very first day. My job was welcoming guests here in our hotel and looking after them while they were with us. It was very different from my job in Johannesburg: there the customers never even looked at me, but in the hotel the guests were happy and thanked me for my work.

As often as possible I went with the guests when rangers organised tours in the wilderness. Each time I learned more about the animals, the rivers, the trees – and I began to wonder if I could become a ranger too. Luckily, the park needed more rangers because more visitors were coming every year – so I did some training and in the end I became a ranger myself. And if you ask me, it's the best job in the world!

Our most important job as rangers is looking after the animals. Not like in a zoo, of course, because the animals can go where they like. What we have to do is check that they are healthy and have enough to eat, especially after natural catastrophes like floods and fires. That can be dangerous – in 2001 four rangers and twenty workers died when a fire reached their camp. I wasn't here then, but some of the older rangers still talk about it. Our big problem today is that we have too many elephants – 13,000 compared with 6600 in 1967. So they don't have enough space and that's one reason why we want to be part of the new Great Limpopo Transfrontier Park which will have 35,000 square kilometres in three countries: South Africa, Zimbabwe and Mozambique. A thousand elephants are already living in the two other countries.

The other part of our job is taking tourists into the wilderness. They can sometimes see animals from their hotel room when they come to the river and drink, but going into the wilderness is much more exciting, of course! Sometimes you can get very close to lions, leopards, buffaloes, hippos, zebras and all our other animals, but it's not dangerous as long as the tourists do what they're told.

I love the animals and that's why I get angry when tourists break the park rules and put the animals in danger – like when visitors started to feed some monkeys near our hotel. The monkeys liked the food and soon became aggressive when there was no food and in the end one of my colleagues had to kill them because they had become dangerous. It was the tourists' fault, really.

My worst experience was when we had a male leopard near the outer fence: crowds of tourists stopped in order to see him, but they came much too close and he became frightened.
I tried to tell the tourists to go away, but I was too late – the leopard tried to jump over the fence. The outer fence is electric – and it killed him. I saw it all and it made me sick. Humans aren't usually in danger from the animals. The biggest danger for them is car accidents – one of the worst was when five Europeans were killed in 2007. They were driving too fast and their car fell into a river.

SKILLS

1 True (T), false (F) or not in the text (NT)?
1. Life was easy for people in Soweto when Dominique was a child.
2. Dominique says that there were social problems in Soweto when she was small.
3. Dominique got a job at once when she left school.
4. The course which Dominique did in Johannesburg was free.
5. Dominique liked her first job in the Kruger Park from the beginning.
6. Dominique has been a ranger for three and a half years.
7. Rangers check that the animals in the park have no disease.
8. Dominique's worst experience was when a male leopard jumped on a tourist and killed him.

2 Who ...   » Your answers do NOT have to be full sentences.
1. wanted Dominique to fetch water for the family when she was small?
2. told Dominique about a course which trained young people in Johannesburg?
3. supported Dominique when she didn't get the job that she had applied for?
4. didn't look at Dominique when she served them?
5. was killed in a natural catastrophe before Dominique began to work as a ranger?
6. caused the death of the leopard, in Dominique's opinion?

3 Questions on the text: Answer in full sentences.
1. What job did Dominique have to do before she was six and why didn't she like it?
2. What were two of the good things in Dominique's life in Soweto?
3. What were three problems with Dominique's first job?
4. What did Dominique have to do in her first job in the Kruger Park?
5. Why is it a problem if the Kruger Park has too many elephants?
6. What, in Dominique's opinion, is the biggest danger for people in the Kruger Park?

4 Adjectives

a) Look at the text again and guess what these adjectives mean.
Write complete sentences in English.
1. serious *(line 13)* – Something is serious if ...
2. confident *(line 43)* – You feel confident when ...
3. disappointed *(line 48)*
4. healthy *(line 78)*

b) Now use a dictionary and check that your answers in 4a) are correct.

5 Look at the text again and explain in German ...
1. why there was a special atmosphere in Soweto.
2. what makes Dominique angry in her job as a ranger.

6 What are important things in a job:
Money? Colleagues? Where the job is?
Customers? Hours of work? ...?
Write what *you* think in three or four sentences.
What's important in a job is that ... •
I'd like to ... • I don't like jobs where you can't ...

"I'm really happy with my job because I meet a lot of people and I see that they're happy."

Dominique Mathebula

▶ W 7–11

Unit 2

🎧 LISTENING – Two radio diaries

1 🔊 44, 45

1 The day that Nelson Mandela came out of prison

a) Listen to Lucinda and her radio diary. What's the right option: a), b) or c)?

1 Lucinda ...
   a) has a husband and children.
   b) is married with no children.
   c) is single.
2 On the day that Mandela came out of prison Lucinda ...
   a) was at work.
   b) was at home.
   c) was with a friend.
3 When he came out of prison, Mr Mandela was ...
   a) 52 years old.   b) 62 years old.   c) 72 years old.
4 When Mandela saw the crowd, he was ...
   a) afraid.   b) surprised.   c) disappointed.

b) Now listen again and finish the sentences.
1 Lucinda works in a ... in Cape Town.
2 On February 11th, 1990 Nelson Mandela came ...
3 At *Victor Verster Prison* Nelson Mandela talked to Mr de Klerk, the ... of South Africa.
4 Some people were standing halfway up trees in order to get the best possible ...
5 Nelson Mandela walked through the crowd for more than ...
6 He said that apartheid has no ...

2 Thembi, a young woman with AIDS

a) True or false?
1 Thembi's boyfriend probably died of AIDS.
2 Thembi got worried and went for an AIDS test.
3 At the hospital she was tested five times.
4 Melikhaya is Thembi's new boyfriend.
5 Melikhaya isn't HIV positive.

b) Listen again: What's the right option?
1 The sister told Thembi that her brother was ill/angry.
2 When Thembi went for a test, the doctor tested her only once / five times.
3 The doctor told Thembi that she had been HIV positive for many years/months.
4 Melikhaya and Thembi love/hate each other.
5 Melikhaya wishes / doesn't wish that he had never met Thembi.
6 They're scared because they won't die / will die at the same time.

Thembi fought against her illness, but died on June 4th, 2009.

▶ W 12, 13

SKILLS

MEDIATION – The 2010 World Cup

1 The 2010 World Cup in South Africa
A foreign newspaper reporter wrote this article in 2008.
Translate it into German.

> **Tipp** Eine Übersetzung gelingt nicht immer beim ersten Aufschreiben. Am besten du fertigst zunächst eine „Rohübersetzung" an und liest diese aufmerksam durch. Dabei merkst du schnell, welche Stellen noch „holprig" klingen und kannst sie ändern.

The 2010 World Cup

» You can use a dictionary to find the meaning of new words.

Everybody I meet here talks to me about the 2010 World Cup. There are[1] posters, flags and pictures everywhere.

International sports events are incredibly important here. Why? Because people remember that South Africa was banned[2] from the Olympic Games from 1964 to 1992 because of the government's policy of apartheid. For this reason, people still talk about the first major international event that took place here after the end of apartheid: that was the rugby World Cup in South Africa in 1995[3]. South Africans are especially proud of it because their country won the final against New Zealand.

But the 2010 football World Cup is of course an even more important[4] event. Port Elizabeth is building a new stadium for it. There is[1] a new high-speed train between Johannesburg city centre and the airport. The decision that the World Cup should take place in South Africa in 2010[3] was taken[2] in 2006 and since then South Africans have felt more confident[4] and less isolated. The World Cup has banished some of the last ghosts of apartheid in sport.

---

[1] Vorsicht! Die richtige Übersetzung von *there is/are* ist „es gibt".
[2] Achtung, Passiv (s. S. 101)!
[3] Achte bei der Übersetzung auf die richtige Stellung von Orts- und Zeitangaben:
   in South Africa in 1995 ➜ 1995 in Südafrika
[4] *More* heißt nicht immer „mehr": a*n even more important event* ➜ ein noch wichtigeres Ereignis

▸ W 14

Unit 2

WRITING – When you have to complain

Dear Sir or Madam,
On May 5th I ordered an XNO2 laptop computer from your catalogue. It arrived on May 8th, but the screen is damaged and the power cable is missing.
Please tell me what I should do. Should I return the computer? When can you send me a replacement?
Please let me know as soon as possible.
Corinna Philpott

Hi,
Five days ago (on May 10th) I bought a Komil EP300 digital camera from you online. I still haven't received it. Have you sent it?
Please let me know ASAP.
Thanks,
Mike

28 Ringwood Road,
Pretoria 0181

Mr G. van Tonder
Owner
SaSa Holidays

December 8th, 2009

Dear Mr van Tonder,
I want to complain about our stay in the Penguin Palace Hotel in Cape Town from November 30th to December 6th.
When we came into our room, the shower was dirty and the television didn't work.
Also, the brochure says that the hotel is near the sea, but the sea is two kilometres away!
When we complained to the manager, he said that we should write to you.
Yours faithfully,
Emily Jackson

1 Find the phrases which mean …

1 broken 2 isn't there 3 send back 4 a different one
5 tell me 6 It hasn't arrived yet. 7 very quickly 8 not clean
9 write angrily that you do not like something

2 Copy and complete the email. Then write what it means in German.

Dear Sir or Madam,
A week ago I ordered a … When it arrived it was a bit … Also, the cable to the computer … Should I … the camera?
Let me know as soon … And please send me a …
Jenny Owen

→ as possible • was missing
damaged • digital camera
replacement • return

3 You ordered a mobile phone online. Write an email and complain about what is missing.

2nd Feb • ordered • mobile phone • from Tommy •
missing: charger, rechargeable battery

rechargeable battery   charger

4 On a holiday in South Africa you stayed in the *Magic* campsite in the Kruger Park. It was terrible. Write a letter (at least 120 words) and complain.

Ideas loud (why?) • dirty (what?) • broken (what?)
closed (pool?) • awful shop (no …?)
unfriendly warden (what did he say?) • …

▶ W 15, 16

35

thirty-five

LOOK AT LANGUAGE

STRUCTURES

 On holiday in Cape Town

1 ⊙ 46 Sabine and Julian from Augsburg have saved money for a holiday in South Africa. On their first evening their guide meets the new groups of tourists in their hotel in Cape Town.

> " Good afternoon, ladies and gentlemen, and welcome to South Africa!
> My name's Boniswa and I will look after you during your stay here in Cape Town.
> First I'm going to tell you about our programme for the week. This evening we have a coach tour of Cape Town, which is spectacular at night, and tomorrow we explore the town together. The day after tomorrow we travel to Hermanus where you'll see whales if you're lucky – so don't forget your cameras!
> The programme on Thursday is that we visit the Table Mountain National Park where you'll see zebras and then we stop at Boulders Beach where you'll see penguins. In the evening we go on a boat trip to Seal Island ... I don't need to tell you what you'll see there!
> On Friday we visit Robben Island with its famous prison. Our boat leaves at 10.30 a.m.
> You're free at the weekend, but on Sunday evening we offer a tour of Langa, a poorer township.
> On Monday our programme is that we cross the mountains and arrive in Oudtshoorn in time for lunch and in the afternoon we then visit an ostrich farm, where you can try riding an ostrich!
> And on Tuesday, your last full day here, you'll probably want to relax on one of our fantastic beaches. "

1 Look at the text and write the tourists' programme for the week. Find the right activity for each day and complete the sentences with the right form of the verbs.

Cape of Good Hope Hotel – *Programme for the next week*

Monday, 12th May .... We *have* a coach tour of Cape Town.
Tuesday, 13th May .... We ... Cape Town together.
Wednesday, 14th May .... We ... to Hermanus.
Thursday, 15th May .... We ... the Table Mountain National Park.
Friday, 16th May .... We ... Robben Island.
Saturday, 17th May .... You ... free!
Sunday, 18th May .... We ... a tour to Langa.
Monday, 19th May .... We ... an ostrich farm.

2 When? Complete the time phrases with the right preposition.

1 *in* the evening   2 ... Monday evening   3 ... the weekend   4 ... night
5 the day ... tomorrow   6 ... eleven o'clock   7 ... the afternoon

3 Checkpoint: Look at Exercise 1 again and complete the sentence and the example.

CHECKPOINT
Mit der *simple present*-Form sprichst du über die Gegenwart. Du kannst sie aber auch verwenden, wenn du über Ereignisse in der ... sprechen willst, die durch einen Zeitplan, z. B. einen Fahrplan, ein Programm oder einen Kalender, festgelegt sind.
Beispiel: *Our boat ... (leave) tomorrow at 10.30 a.m.*

▶ W 17

Unit 2

 Sabine has a friend, Terry, in Cape Town and she'd like to meet him on one of her free days.

1 ◉ 47

SABINE Hi, Terry. It's Sabine here.
TERRY   Oh, hi Sabine! Great to hear you! Where are you?
SABINE I'm here in Cape Town, at the *Cape of Good Hope Hotel* and I …
TERRY   Listen, we must meet while you're here in Cape Town. When are you free?
SABINE Well, tomorrow, for example …
TERRY   Tomorrow's difficult. I'm working during the day and some friends have invited me in the evening. We're having a braai. What about Friday?
SABINE I don't know … On Friday we visit Robben Island and I don't know when we come back. What about at the weekend?
TERRY   At the weekend? Great! I'm helping a friend on Sunday – he's moving into a new flat – but what about Saturday? We could spend the day together.
SABINE Sounds great. If you have time …
TERRY   Of course I have time! I can come to your hotel at about ten o'clock, OK?
SABINE Fine … Oh, err, Terry, I should tell you. My boyfriend Julian is here too. I hope that's OK?
TERRY   Oh!

4 Look at the text again: What are Terry's plans for tomorrow and Sunday?

Tomorrow *he's working* during the day. And in the evening they … a braai. On Sunday …

5 Now complete the checkpoint. Finish the sentence and the examples.

CHECKPOINT

Mit der *present progressive*-Form kannst du sagen, was gerade passiert. Aber du kannst damit auch über die … reden und sagen, was jemand plant oder vorhat.
Beispiele: When **are** you **leaving** tomorrow? – I'**…** after lunch.
How long **…** your friends **staying** here? – Dave **…** (leave) tomorrow, but Lucy **…** (stay) longer.

6 You don't want to meet Sally: Look at the pictures below and tell her why.

SALLY	YOU
Hi! Are you free on Monday evening?	No, sorry, Sally. On Monday I'*m …ing* …
Well, what about Tuesday evening?	No, sorry, Sally. On …

Monday evening

Tuesday evening

Wednesday evening

Thursday evening

▶ W 18

LOOK AT LANGUAGE

WORDPOWER

1 Parts for a laptop computer: What are they?

> **Tipp** Im Prüfungsteil *Use of English* darfst du kein Wörterbuch benutzen. Löse die Aufgaben also ohne Wörterbuch. Später kannst du deine Antworten mit Hilfe des Wörterbuchs überprüfen.

2 A fishing trip: Write words which mean the same.

A group of wealthy[1] tourists from Johannesburg had a bad time yesterday when they went fishing near Cape Town. They had caught some enormous[2] fish when they felt that the wind was stronger. They had almost[3] reached Robben Island when the storm exploded around them and they really felt afraid[4]. Luckily[5], however, they reached a small port[6] not far from Cape Town.

1 rich   2 h▇▇▇   3 n▇▇▇▇▇   4 f▇▇▇▇▇▇▇▇   5 f▇▇▇▇▇▇▇▇▇   6 h▇▇▇▇▇▇

3 Opposites

a) Write opposites with *in-*, *un-* or *im-*:
1 possible   2 dependent
3 armed   4 happy

b) Write the opposites of these words:
1 war   2 narrow   3 minority
4 huge   5 go up   6 well-paid

4 Animals

1 South Africa's "Big Five"	2 Pets	3 On the farm	4 South African birds
rhinoceros	fish	...	...
...	...	...	...
...	...	...	...
...	...	...	
...	...		

5 Social problems: Write what the words and phrases mean.
1 We have too many thieves in our area.   Thieves are people who ...
2 Many houses don't have running water.   Running water is ...
3 There is too much violence in some areas.   There is violence when people ...
4 Too many people suffer from unemployment.   Unemployment is when ...

Unit 2

REVISION

» If you need help on this page, look at the *Summary Pages* (92–101).

1 An email from the Kruger Park
Copy and complete the email. You won't need all the words in the box.

→ any • anybody • anywhere • no • nobody • nothing • some • somebody • something

> Hello from the Kruger Park! We saw … zebras and hippos this morning, but we haven't seen … lions yet. … told us that they sometimes drink from a lake near here, but when we went there we saw … animals at all! The park is great and there aren't many tourists – you can drive for miles and not see …!
> Best wishes, Tim

2 In a restaurant in the Kruger Park
Write the right form of the twelve verbs (P = passive).

“ It's lunchtime here in the *Khoka Moya Camp* in the Kruger Park and all around me customers (enjoy) their meals in this fine modern restaurant. I (just order) an ostrich steak. Mm! I'm hungry and I (really look forward) to it!
All the food here (prepare: P) by Mosola Manyi who (work) in the kitchen since 1997. At first he (not know) much about work in a large kitchen. "But I've been able to learn very fast," says Mosola. "And now I (be) very happy with my job."
Before Mosola (come) to the camp he (live) in a small village where he (have to) carry the water 500 metres into the family house. Mosola's parents still (live) in the village and Mosola (visit) them as often as he can. ”

Mosola Manyi

3 Quick check

a) What's …
1 kwaito?   2 a braai?   3 a township?   4 apartheid?

b) Present tense with future meaning: Complete the two sentences.
1 Mit dem *simple present* kannst du über die Zukunft reden, wenn es um … geht.
2 Mit dem *present progressive* kannst du über die Zukunft reden, wenn es um … geht.

c) Now copy and complete the dialogue. Put the verbs in the right form.
   SARAH   What … you … (do) at the weekend, Michael?
   MICHAEL I … (visit) my uncle and aunt in Pretoria.
   SARAH   Oh! And when … your plane … (leave)?
   MICHAEL It … (leave) at 8.42 on Saturday morning.

▶ W 19–21

Unit 3

India

1 Introduction to India

a) What comes to mind when you think about India?

b) Listen: Which five topics are discussed?
1 industries   2 food   3 languages   4 music
5 population   6 religion   7 rivers   8 weather

c) Look at the map of India at the front of the book.
1 India is about   a) three   b) nine   c) twenty   times bigger than Germany.
2 The highest mountains in India are in the   a) south   b) north   c) east   of the country.
3 The capital of India is   a) Mumbai.   b) Kolkata.   c) New Delhi.
4 In the northwest India has a border with   a) Pakistan.   b) Afghanistan.   c) Russia.
5 From the north to the south India is about   a) 1000 km.   b) 1600 km.   c) 3200 km.

▶ W 1

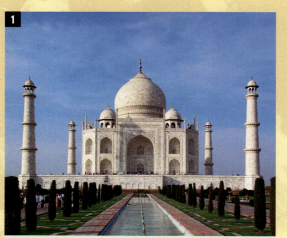

India has many beautiful buildings and monuments. Its most famous building, the Taj Mahal, was built in 1648 by a Muslim prince.
Today 80% of Indians are Hindus and 13.4% are Muslims. That's more than 180 million people – the third largest Muslim population in the world.

- Are Muslims a majority or a minority in India?

India's national parks have lions, leopards, rhinoceroses, buffaloes and elephants and the country is especially proud of its tigers. Tigers were once almost extinct and *Project Tiger* was started in 1972 in order to protect them. The project began with 268 tigers in nine reserves; in 2003 there were 1576 tigers in 27 reserves.

- How do we know that *Project Tiger* seems to be successful?

India has the second biggest population in the world (about 1.13 billion people). It has many very large cities: Mumbai (in the past called Bombay), with 19 million people, is one of the five biggest cities in the world.
Indian city streets are full and busy. Cars, buses and bikes fight for space with people and animals. Many shops and street stalls have signs in different languages. City centres have banks, offices, parks and department stores, but many suburbs are very poor.

- **Why are Indian city streets often noisy?**

70% of Indians live and work in villages and many earn only 50 rupees (one dollar) a day. But most villages now have electricity and running water and modern technologies are helping farmers to grow more crops. And with mobile phones farmers can compare prices in different markets and get better prices for their crops.
Monsoon winds bring rain between June and September, but the rain can cause floods which destroy the crops and damage buildings in both villages and towns.

- **When's the monsoon season and what damage can the monsoon winds cause?**

2 Read the texts again and then write three questions about India for your partner. Can he/she answer them?
▶ W 2

3 **Picture-based conversation**
» The tips on page 12 can help you.
Compare photos 3 and 4. Talk about e.g. the people, buildings, noise, colours, traffic, work, lifestyle, etc.

→ LEAD-IN

🎧 Different faces of India
1⏺ 51–54

"Bollywood" is the nickname for India's film industry which began in Mumbai when the city was still called Bombay. Bollywood, the world's largest film industry, now produces more films than Hollywood.

Bollywood's new queen?
Katrina Kaif, who has a British mother and a father from the north of India, came from Britain to Mumbai in 2003 to make a career in Bollywood. She now has six box-office hits behind her and last year became the most downloaded film star in India.

Bollywood is famous for its romantic films with brilliant dancing scenes and Katrina's good looks make her a perfect Bollywood star – now that she has lost her British accent.

1 India's film industry
1. Why is India's film industry called Bollywood? » Think of the city where it began!
2. What sort of films does Bollywood typically produce?

Police save 17 sweatshop children
A clothing factory in a suburb of Mumbai was closed yesterday when the police found that 17 children between the ages of 8 and 13 were working there illegally. The children were making clothes for an international clothing company.

They were earning little more than their food and were working in terrible conditions.

The police said that they would try to send the children back to their families who were probably in poor villages near Mumbai.

Child labour for children under 14 is banned in India (except for work in the family), but according to the United Nations 55 million children under 14 work in Indian factories.

On the other hand, as Indian companies and businesses grow, some people in India have become very rich.

MORE MILLIONAIRES IN MUMBAI THAN MANHATTAN

2 What do the texts tell you about India? Choose the right option: a), b) or c).
a) While poverty was once a problem in India, it isn't a problem in India today.
b) One of India's problems is that it doesn't have any rich people.
c) India has some very wealthy people, but also many people who are very poor.

42
forty-two

Unit 3

Most Indian parents arrange marriages for their children. Possible partners are found in newspaper adverts or on the Internet. Partners are then chosen according to religion, education, family, looks – and even horoscopes.
The children can usually say no if they disagree with their parents' choice.

Name: Hasina Bai
Height: 160 cm
Mother language: Hindi
Religion: Hindu
Smoker: no
Work: computer worker
Age: 23 years
Living in: Bangalore

Education: secondary school, college
Hobbies: dancing, music, films
Eating habits: vegetarian
Dress style: Indian/ethnic clothes

Father works for the Tata company, mother is a nurse. As a family we believe in hard work and we believe that we must love and help each other.

3 Arranged marriages
1. Who usually chooses a husband or wife in India?
2. What do you think of arranged marriages? What's good about them? What's bad?
3. Write your own Internet advert – for yourself or a friend of yours.

Parts of India suffer from natural catastrophes like floods

More floods in Bihar
Bihar province is suffering from the worst floods in fifty years. Hundreds of villages have been damaged and two million people have left their homes. Half the population of Madhepura has left and the city of 50,000 people now looks like a ghost town. The people who have stayed in their homes have no clean water or electricity and the government has warned that the terrible conditions could lead to diseases like cholera.

Floods this year have also damaged roads and railways on both the east and west coasts of India.

4 The floods of 2008
1. How do we know that the floods of 2008 were especially bad?
2. What's usually the population of Madhepura and why did half the people leave the city in 2008?
3. What were the problems and dangers for the people who stayed in the city?

5 With the information from pages 40–43 write an info box for India,
e.g. population, climate, industry, lifestyle, cities, languages, poverty, religion and animals.

▶ W 3-5

→ SKILLS

SPEAKING – Interpreting: In India

While Tobias from Germany is travelling in India by train, a young Indian man called Govind asks him some questions. Tobias asks you to interpret.

1 Work with two partners.

a) Read the sentences below and agree together how you should interpret them.

GOVIND I'm glad to meet you, Tobias.
STUDENT *Govind sagt, dass …*
TOBIAS Und ich freue mich, dass ich nach Indien gekommen bin.
STUDENT *And Tobias says …*
GOVIND Tell me, what do you like especially in India?
STUDENT *Er fragt, was …*
TOBIAS Ich liebe das Essen hier.
STUDENT *Tobias says that …*

Tipps
- Nicht Wort für Wort übersetzen, sondern sinngemäß übertragen. (Aus diesem Grund kann die vorgeschlagene Lösung, die ihr in 1b) hören werdet, von eurer Übertragung abweichen.)
- Den Pronomenwechsel nicht vergessen! Beispiel:
  Tobias: „Ich freue mich, dass ich …"
  → *Tobias says he's happy that he …*
- Wenn du etwas nicht verstanden hast, frage noch einmal nach und bitte um Wiederholung:
  I'm sorry. Can you repeat that, please?

b) Now listen and check your answers.
1 ⦿ 55

2 Work again with two partners.

a) Partners B and C:
Look at page 88 and read part a) of Govind and Tobias's dialogue.
Partner A: Listen to Govind and Tobias and interpret for them.

b) Now change roles.
Partners A and C read part b) of Govind and Tobias's dialogue on page 88, partner B listens and interprets.

c) Change roles again.
Partners A and B read part c) of Govind and Tobias's dialogue on page 88, partner C listens and interprets.

d) Now listen to Govind and Tobias's full dialogue – especially the parts which you found difficult.
1 ⦿ 56

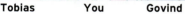
Tobias   You   Govind

Unit 3

SPEAKING – A topic-based talk about India

1 Before you talk

a) First choose one of the three topics below for your talk.

The geography of India	Work and industry in India	Bollywood

b) Then find information about your topic.
- Use information on pages 40–43, in the reading text (pages 46–47) and in books in the library.
- Find information on the Internet, e.g. at **www.new-highlight.de**. Put in **NHL-BY-6-45**.

c) Prepare your talk.
- Divide your topic into three or four parts, e.g.:   » These are examples only!

The geography of India	Work and industry in India	Bollywood
1 Big rivers, big mountains	1 Modern industries	1 How it began
2 The monsoon winds	2 Child labour	2 ...
3 Big cities, small villages	3 ...	3 ...
4 ...	4 ...	4 ...

- Find examples for each part.
- Say what you think about each topic. *Your* opinion is important!

2 When you're ready for your talk

a) First look at the card for your topic.   » The tips on page 29 can help you.

"India is not really a country – it's a whole continent."	"Indian industry will soon be a model for Europe."	"Bollywood comes to Germany."
• How is the north of India different from the south? • What natural catastrophes does India suffer from?	• Give examples of modern industries in India. • Describe some problems. • Do you agree with the title?	• How are Bollywood films different from Hollywood films? • Do you think they could be successful in Germany?

b) Now work with a partner.
- Give your talk and include answers to the questions on your card.
- Your partner then asks you two more questions (which she/he will find on page 89).
Listen and give full, interesting answers.

c) Change roles. Your partner gives her/his talk and you ask the questions on page 89.

Tipp Aus den Fragen und deinen Antworten soll sich ein Gespräch entwickeln. Je ausführlicher du antwortest und je mehr du zum Gespräch beitragen kannst, desto mehr Punkte bekommst du! Wichtig ist auch, dass du deine Meinung darlegen und begründen kannst.

45

forty-five

SKILLS

READING – A magazine article

Why India matters – to you! by Nandila Das

OK, so you think that India is a country which is far away and has nothing to do with you? Well, sorry – you're wrong. If you're under 30 and interested in sport or films or if you'll soon be looking for a job, India will almost certainly be an important country for you.

1 Hard to believe? Then consider this: India has a population of over a billion people. More importantly, it has a growing wealthy middle class of 350 million people. That's an enormous number of people and in the next few years they're going to buy themselves cars, watch films and buy tickets for sports events. That will pump billions of dollars into the Indian motor industry, the Indian film industry and into sport in India. The result? India and Indians will become more and more important in all these areas.

2 The change has already begun. Years ago the world's biggest makers of steel were German, American or Japanese. Then, in 1976, an Indian businessman called Lakshmi Mittal founded a new steel business – and today Mr Mittal's business is easily the world's biggest steel company with steel plants in Asia, Europe, America and Africa. His company is building two new huge steel-making plants in India and Mr Mittal himself is the richest person in Asia and the fourth richest person in the world. Oh, and by the way: Mr Mittal's company is not alone – the world's sixth largest steel-making company, *Tata Steel*, is Indian too.

3 Never heard of *Tata*? Well, perhaps you've heard of *Jaguar* cars and *Land Rovers*, and perhaps you thought they were British companies – wrong again. They used to be British, it's true, but now they belong to *Tata*, India's second biggest company. And *Tata* has big plans. It makes the *Nano* which costs 1540 euros in India and is one of the world's cheapest cars. The price of a *Nano* will be very attractive in other countries too – who knows, perhaps *your* first car will be built in India?

4 India's influence is growing in the world of entertainment too. In the past Bollywood films were not successful outside Asia. But that's changing fast. A Hindi film is now often in the Top Ten of films in Britain. In Germany, Stuttgart's festival of Indian films gets more visitors every year and in 2008 Bollywood's biggest star, Shah Rukh Khan, took his show on a successful tour of Berlin, Munich and Frankfurt. Bollywood films are now shown on German TV and more and more Germans like the emotions, the exotic locations, the dances, the singing and the happy endings in Indian films.

5 Something else happened in 2008: for the first time an Indian company tried to buy a Hollywood studio – *Culver Studios*, the studio where famous films like *Gone with the Wind*, *Extra Terrestrial*, *What Women Want* and *Stuart Little* were made. Is this perhaps the start of a new trend? Will Bollywood's influence on Hollywood grow?

6 And what about sport? OK, India only won one gold medal at the Olympic Games in 2008 (its first in 28 years) and its football team has never played in the World Cup. True – but consider the Commonwealth Games and that India's first Formula One Grand Prix race could take place in the next few years ... No doubt about it, from now on India will play a bigger role in world sport.

7 Actually India already plays a big role in an international sport which you've probably not considered – cricket. It's the only world sport not dominated by Europe. In football, foreign players want to play in European clubs; in cricket, it's the other way round: British cricket players want to play in India because they can earn more money there. Salaries are higher in India because 350 million wealthy middle class Indians can pump money into the game. Incredibly, 80% of all the money in world cricket comes from India.

8 OK, you're not interested in cricket – but wait a moment. What has already happened in cricket could happen in other sports too. Wealthy Indians have already started to buy European football clubs, for example, Mr Mittal owns 20% of London's *Queen's Park Rangers* football club. What if European football players start playing in India? How will you feel if your favourite football player stops playing in Bavaria and goes to play in India instead?

So what do you think: is India perhaps more important than you thought?

SKILLS

1 Find a title for each paragraph 1–8.
Example: Paragraph 1: **E**

- A A country with low unemployment
- B Indian influence is growing in the USA.
- C Indian culture is spreading in Europe.
- D India – important in world sport?
- E A large population = a greater influence
- F A sport where India is king
- G An Indian company with an exciting project
- H A successful Indian businessman
- I How Bollywood began
- J A possible future for sport

2 Questions on the text: Answer in full sentences.
1. How many people live in India?
2. What has changed in the world order of steel-making companies in the last few years?
3. Why is the *Nano* a special car?
4. How is the influence of the Indian film industry changing in the world?
5. Why is India important in world cricket?

Tipp Antworte so ausführlich wie möglich – manchmal gibt es mehr als eine Begründung.

3 India's influence in the world

a) Translate the following two sentences into German.
1. So you think that India is a country which is far away and has nothing to do with you? *(line 1)*
2. What has already happened in cricket could happen in other sports too. *(line 93–95)*

b) Choose one topic (industry, films or sport) and then write a few sentences about it.
1. Describe India's influence on your topic according to the text.
2. What's your own experience? Do you agree with the text? Why (not)?
   Example: I agree / don't think that India has a big influence in … because …

4 Explain the six verbs in complete sentences. You can use a dictionary.

1. believe *(line 4)*
2. consider *(line 4)*
3. found *(line 21)*
4. grow *(line 67)*
5. dominate *(line 81)*
6. own *(line 97)*

Tipp Bei Verben kannst du deine Definition oft mit *When you* einleiten, z.B.: *When you believe something, you think it's true.*

5 And you?
If you've seen a Bollywood film: Did you like it? Why (not)?
If you haven't: Do you think that you would like to see one? Why (not)?
Look at the texts and photos on pages 42, 46 and 47 and then write a few sentences.
Useful words:

colours • songs • dancing scenes • happy endings • emotions

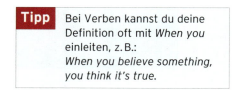

▶ W 6–9

Unit 3

📖 LISTENING – Indian culture in Britain

2 ⦿ 10, 11

India was a British colony for many years – and today Indian culture has a big influence in Britain.

1 Indian food is very popular in Britain. You can buy it in supermarkets, but many people buy it as take-away food in Indian restaurants. There are over 8000 Indian restaurants in Britain and the most popular Indian meal, chicken tikka masala, is now more popular than fish and chips.

a) Listen and match each food on the menu with a picture.

1 Dahi
2 Gosht
3 Kofta
4 Aloo
5 Sabzi
6 Mithai
7 Kulfi
8 Lassi

b) Now listen again and take notes on how the following foods are sometimes used.
1 yoghurt *(two uses)*   2 potatoes   3 carrots

2 Gurinder Chadha is a British film director of Indian origin. One of her most famous films was *Bend it like Beckham*. Listen to an interview about Gurinder and answer the questions.
1 Gurinder Chadha was born in   a) Britain.   b) India.   c) Africa.
2 Southall is a suburb of   a) London.   b) Mumbai.   c) Nairobi.
3 Gurinder's parents wanted her to learn Indian dance routines and
   a) play Indian music.   b) speak Indian languages.
   c) cook Indian food.
4 In the film *Bend it like Beckham* Jess Bhamra wants to
   a) visit India.   b) play football.   c) go to a disco.
5 Gurinder's husband is half American and half
   a) British.   b) Indian.   c) Japanese.

▶ W 10, 11

SKILLS

MEDIATION – Information about Mohandas Gandhi

Mohandas Gandhi

» You can use a dictionary to find the meaning of new words.

Mohandas Gandhi, one of the most important leaders of the twentieth century, was born when India was a British colony. Gandhi was known as 'Mahatma' ('Great Soul'). He led his country to independence and his policy of non-violence inspired later leaders such as Martin Luther King and Nelson Mandela.

When Gandhi joined a group of Indians who were fighting for independence in 1915, the British army was using more and more violence in India. In the worst massacre about a thousand Indians were killed and two thousand were injured at Amritsar in 1919. Many Indians replied with violence, but Gandhi insisted that non-violence would be more effective. For example, in order to protest against the tax on salt which even poor Indians had to pay, Gandhi organised a march of several hundred people to the sea. There they made salt from sea water. The British put Gandhi in prison – but the publicity of the march persuaded many people (both Indian and British) that the British were losing control of their colony.

Gandhi wanted one independent country with equal rights for people of all religions, but many Muslims wanted their own country. So when independence came in 1947, two independent countries were born: India (majority Hindu) and Pakistan (a Muslim country). Soon afterwards Muslims and Hindus fought each other in both countries. Thousands of people were killed, millions had to leave their homes.

Could one man stop all this violence? Gandhi tried. On January 18th, 1948, at the age of 78, he stopped eating. He said he would not eat again till all the fighting stopped. And amazingly five days later there was peace. It was perhaps Gandhi's greatest victory. But he paid for it – on January 30th a Hindu extremist who wanted violence shot Gandhi and killed him.

Tipps
- Du brauchst die Informationen im Text nicht Wort für Wort zu übersetzen.
- Teile dir die zur Verfügung stehende Zeit gut ein.

---

1 Du hast im Internet diesen Text über Mohandas Gandhi gefunden.
Erkläre auf Deutsch, ...

1 warum Gandhi eine der bedeutendsten Persönlichkeiten des 20. Jahrhunderts ist.
2 warum die Situation in Indien nach 1915 von Gewalt geprägt war.
3 warum Gandhi 1930 den Salzmarsch organisierte und welche Wirkung er bei Briten und Indern hatte.
4 warum aus der britischen Kolonie Indien nicht ein Land, sondern zwei Länder gebildet wurden.
5 warum Gandhi 1948 in einen Hungerstreik ging und was er damit erreichte.
6 wie Gandhi starb.

▶ W 12

Unit 3

WRITING – A keyword story

1 **A writing competition: Can you win a free holiday to India?**
The Indian tourist office has a writing competition – the person who writes the best story will win a free holiday to India.

a) Choose at least six words and then write a story which includes them.

- travel
- colourful
- taste
- laugh
- spectacular
- surprise
- meet
- accident
- fortunately
- break

- Write at least 120 words.
- Give your story a good title.

Tipps
- Dir fällt zu den vorgegebenen Wörtern keine interessante Geschichte ein? Vielleicht hast du selbst schon einmal etwas erlebt, was du hier erzählen könntest? Oder du lässt dich von einer Geschichte oder einem Film inspirieren!
- Baue deine Geschichte sinnvoll auf und achte darauf, dass sie eine Einleitung, einen Hauptteil und einen Schluss hat.
- Erzähle die Geschichte in der Vergangenheit.
- Achte darauf, die Schlüsselwörter möglichst gleichmäßig auf die Geschichte zu verteilen.
- Es ist oft einfacher, zuerst die Geschichte zu schreiben und erst danach einen passenden Titel zu suchen.

b) OK, you've written your story. Can you now improve some sentences? First look at these examples.

We walked along the road back to our campsite. *1	*1 Hier könntest du noch eine Zeitangabe ergänzen, z. B.: *in the evening, three hours later* oder *when we had said goodbye*.
It was a long, long way. *2	*2 Beschreibe auch wie die Personen sich fühlen, z. B.: *We felt very tired*.
It was night. It wasn't cold. *3 But it was dark.	*3 Verbinde die ersten beiden Sätze mit *although*.
Tim's foot hit something – he couldn't see it. *4	*4 Kannst du daraus einen Relativsatz machen?
Tim fell. *5 He lay on the road.	*5 Adverbien machen die Erzählung lebendiger, z. B. *Tim fell heavily*.
A boy came to us. *6	*6 *Suddenly* würde die Spannung erhöhen.
He saw Tim. He said, "I can help you." *7	*7 Verbinde die beiden Sätze, z. B. mit *when*.

c) Now work with a partner. Can you improve your partner's sentences and can your partner improve yours? Think of the examples above.

▶ W 13, 14

LOOK AT LANGUAGE

STRUCTURES

What's life like for young people in India?
At the weekend a conference in Kolkata discussed "What's life like for young people in India?"

Here's what some people at the conference said: And here's a report about the conference:

Kala

Families **are** very important. Young people **are born** into large families and everywhere they **go**, they **find** a relative who **helps** them.

Kala said that families **were** very important. She explained that young people **were born** into large families and said that everywhere they **went**, they **found** a relative who **helped** them.

1 Read what Dinkar said. Can you complete the report?
» The conference report about Kala at the top of this page will help you to find the right form of the verbs!

Dinkar

About 40% of the population **earn** less than $1.25 a day. Young people in these families **have** to work hard. Some of them **work** in sweatshops.

Dinkar explained that about 40% of the population ... less than $1.25 a day. He added that young people ... to work hard. And he said that some of them ... in sweatshops.

Uttam

I have relatives who **are living** in Britain. **I visit my** relatives once a year.

Uttam told the conference that **he had** relatives who **were living** in Britain. He added that **he visited his** relatives once a year.

2 Now read the report. Can you write what Neela actually said?
» You have to change the verbs and the pronouns! The conference report about Uttam will help you.

Neela

I text ... friends when ... ... to tell them something. All ... friends ... computers and mobile phones and they ... to music on their MP3 players.

Neela said that **she texted her** friends when **she wanted** to tell them something. She added that all **her** friends **had** computers and mobile phones and said that they **listened** to music on their MP3 players.

CHECKPOINT
Mit der indirekten Rede *(reported speech)* berichtest du, was jemand gesagt hat.
Meist wird das Gesagte durch *say, tell* oder ein ähnliches Verb eingeleitet.
Beispiel: Uttam said, "**I have** relatives who **are living** in Britain."
Uttam said that **he had** relatives who **were living** in Britain.

Unit 3

When I left my family's village and found a job in Kolkata, the contrast was enormous. It wasn't easy and I often felt lonely.

I know many young people who have left their families. They have tried to find work in a big city, but many have been unsuccessful.

Ela reported that when she had left her family's village and had found a job in Kolkata the contrast had been enormous. She insisted that it hadn't been easy and complained that she had often felt lonely.
Ela added that she knew many young people who had left their families. She explained that they had tried to find work in a big city, but she thought that many had been unsuccessful.

3 What did Ela say?
Replace "said" with another verb and put the verb in brackets in the right tense.

Ela said that when she (leave) her family's village and (find) a job in Kolkata the contrast (be) enormous. She said that it (be/not) easy, and said that she (often/feel) lonely. Ela said that she (know) many young people who (leave) their families. She said that they (try) to find work in a big city but she said that many of them (be) unsuccessful.
Ela reported that when she ...

| Tipp | Die ständige Wiederholung von *said* klingt langweilig – versuche deshalb *said* durch andere Verben zu ersetzen, z. B. *added, explained, reported, insisted, complained* oder *told*. |

Next year my family will move into a new house. We'll have running water and electricity, and I hope that each member of the family will have more room.

Lalit said that his family would move into a new house next year. He added that they would have running water and electricity, and he hoped that each member of the family would have more room.

4 Finish the checkpoint.

CHECKPOINT

Die indirekte Rede *(reported speech)* wird oft durch ein Verb im *simple past* eingeleitet (z. B. *said, told, explained*). Das Gesagte wird gegenüber der direkten Rede *(direct speech)* meist um eine Zeitstufe in die Vergangenheit „zurückverschoben".

direct speech | | reported speech
1 simple present: Kala: "They **find** ..." → simple past: Kala said that they **found** ...
2 simple past: Ela: "I **left** my village ..." → ...: Ela reported that she ...
3 present perfect: Ela: "They **have tried** ..." → ...: Ela added that they ...
4 will: Lalit: "We **will have** ..." → ...: Lalit hoped that they ...

▶ W 15–17

LOOK AT LANGUAGE

WORDPOWER

» Achtung: Kein Wörterbuch erlaubt (wie in der Prüfung)!

1 A country of contrasts
Use the right prepositions.

→ against • for (2x) • from • in (2x) • of • on (2x) • to

"When I think ... India I see a land of contrasts. While a majority suffers ... poverty and disease, many millions spend their money ... the latest gadgets. ... the country poor farmers have to wait ... the right weather conditions and depend ... each other for help, while in modern city centres the rich can apply ... well-paid jobs and look forward ... successful careers. At the same time some families and communities are very traditional, while other people believe ... equal rights for men and women and fight ... injustice."

2 Explain what these people do.
1 Students are people who go to ...
2 Fishermen are people who ...
3 Actors are people ...
4 Farmers ...
5 Artists ...
6 Thieves ...

3 Sounds

a) Do the three words rhyme – yes or no?

1 height, sight, kite
2 draw, war, sure
3 peace, kiss, piece
4 coast, ghost, cost
5 head, said, led
6 would, wood, flood
7 near, hear, here
8 road, loud, crowd
9 hour, shower, your
10 aunt, plant, can't
11 steak, speak, make
12 word, third, heard

b) Now listen and check your answers. Were you right?

4 Explain the blue words or phrases in English.
1 Kareena Kapoor was born in 1980 into a family of actors and is now one of *the wealthiest celebrities in Bollywood*. *This means that Kareena is one of the ... in ...*
2 She has acted in several *box-office hits*.
3 She has won lots of *awards*.
4 *Her dress style is perfect.*
5 She *was educated* in Mumbai and Dehradun.

Unit 3

REVISION

» If you need help on this page, look at the *Summary Pages* (92–101).

1 Use the right forms of the adjectives and the adverbs.
1 Driving in India is (exciting) than in Germany.
2 Some of the cars on the roads are (incredible) (old).
3 Others are some of (modern) cars in the world.
4 Luckily most drivers drive (safe) and (good).
5 But there are some (crazy) drivers too, of course.
6 And traffic isn't (organised) as in Germany.

2 *Simple past* or *past perfect*?

Hi! We (move) to Mumbai three years ago after I (live) all my life in a village. At first I (find) life in the city very difficult. Before we (come) to Mumbai, my school (be) near our house. In my first year in Mumbai, I (have) to go to school by bus. But luckily I quickly (make) new friends and my friends soon (say) that I (become) a true *Mumbaikar* – a person who is from Mumbai.

3 Connect the sentences with the right word.
Project Tiger was founded (in order to / so that) help tigers in India. Tigers were almost extinct (although/ because) people needed more and more land. *Project Tiger* has opened 27 tiger reserves (since/for) it began in 1973. The tigers (which/who) live in reserves are protected. Their number has grown to 4000 (while/during) the project has existed – and the project now wants to open more reserves (so that / for) the tiger population can grow even bigger.

▶ W 18–20

4 Quick check

a) **India**
1 Explain these words: **a)** monsoon **b)** sweatshop **c)** Bollywood **d)** Taj Mahal
2 Why is India's influence growing in the world? Give two examples.
3 India is a country of contrasts. Give some examples.

b) **Complete the sentences: Use *reported speech*.**
1 "My parents have chosen a wife for me," explained Lalit.
   Lalit explained that …
2 "We have already met several times," he said.
   He said that …
3 "I hope we'll be happy together," he added.
   He added that …

EXTRA PAGES

A SHORT STORY

Nightmare

by Indian author Meenal Dave

» Use a dictionary to find the meaning of new words.

[...] My boss, Mrs Rao, is really the limit! She has to give me this assignment at the very last minute, just when it's time to leave! [...] And if I miss my train, I have to wait at the station for a good hour, and then ride in the train for another two [...] – and what's more, probably in an empty compartment [...]

Hurry up, please! [...] Good God, did this light have to turn red now? [...] All these people coming out of the station, but, please, would you make way for those who have trains to catch? And then, these railway people, they're just too much. Trust them to put the staircase right at the end of this long platform, and my train is from Platform 4 and about to leave. Let me run ... just the last two steps and ... there! Damn. Missed it. [...]

The man selling tea says, "Now you'll have to wait for an hour." Why's he looking at me like that? And now there's not a single passenger on the platform [...] The smell of fear [...] hangs in the air. Even when the man selling tea looks at me, I'm afraid, who knows, he might throw his tea things at me [...] I'm thirsty. Where's that bottle of water – I think I put it in my bag ... oh, there it is, but it's empty!

Maybe I should call home [...] and also pick up some water. And a magazine. Vikram answers the phone. He's upset that I haven't made the first train [...] I pick up two magazines and settle down on a bench.

The platform is deserted. Cooking fires are being put out at tea stalls. [...] Bottles of [...] drink have been returned to their crates. The lame boy who polishes shoes is peacefully asleep. [...] But the dog near my bench is restless. He [...] stands, looks around, pricks up his ears and seems to be listening. [...] There are two dogs fighting on the platform across. Is he frightened of them?

I notice that there is a woman sitting next to me now. She wears a thick black burkha, only her hands are visible. And she carries a large cloth bag. [...]

So many benches free on the platform, why did she have to come and sit next to me? What does she have in mind? Is she carrying a bomb in that bag of hers? What if she leaves the bag here and walks away and the bomb goes off, what will happen to me? That would be the end of my poor husband and children. No, let me not think that will happen. Poor thing, she's just sitting quietly there. But does that mean she's harmless? Should I move away? Go elsewhere? [...] My fingers are clutching my handbag [...]

The food seller descends like a saviour. [...] "You're late, [...] the first train has left. [...] Why are you sitting here? [...] At such times you shouldn't be sitting here." [...]

EXTRA PAGES

He's right. I should get up from here. You never know what she might do, this woman. She could pull a knife out of that
70 bag and stab me and no one would know anything. Look at her hands, how big and masculine they are. Is there a criminal hiding behind that burkha? How do I get up? Why did I have to decide to travel at
75 this time? [...] Should she try anything, I will tell her, listen woman, take what you want but don't kill me. [...] My hands are frozen. The moment I see someone coming, I'll get up. I search around the
80 platform, [...] moving my eyes this way and that. Not a soul now. Where have all the people gone?

It seems like it was only yesterday that this platform buzzed with life – trains coming
85 and going all the time, people rushing from here to there, difficult to find a spot to stand. And the ladies' compartment in which I travel every day – at every station women pour into it, and some get off. [...]
90 Then once they have found somewhere to sit, handbags and baskets are opened and out come beans, peas, garlic [...] But where are all these faces today? [...] How can I get away from here? [...]

The train's late. I didn't even notice its 95
arrival. Okay, now straight into the ladies' compartment. Oh dear, the burkha-clad woman is climbing in after me.
Why doesn't she leave me alone? The compartment's virtually empty – barely 100
two or three women. A fisherwoman fast asleep with her empty basket lying next to her. It's stinking, but never mind, at least there's another human being in here.
And that other woman is sitting facing me. 105

It is dark and black outside just like the burkha she's wearing [...] What shall I do? I shut my eyes, hoping the darkness will go away. [...] What must she be doing now? People say that you can't trust them. You never know when they might draw a knife. I remember a classmate called Hasina from college. Her brother stabbed his wife. I couldn't help wondering if this woman might also do that.

Oh God, someone's shaking me. I open my eyes – it's the woman in the burkha! Oh no, what will she do to me? Should I shout for help? The fisherwoman is fast asleep. So she won't know if I get killed. Should I jump off the moving train? Oh God, please, please come to my rescue! I promise never to get onto this train again. I'll even give up my job [...] Better to starve than to suffer this nightmare!

"[...] Sister," the burkha woman is calling me, "I'm getting off here. I'm so grateful that you were around, imagine travelling alone at such a time. I was so scared ... you know ... so difficult ..." I can't believe it! She's frightened like me! I burst out laughing! [...]

She places her hand on mine and says [...] *May God be with you.* [...] The train stops. I help her with her bag, which suddenly seems light and harmless. She melts away in the faint light of the station. The fisherwoman yawns. [...] The stars begin to shine in the dark and show me the way home.

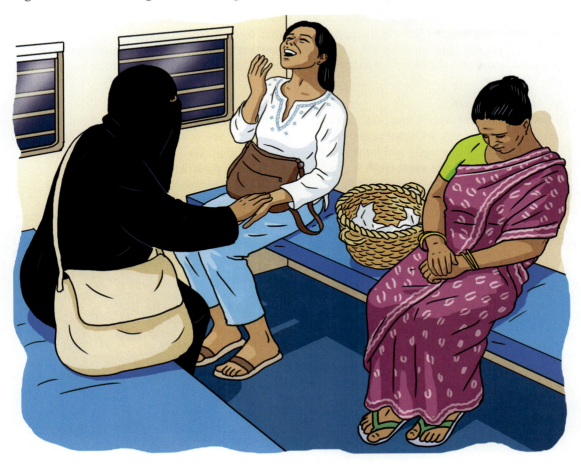

Unit 4

Young adults

In this Internet forum teenagers are discussing how young people in Britain feel about their lives.

#1 Selma, Germany (6.15 p.m.)
According to an international report, conditions are bad for young people in Britain. Compared with other European countries, the UK apparently has the most young people who live in poverty, the highest number of teenage girls who have babies and the worst problems with
5 alcohol. So I wonder: what's it like being a young person in Britain today?

#2 Loren (6.45 p.m.)
Hi, Selma! I live in Leeds, I've just had my 17th birthday and no – I'm not pregnant, I don't get drunk every weekend and I don't always have rows with my parents and teachers. I have good friends. Of course we argue sometimes, but we get on pretty well and when one of us has a
10 birthday, we go to a concert together or have a meal together in a restaurant or pizzeria.
Life for young people like me is pretty good – but I know I'm lucky: I live in a nice part of Leeds. If I lived in an area with crime, unemployment and poverty, life would be much more difficult.

#3 Kevin (7.30 p.m.)
Well said, Loren! If you believed the media, you would think all young people in Britain carry
15 knives and mug people. Actually the number of crimes committed by young people is lower now than ten years ago, and ten times more young people do all kinds of voluntary work than commit a crime. Instead of only reporting the bad news, the media should report the good news for once!

#4 Jake (8.30 p.m.)
20 If we young people were under less stress, we wouldn't drink so much alcohol! At school we have too many exams. At home parents don't have time for their children. Older people say that we're addicted to designer clothes and the media are prejudiced against us and portray us as chavs: stupid and aggressive. And we can't travel, take the driving test or just go out in the evening unless we have a job because everything is so expensive. Then there are
25 problems like falling ill, parents splitting up or the end of a relationship with a boyfriend or girlfriend … It can all be too much.

1 Young people in Britain

a) Who says that ...
1. many young people help other people and are not paid for this work? *Kevin*
2. your life is probably good if the area where you live is good? *Loren*
3. many things that young people want to do cost too much? *Jack*

b) Now find the phrases which mean:
1. a woman's condition when she's going to have a baby — *pregnant*
2. drink too much alcohol — *drunk*
3. hurt people and steal their money — *criminal*
4. all sorts of work which isn't paid — *voluntary work*
5. silly and aggressive young people

2 An interview: Teenage mothers

Listen and answer the questions.
1. How many babies are there for every 1000 girls in the United Kingdom? *27 babys*
2. And what's the number in Germany? *13 babys*
3. How has the number of babies changed in the last 30 years in the United Kingdom? *fallen, half*
4. What are often problems for the teenage mothers? *mother leat school, un well paid, unhealthy*
5. What are problems for the children of teenage mothers? *more disatvantage, provety, no father, school problems*

3 Comparing the lives of young people in different countries

**a) Look at the information from an international report.
Then write four sentences about it.**

Young people (aged 11, 13 and 15) who say that they have got drunk twice or more in their life:	
Germany	17.7 %
France	8 %
UK	30.8 %

Young people who eat at a table with one or two parents several times a week:	
Germany	81.5 %
France	90.4 %
UK	66.7 %

Example: The number of young people in ... who ... is higher/lower than in ...

**b) The international report looked at other aspects of young adults' lives.
How important do *you* think they are?**

Young people who ...
- live with only one parent.
- feel that they are outsiders.
- live in families which are poor.
- have one parent who is unemployed.
- have taken cannabis in the last 12 months.
- have been in a fight in the last 12 months.

1. Rank the aspects from A to F (A = most important, F = least important).
2. Look at A and B in your list and explain why you think these aspects are important.
3. Compare your results with a partner and then in class.

▶ W 1–3

→ SKILLS

SPEAKING – Talking about driving lessons

1 Learning to drive

What's different in Britain and Germany – and what's the same?
Loren, who lives in Leeds, tells Elias from Germany about her driving test.

LOREN I'm taking my driving test next week. Wish me luck!

ELIAS Taking your driving test? But I thought you were only 17?

LOREN Yes, I am. But you can drive a car in Britain if you're 17.

ELIAS Oh, right. And are the driving lessons expensive?

LOREN Well, they cost about £20 per lesson. But what's much worse is the car insurance after you've passed your test. If you're under 21, it can cost £2300 a year – even if you drive your parents' car and it's a pretty small one.

ELIAS Have you had some lessons at night?

LOREN No, we don't usually do that here. And we never have any lessons on the motorway either.

ELIAS And how are you feeling about the test? Are you confident?

LOREN Hm, I'm a bit nervous – but it's no use being frightened, is it? I'm really looking forward to being able to drive. I'll feel more independent as soon as I can drive!

ELIAS Well, good luck! I'll cross my fingers for you!

2 Find these expressions in the text. (They're not in the same order!)

1 die Autoversicherung   **2** auf der Autobahn   **3** ein ziemlich kleines
4 nachdem du deine Fahrprüfung bestanden hast   **5** Ich drücke dir die Daumen.
6 Fahrstunden   **7** zuversichtlich   **8** sogar wenn du das Auto deiner Eltern fährst

3 Partner work: And you? Answer your partner's questions.

PARTNER A Are you looking forward to learning to drive?

PARTNER B *I'm not sure. On the one hand I'm a bit frightened, but on the other hand ...*

PARTNER A Are lessons and car insurance expensive in Germany?

PARTNER B ...

PARTNER A Are you going to learn to drive when you're 17 or 18?

PARTNER B ...

Now partner B asks the questions and partner A answers.

4 More partner work: Now work with two partners.
Lena from Germany has met Ben from Cardiff. She wants to ask him some questions.

a) Partners B and C: Look at page 89 and read Lena and Ben's dialogue.
Partner A: Listen to Lena and Ben and interpret for them.

b) Now change roles. Partners A and C read the dialogue on page 89, partner B interprets.

c) Change roles again. Partners A and B read the dialogue on page 89, partner C interprets.

► W 4

Unit 4

SPEAKING – Picture-based conversation

1 Party time

a) Look at picture A and describe it.

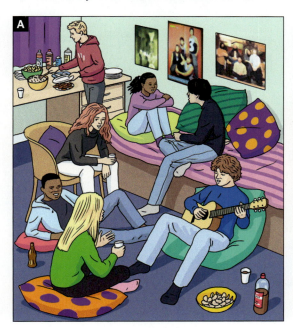 

> **Tips**
> 1 Describe the scene: say where the young people are and what they're doing.
>   Use the *present progressive* as you're describing a scene, e.g. some of them *are lying* lazily, some *are singing*, some *are chatting* ...
> 2 Describe the atmosphere and some of the people: use adjectives and adverbs.

b) Now describe picture B and compare the two pictures.

Examples:
In picture B the people ...   In picture A, on the other hand, the people ...
In picture B the atmosphere ... while in picture A the atmosphere ...
In picture B the people are wearing ...   In picture A, in contrast, the people are wearing ...
The picture on the right shows ... whereas the other one ...

c) Give your opinions.

Examples:
The party in picture A is perhaps / is probably / could be a birthday party.
I prefer parties like the one in picture A because ...
However, I sometimes like more formal meals like the one in picture B, especially if ...

d) Compare both scenes with your own experiences.

Examples:
The first picture reminds me of a party which I had ...
When I look at the second picture, I think of a meal which I had ...

▶ W 5

sixty-three

SKILLS

READING – A story

About a boy

Nick Hornby's "About a boy" is a best-selling book and has been made into a film.
Here, at the beginning of the book, we meet Marcus, a teenager who lives with his mother.
They have just moved from Cambridge to London.

"Have you split up now?"
"Are you being funny?"
People quite often thought Marcus was being funny when he wasn't. He couldn't understand it. Asking his mum whether she'd split up with Roger was a perfectly sensible question, he thought: they'd had a big row, then they'd gone off into the kitchen to talk quietly, and after a little while they'd come out looking serious, and Roger had come over to him, shaken his hand and wished him luck at his new school, and then he'd gone. [...]
"It looks to me like you've split up. But I just wanted to make sure."
"We've split up."
"So he's gone?"
"Yes, Marcus, he's gone."

He didn't think he'd ever get used to this business. He had quite liked Roger, and the three of them had been out a few times; now, apparently, he'd never see him again. He didn't mind, but it was weird if you thought about it. He'd once shared a toilet with Roger. [...] You'd think that if you'd peed with someone you ought to keep in touch with them somehow.
"What about his pizza?" They'd just ordered three pizzas when the argument started, and they hadn't arrived yet.
"We'll share it. If we're hungry."
"[...] Didn't he order one with pepperoni on it?"
Marcus and his mother were vegetarians. Roger wasn't.
"Well, throw it away then," she said.
"Or we could pick the pepperoni off. I don't think they give you much of it anyway. It's mostly cheese and tomato."
"Marcus, I'm not really thinking about the pizzas right now."
"OK. Sorry. Why did you split up?"
"Oh, this and that. I don't really know how to explain it."
Marcus wasn't surprised that she couldn't explain what had happened. He'd heard more or less the whole argument, and he hadn't understood a word of it; there seemed to be a piece missing somewhere. When Marcus and his mum argued, you could hear the important bits:

40 too much, too expensive, too late, too young, bad for your teeth, the other channel, homework, fruit. But when his mum and her boyfriends argued, you could listen for hours and still miss the point. [...]
"Did he have another girlfriend?"
"I don't think so."
45 "Have you got another boyfriend?"
She laughed. [...]
"No, Marcus, I haven't got another boyfriend. [...] Do you mind me having boyfriends?" [...]
"No. Course not."
"You've been really good about everything. Considering you've had two different sort of
50 lives."

He understood what she meant. The first sort of life had ended four years ago, when he was eight and his mum and dad had split up: that was the normal, boring kind, with school and holidays and homework and weekend visits to grandparents. The second sort was messier, and there were more people and places in it: his mother's boyfriends and his
55 dad's girlfriends; flats and houses; Cambridge and London. You wouldn't believe that so much could change just because a relationship ended, but he wasn't bothered. Sometimes he even thought he preferred the second sort of life to the first sort. More happened, and that had to be a good thing.

Apart from Roger, not much had happened in London yet. They'd only been here for a few
60 weeks – they'd moved on the first day of the summer holidays – and so far it had been pretty boring. He had been to see two films with his mum, *Home Alone 2*, which wasn't as good as *Home Alone 1*. [...] And they'd been to have a look at his school, which was big and horrible. [...]

The pizzas arrived and they ate them straight out of the boxes.

65 "They're better than the ones we had in Cambridge, aren't they?" Marcus said cheerfully. It wasn't true: it was the same pizza company, but in Cambridge the pizzas hadn't had to travel so far, so they weren't quite as soggy. It was just that he thought he ought to say something optimistic.
70 "Shall we watch TV?"
"If you want."

He found the remote control down the back of the sofa and zapped through the channels. He didn't want to watch any of the soaps, because soaps were full of
75 trouble, and he was worried that the trouble would remind his mum of the trouble she had in her own life. So they watched a nature programme. [...]

If you want to know how the story goes on, read the book or watch the film!

SKILLS

1 Answer the questions in full sentences.
1 Who's Roger?
2 What did Roger and Marcus's mother do just after they argued with each other?
3 Why didn't Marcus and his mother want to eat Roger's pizza?
4 When did Marcus and his mother come to London?
5 How do we know that Marcus didn't like his new school?

2 What do you think: Why isn't Marcus's mother very interested in talking about pizzas?

3 Marcus tries to help his mother because she's sad.
Explain how he does this …
1 when they eat their pizzas.
2 when they watch TV.

4 Explain the following phrases in English.
You can use a dictionary.
1 a little while *(line 13)* – *a short time*
2 We've split up. *(line 17)*
3 had been out a few times *(line 21)*
4 Do you mind …? *(line 47)*
5 zapped through the channels *(line 73)*

5 Explain in German …

a) how the arguments between Marcus and his mother are different from the arguments between Marcus's mother and her boyfriends.

b) why Marcus has had "two different sorts of lives" and what they're like.

6 Arguments with parents

a) Look at lines 40–41 *(too much … fruit)*.
Then write what you think Marcus's mother said when they argued.
Write eight sentences and use your own ideas.
Examples:
1 too much: "You eat too much chocolate, Marcus! It's not good for you."
2 too expensive: "You want to buy this phone? You must be crazy, Marcus! It's much …!"
3 too late: "You go to bed …, Marcus! …"
4 …   5 …   6 …   7 …   8 …

b) What do you argue about with your parents? Write 5–6 sentences.

- We sometimes argue about …, especially if …
- My parents and I argue if I …
- They often argue with me when …

Unit 4

🎧 LISTENING – Two audio messages

2 🔊 27, 28   Your school exchanges audio messages with young people in Britain.
In this month's messages two British teenagers complain about something.

1 Sarah talks about "hoodies".

a) Listen to Sarah. Which picture shows a hoody?

A

B

C

b) Listen again: True or false?
1 Sarah sometimes steals cars and mugs people.
2 She gets on well with her parents and teachers.
3 She wears a hoody because she wants to be warm.
4 The media says that young people wear hoodies
   so that the cameras in shops can't see their faces.
5 A big sports centre in London banned young people
   with hoodies in 2005.

c) What exactly is Sarah complaining about? Explain in German.

2 William talks about "mosquitoes".

a) Listen and answer the questions.
1 When did William first see a mosquito?
2 In what year was the first mosquito put up?
3 Outside what kind of places are mosquitoes used?
   Give two examples.
4 How many mosquitoes are there apparently in the UK?
5 In what country are gadgets like mosquitoes banned?

b) Listen again and take notes. Then explain:
1 What are mosquitoes and why are they used?
2 Why does William think that they're unfair?

3 Problems for young people in Bavaria

a) Discuss in class: Are hoodies or mosquitoes a problem in Bavaria?

b) Group work: Write an audio message for a school in Britain and describe the
problems that young people have in Bavaria.

▶ W 11, 12

sixty-seven

SKILLS

MEDIATION – An online book review

The confessions of Georgia Nicolson

» You can use a dictionary to find the meaning of new words.

The confessions of Georgia Nicolson by Louise Rennison is one of the most popular series of books among British teenage girls. The books are the very funny diaries of a girl who loves complaining about school, her parents, her cat and, especially, boys. In 2008 the first two books were made into a film by Gurinder Chadha, the director of *Bend it like Beckham*.

Here's an online review of the book:

"When I started reading this book I couldn't stop until I had read it all. Georgia is crazy. And no wonder! She has to look after a little sister, her parents don't understand her and she has a mad cat called *Angus*.

So many things in her life are embarrassing – like her uncle Eddie who thinks it's so cool to ride a motorbike even though it's ancient. Or her dad who thinks his lame jokes are so funny. It's not easy being a teenage girl in Britain – Georgia's diary will tell you that. You'll read how she uses false eyelashes in order to attract a guy who is several years older than her and how she almost destroys her eyebrows when she accidentally shaves them off. You'll certainly laugh louder than you've ever laughed before.

I can really recommend this book! It's hilarious and when you read it you'll realise that although you probably sometimes feel that you're an outsider, there are people in the world who are far weirder than you are. Author Louise Rennison is brilliant at capturing the feelings of teenage girls."

1 Erzähle deiner Freundin, die gerade im Internet ein „Georgia Nicolson"-Buch gesehen hat, was du über die Buchreihe weißt.

Erkläre auf Deutsch, ...

1. warum man sagen kann, dass die Buchreihe *The confessions of Georgia Nicolson* erfolgreich ist.
2. welche Georgias auffälligste Charaktereigenschaft ist und womit sie sich zu Hause auseinandersetzen muss.
3. welche Gefühle ihr Onkel Eddie und ihr Vater bei ihr auslösen und warum.
4. was du über die Sache mit den Wimpern und den Augenbrauen weißt.
5. warum das Buch besonders für Menschen, die sich als Außenseiter fühlen, empfehlenswert ist.
6. was der Autorin besonders gut gelingt.

► W 13

68
sixty-eight

Unit 4

WRITING – Formal letters and emails

1 Why did Thomas write his letter and why did Rebecca write her email?

35 Maxwell Avenue
Liverpool
L26 1XY
June 24th, 2009

Dear Sir or Madam,
I saw your advert for a job in your "After School Club" and I would like to apply for the job.
I'm 17 years old and I go to Faxford School. I could work in the afternoon twice a week.
I've helped younger pupils in my school's "Be a friend" scheme.
I enjoyed it and Mr Timms, the teacher who organised the scheme, would be happy to be my referee.
Please let me know how much you pay.
I'm looking forward to hearing from you.

Yours faithfully,
Thomas Bailey

Dear Ms Cummings,

Thank you for your email of 23rd June. I'm glad that you have rooms available and I would like to book two double rooms for my parents, my sister and me for two nights. We'll arrive on Tuesday August 1st and we'll leave on Thursday August 3rd. We would like the evening meal on 1st August, half board on 2nd August and breakfast on 3rd August. Could you please tell me if we should pay a deposit? And could you tell me if the hotel has a car park?
Many thanks.

Best wishes,

Rebecca Harrison

2 How does ...
1. Thomas say who could recommend him for the job?
2. Thomas ask what he'll earn?
3. Rebecca say she's happy that there are some rooms free in the hotel?
4. Rebecca describe what rooms and meals she wants?
5. Rebecca ask if she should pay some money in advance?

3 Email the *George Hotel* in Eastbourne.
1. Book a double room and a single room from August 29th – September 1st; you want B&B only.
2. Your questions: cost? • deposit? • car park? • far to the sea?

4 You and your best friend decide to apply for this job.
Write a letter for both of you (at least 120 words).
1. Give information about yourselves, your experience and explain why you want the job.
2. Your questions: where's the camp? • when? • earn how much? • travel paid? • letter from parents necessary?

Youth camp near Munich
We need young people who can help us to look after children from all over the world!
• go with them on trips (Munich, mountains, etc.)
• help in the kitchens, clean the rooms, etc.
For more information please contact:
World Camps, 25 Barrett Way,
Woking GU23 6QZ

▶ W 14

LOOK AT LANGUAGE

STRUCTURES

Agony aunts

Some people write to agony aunts in magazines or on special websites when they have problems and need advice. And many people enjoy reading the letters, even if they don't have the same problems!

1 Two typical letters to an agony aunt

> I have a boyfriend (he's called Dan), but my parents don't know about him. They love me very much – but *if* I *tell* them about Dan, they*'ll say* that I'm too young (I'm 16). But *if* I *don't tell* them, Dan and I *will have to meet* secretly. What should I do? Please help me!
> Emma

Complete James's letter.   » Emma's letter can help you to find the right form of the verbs.

> My friend Jessica has taken cannabis for several months and now she wants to stop.
> But she needs help – and she doesn't know who she can talk to.
> If she (talk) with her parents, they (have) an awful row.
> But if she (not talk) with anybody, she (not stop) taking cannabis.
> I'd like to help her – what can I do?
> James

2 The agony aunt's answers to Emma and James

> Dear Emma,
> Of course you must tell your parents about your boyfriend. You never know – perhaps they won't be as surprised as you think! *If* they *say* you're too young, you *can tell* them that many sixteen-year-olds have boyfriends and girlfriends. But you *must talk* with them, even *if* they *argue* with you at first. It's your life – and not telling them now will only make things worse later. Good luck!

Now complete the agony aunt's answer to James's letter. Use your own ideas.

> Dear James,
> Thank you for your letter.
> If Jessica can't talk with her parents, perhaps she can talk with …
> And if you really want to help your friend, James, you should …

3 Read and complete the revision box.

REVISION

Mit *if*-Sätzen vom Typ I sagst du, was unter bestimmten Bedingungen geschehen wird. Der *if*-Satz steht im *simple present*, der Hauptsatz enthält eine Zukunftsform mit … oder ein modales Hilfsverb (z. B. *must*, … oder *should*).
Beispiele: If I **don't tell** them, we**'ll have to meet** secretly.
You **must talk** with them, even if they **argue** with you.

Unit 4

4 Read what Emma and James say.

Emma isn't happy with the advice which the agony aunt gave her.

> The agony aunt said that I should tell my parents about Dan. But she's wrong and if she were here, I would tell her so. If I told mum and dad about Dan, they would hit the roof. And if I invited him home, they wouldn't talk with me for days. It's not as easy as the agony aunt thinks!

Emma talking to a friend

But James has decided to talk with Jessica about her problem.

> If I were you, I would tell your parents about the cannabis, Jessica. OK, if you just say you're taking drugs, they'll be angry, but if you said that you wanted to stop taking cannabis, they would help you. They love you, don't they? I think that they would be disappointed if you didn't tell them.

James   Jessica

a) Find examples of *if*-sentences and copy them into the table.

if-Satz	Hauptsatz
If she were here,	I would tell her so.
If I ... mum and dad about Dan,	they ... hit the roof.
...	...

b) Answer the questions about Emma and Jessica. Begin your answers with "If ..."
1. What (according to Emma) would happen if she told her parents about Dan?
   If she told her parents about Dan, her parents ...
2. What would happen if she invited Dan home?   *If ...*
3. What would Jessica's parents do if she told them she wanted to stop taking cannabis?
4. How would they feel if their daughter didn't talk with them about her problem?

c) Now find three examples of *if*-sentences on page 60, one each for Loren, Kevin and Jake. Write the sentences in your table from Exercise 4a.

5 Read and complete the checkpoint. Finish the sentences.

CHECKPOINT

Mit Bedingungssätzen vom Typ II kannst du ausdrücken, was unter bestimmten Bedingungen passieren würde. Es ist jedoch ziemlich unwahrscheinlich, dass die Bedingung erfüllt wird.
Beispiele: If you **were** the queen/king of England, you **would live** in Buckingham Palace.
          If parents **listened** more to their children, life **would be** much easier.

Für solche Sätze gilt: • Der *if*-Satz steht in der ...
                          • Der Hauptsatz enthält ... und einen Infinitiv.

In folgenden Wendungen wird statt *was* im *if*-Satz des Typs II *were* gebraucht:
if I were you: an deiner Stelle (wenn ich du wäre)   **if he were here:** wenn er hier wäre

▶ W 15, 16

LOOK AT LANGUAGE

WORDPOWER

» Achtung: Kein Wörterbuch erlaubt (wie in der Prüfung)!

1 Which words or phrases don't belong in the groups – and why?

Dutch?

1	Poland	2	path	3	trousers
	Dutch		motorway		coat
	Belgium		street		biro
	Austria		road		shirt

4	shout	5	steal	6	weird
	discuss		mug		crazy
	have a row		kill		mad
	hit the roof		look after		sensible

1 *Dutch doesn't belong to group 1, because it's a nationality. The others are all countries.*
2 ...   3 ...   4 ...   5 ...   6 ...

2 Match each sound with two words from the green box. You won't need two of these words.

1 [ʊə]: ...   2 [uː]: ...   3 [ɜː]: ...   4 [ʌ]: ...

→ disease • double • flood • girl • insurance • poor • roof • several • turn • youth

3 Write the appropriate noun for each verb.

Example: 1 I *live* in Wimbledon, a suburb in the southwest of London.
It's a wealthy suburb and *life* isn't difficult there.

2 But last year I *stayed* with my cousins in Hackney.
I learned a lot during my ... in this poorer part of London.
3 In Hackney too many young men *choose* to join gangs.
They make this ... because they're bored, lonely or afraid.
4 The different gangs sometimes *argue* with each other.
And their ... sometimes lead to violence.
5 Once two gangs *fought* each other in a street not far from us.
One of my cousin's friends saw the ...
6 I think the people who *govern* the country should help people in Hackney.
In Hackney people feel that the ... doesn't do enough for them.

4 Use your own ideas and give examples of ...
1 voluntary work.
2 an illegal activity.
3 something really embarrassing.
4 something which you and your parents (or you and a friend) have rows about.

Example: 1 When you help old people or ... and earn nothing for your work.

Unit 4

REVISION

» If you need help on this page, look at the *Summary Pages* (92–101).

1 Young adults in Nigeria: Write the right form of the verbs.

Hi! My name's Lami – the name Lami (mean) that I am a female who (born) on a Thursday. I live and go to college in Lagos, Nigeria's largest city. I love it here. I (live) here for ten years – before that we (live) in Katsina, in the north of the country.

Till last year my mother (work) in a hospital here in Lagos, but she (lose) her job two months ago. At the moment she (help) in a centre which (look) after young women who (just arrive) in Lagos. Many of the girls in the centre (never be) in a big city before and some of them (not have) any money. In the centre they (learn) how to make clothes. If the centre didn't look after them, some of the girls (certainly live) in the streets. Some of the girls in the centre are now my best friends. One of them, Yetunde, who (be) in the centre for two years, (get married) next week and of course I (go) to her wedding. She (tell) me yesterday that she (be) very, very happy. And she (say) that the centre (change) her life.

2 Lami's college organises online discussions with Sarah's school in England. When the discussion is finished, Lami and Sarah sometimes chat together. Replace the words in blue with *yours, hers*, etc. (possessive pronouns without nouns).

LAMI   What's your mother like, Sarah? (My mother) is kind, but very strict.
       Is (your mother) very strict too?
SARAH Sometimes, especially when she's under stress from her work.
       She doesn't like her job.
LAMI   My mother likes (her job). But she doesn't earn much and that's hard because
       although my college is free, my brother goes to a different school and (his school)
       is expensive. Is your school free, Sarah?
SARAH Yes, (our school) is free. But I have two friends who go to a private school.
       (Their school) is very expensive. It costs about £14,000 a year.

▶ W 17–19

3 Quick check

a) Young people in Britain
1 Explain …
   a) chavs.   **b)** hoodies.   **c)** which social problems are especially bad in Britain.
2 Name two writers of books which are popular with teenagers in Britain.

b) Complete the sentences.
1 "If you buy the DVD in a shop," said Mark, "it (cost) £19.99."
2 "But if you bought it online," he added, "it (cost) much less."

73
seventy-three

Unit 5

One world

1 Pupils at Elgin School in Scotland discussed problems in the world.

What do you think are the biggest problems in the world? Work with a partner and write your ideas in a list:

Problems in the world
pollution
...

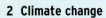

1 Global warming
Most scientists agree that global warming is happening because we're producing too many greenhouse gases, e.g. carbon dioxide. Because of global warming the ice in the Arctic Ocean is melting. If this continues, polar bears and other animals will be threatened with extinction.

2 Climate change
The Gulf Stream, which brings warm water across the Atlantic Ocean to Europe, is now 30% weaker than twelve years ago. If this continues, people in Europe will have to get used to colder winters.

3 Food shortage
As deserts expand people have less clean water and diseases spread. They can grow less food and so the price of food goes up. This hurts people in the poorest countries most because they spend up to 80% of their money on food (in Britain, for example, people spend only 15% of their money on food).

4 Deforestation
The Amazon rainforests are the world's "lungs" because they absorb carbon dioxide and release oxygen. But 13,000 square kilometres of forest (an area three-quarters of *Oberbayern*) are cut down each year. The land is then mostly used for farms – especially cattle farms.

2 Read the eight texts and answer the questions. Why ...
1 are the rainforests the world's "lungs"?
2 are China's deserts becoming bigger?
3 will Europe perhaps soon be colder in winter?
4 do wealthier countries have a larger carbon footprint than poorer ones?
5 is food becoming more expensive?
6 did Syria and Turkey almost have a war?
7 is the ice in the Arctic Ocean melting?
8 is the government of the Maldives looking for land in other countries?

5 Population explosion

The world's population is rising fast: India, for example, will probably have 200 million more people in 2020 than in 2000. However, a rich country with a smaller population often has a bigger carbon footprint. This means that it produces more carbon dioxide than a poorer country with a larger population because richer people have a lifestyle which uses more energy and produces more greenhouse gases.

6 Expanding deserts

China had 100 million sheep and cattle in 1960. It now has 400 million because more Chinese people are eating meat. All of the grass next to the Gobi desert has been eaten and this is one reason why the deserts are expanding. The Gobi desert is now 52,000 square kilometres bigger than in 1994 and the sand is now only 100 km from Beijing.

7 Water shortage

31 countries, mostly in Africa and the Middle East, suffered from water shortages in 2000 – by 2025 it will be 48 countries. When Turkey built dams on its rivers, it nearly had a war with Syria because the amount of water which passed through Syria was reduced.

8 Rising sea level

The Maldives is the lowest country in the world: its highest "hill" is 2.3 metres high. The sea level has risen 15 cm in the last 100 years; if it rises much more, the country could disappear. The government is saving money in order to buy land in a larger country where its people could live if they had to leave the Maldives.

3 On her way home from Elgin School, Ruby is telling her friend Oliver about a TV programme which she has seen.

a) Listen to the discussion. Which five of the eight topics (global warming, climate change, etc.) does she talk about with Oliver?

b) Read the sentences below. Then listen again. Are the sentences true or false?
1 The TV programme was about the Amazon.
2 Oliver thought the programme was scary.
3 He laughs at Ruby because she's so serious.
4 Oliver likes hot weather.
5 Ruby explains why food will become expensive.
6 The TV programme about deserts is on Friday.

4 And you?

a) Which three problems do you think are the most important?

b) What can *you* do in order to help against global warming?
Example: I can cycle to school. This produces no carbon dioxide and so it helps against global warming.

▶ W 1–3

SKILLS

SPEAKING – Talking about the environment

1 Ruby has been reading a magazine and now she's angry. Why?

RUBY Look at this advert: "Flights to New York for less than £200"! It makes me sick! Cheap flights are destroying the environment. People should spend their holidays at home instead of going abroad!

OLIVER Oh, come on, Ruby. That's totally unrealistic. Many people would rather have a holiday abroad and you know it.

RUBY Well, did you know that every flight from Europe to New York produces 500 kilos of carbon dioxide?

OLIVER No, I didn't. But actually what I find even more frightening is how much carbon dioxide we produce in our own homes. You simply can't live without producing carbon dioxide, even if you try.

RUBY That's no excuse for not trying to reduce your carbon footprint as often as you can.

OLIVER That's easy to say, but the trouble is that what each person can do has so little effect.

RUBY So what? It's worth doing what you can. It's no use just complaining, is it?

2 Now practise this dialogue with your partner. Change roles when you finish.

PARTNER A Look … this advert: "Buy a bigger, faster car"! It makes me …!
Cars are … the environment. People … travel by bus instead … going by car!

PARTNER B Oh, … on, … That's … unrealistic. Many people need a car and you know it.

PARTNER A That's no … for buying bigger, faster cars. They produce more carbon dioxide.

PARTNER B But you simply can't live … producing carbon dioxide.

PARTNER A My point is that it's … doing what you can. It's no … just complaining!

3 Group work: Tell the students in your group what you think about cheap flights.

4 Interpreting: Ruby has come to Bavaria on a school exchange and is staying with you. Your mum doesn't speak English very well.
Work with two partners and interpret for them.

a) Partners B and C: Look at page 90 and read part a) of the dialogue.
Partner A: Listen to Ruby and the mother and interpret for them.

b) Now change roles. Partners A and C read part b) of the dialogue, partner B interprets.

c) Change roles again. Partners A and B read part c) the dialogue, partner C interprets.

Unit 5

5 You're going to give a topic-based talk about a problem in the environment.

a) First choose a topic, e.g.

| world population | rising sea level | extinction of animals |

b) Then find information about your topic.
Find information on pages 74–75, in books in the library and on the Internet,
e.g. at **www.new-highlight.de**. Put in **NHL-BY-6-77**.

c) Prepare your talk.   » If you need help with this, look at page 45 in Unit 3.
- Divide your topic into three or four parts and find examples for each part.
- Give your opinion. Sentences from the dialogue on page 76 will help you, e.g.
  Cheap flights / ... is/are destroying ... And what I find really frightening is ...
  People can say that I'm totally unrealistic/..., but I think that ...
  The trouble is that ..., but it's worth trying/doing ...

d) Now work with a partner.
- Partner A: Show your partner one of the cards on page 91. Listen to your partner's talk and then ask two of the questions at the bottom of page 91.
- Partner B: Look at the card for one minute. Give your talk and include answers to the questions on your card. Then answer your partner's questions with full, interesting answers.
- Now change roles. Partner B shows a card, listens to partner A's talk and then asks two questions on page 91.
- Partner A gives the talk and then answers the questions.

6 A picture-based conversation

a) Look at the pictures below and plan what you can say about them.

b) Now talk to your partner about the two pictures and compare them.

» See page 63 for useful phrases. Don't forget that you can say what you **can't** see!

A street in Beijing

A sand storm in Beijing with sand from the Gobi desert

SKILLS

READING – An Internet article

1 Describe the two photos. Then read quickly through the text and say why there aren't any people in the photos.

Life after the end of the world

It's a warm summer day. The sky is blue and birds are singing in the trees which grow from the balconies of empty apartment blocks. There are pretty red and white flowers on the bushes between abandoned lorries in the city square. The sun is shining on the sports centre and through its broken windows you can see a swimming pool with no water in it. The hospital is empty. No new buildings are being built and there's no laughing or shouting in the fun park where bumper cars and a big wheel wait silently. At school, pupils' books lie open on the floor. Welcome to Prypiat, a busy, modern town where fifty thousand people used to live, learn, love and work. Since 1986 it has been a ghost town.

Prypiat was built in the north of Ukraine, when the country was part of the Soviet Union, for workers at the Chernobyl nuclear power station. Early on April 26th, 1986, the people of Prypiat heard two explosions at the power station, but nobody knew that clouds of dangerous radioactive gases were already in the air – and that people who breathed the gases could fall ill or even die. Even the firefighters at the power station had no idea of the danger. "We didn't know much about radioactivity," Grigorii Khmel, one of the firefighters, said later. They had no special protective clothing. They saw a huge fire and sprayed water onto the building. Then some of Grigorii's colleagues climbed onto the roof. "I never saw them again," said Grigorii.

While the firefighters were working in Chernobyl, a cloud of radioactive gases began a slow journey across Europe. On April 27th safety equipment at a nuclear power station in Sweden, 1100 kilometres away, found radioactivity in the workers' clothes. First people thought that there had been an accident in Sweden, then they found that the radioactivity had come from Ukraine. The radioactive cloud crossed Poland to Germany, Austria, Switzerland and then on to France, Italy, Britain and Norway. In these countries people stopped eating fresh vegetables in case they had been contaminated and ate tinned vegetables instead. Children played indoors in case the sand in outdoor playgrounds had been contaminated too. Still today some meat from Sweden, Germany, Poland and other countries can't be sold because the radioactive levels in the meat are too high.

Back in Prypiat, workers who had been injured in the explosion were brought to the hospital and people said that some workers had been killed – but life on April 26th was still normal. People even had their windows open because it was a sunny day. But the next day the atmosphere changed dramatically: a thousand buses suddenly appeared and everybody had to leave the city at once. There was no time for packing. Soon, more towns and villages were abandoned and in the end about 130,000 people were evacuated from the area. Today nobody is allowed to live in a zone of 30 kilometres around the power station.

Incredibly, most of the people of Prypiat continued to work in the nuclear power station till it was closed in December 2000. They travelled from Slavutych, a new town which had been built for them, and they worked in the parts of the power station which had not been damaged. A thick wall of concrete around the reactor which had exploded protected the workers from the radioactivity. And 3800 people still work there today, making sure that the area stays safe. Some repair cracks in the concrete wall so that the building doesn't collapse – if it fell, more radioactive gases would be released.

The experts disagree on how many people died in the disaster. Some say that hundreds died and thousands still suffer from diseases like cancer and leukaemia which were caused by the radioactivity. Other reports say that the numbers are really much lower. Some reports say that future generations will not suffer much; other reports disagree. Nobody knows how long the region will be uninhabitable, but everybody agrees that it will cost billions of euros before the area is totally safe again.

Today the area around the power station is quiet, but surprisingly full of life. Wild horses live in the fields, wolves hunt in the forest – and they move freely because nobody comes near them. Nobody? That's not absolutely true. Prypiat has become a macabre tourist attraction. About a hundred tourists a year come in order to see what the world will look like "after the end of the world" – when there are no more people.

Your comments

Thanks, your article is really interesting! It proves that nuclear power stations are dangerous – we should certainly close them all as soon as possible.
Chris

Nice report, but our nuclear power stations in Europe are safer than the one in Chernobyl and they have a smaller carbon footprint than power stations that burn coal, gas or oil.
Julia

SKILLS

2 In lines 1–12 we slowly learn that Prypiat is a ghost town.
What are five signs that nobody lives or works here?
Example: The apartment blocks are empty. ...

3 Answer the questions in full sentences.
1 What was the first sign for the people of Prypiat that there had been an accident?
2 How did people in Europe change   a) how they ate?   b) how children played?
3 What's special about the zone around the Chernobyl power station?
4 Why was the town of Slavutych built?
5 Why must workers still work at the Chernobyl power station today?
6 Give two examples of life in the zone around the Chernobyl power station.

4 Explain the following phrases in English.
You can use a dictionary.
1 a balcony *(line 2)*
2 abandoned *(line 4)*
3 big wheel *(line 9)*
4 evacuate *(line 40)*
5 uninhabitable *(line 55)*
6 carbon footprint *(line 69)*

5 Explain in German ...

a) why the work of the firefighters was so dangerous.

b) why tourists now come and visit Prypiat.

6 And you?

a) Which paragraph in the article do you find the most frightening? Why?

b) Would you want to visit Prypiat? Why (not)? Write 3–4 sentences.

7 The (dis)advantages of nuclear power:
Do you agree with Chris or Julia?

a) Work in a group. Collect ideas about the
advantages and disadvantages of nuclear
power compared with coal, oil or wind power.

b) Then write eight sentences with your own
opinions about nuclear power.
Example:
One big advantage of ... is that ...
However, ...
It's true that ..., but what is frightening is that ...
All in all I think that ...

Unit 5

🎧 LISTENING – Big yellow taxi

38, 39

1 A radio show

a) Listen to the talking before the song *Big Yellow Taxi* is played. Complete the three sentences below.

→ Adele • Amy Grant • Counting Crows • Joni Mitchell • Madonna • R.E.M.

1 The song was written by ...
2 The version chosen by David is sung by ...
3 It has also been sung by ...

b) Listen again. Then answer the questions.
1 Where in Ireland does David live?
2 Where did the writer have the idea for the song?
3 What's the British English for 'parking lots'?
4 What does David say about Amy Grant's voice?

2 Big yellow taxi
Now listen to the song. What are the missing words (🎵🎵🎵)?

Big Yellow Taxi

They paved paradise and 🎵🎵🎵 up a parking lot
With a pink hotel, a boutique and a swinging hot spot.
Don't it 🎵🎵🎵 seem to go
That you don't know what you've got till it's gone,
They paved paradise and put up a parking lot.

They 🎵🎵🎵 all the trees and put 'em in a tree museum
And then they charged all the people twenty-five bucks just to 🎵🎵🎵 'em!

Don't it 🎵🎵🎵 seem to go
That you don't know what you've got till it's gone,
They paved paradise and put up a parking lot.

Hey farmer, farmer, put away your DDT now:
Give me spots on my 🎵🎵🎵, but leave me the birds and the bees, please!

Don't it 🎵🎵🎵 seem to go
That you don't know what you've got till it's gone,
They paved paradise and they put up a parking lot.
I say, they paved paradise and they put up a parking lot. *(repeated)*

Late last night I 🎵🎵🎵 the screen door slam
And a big yellow taxi 🎵🎵🎵 off my old man.

Don't it 🎵🎵🎵 seem to go
That you don't know what you've got till it's gone,
They paved paradise and they put up a parking lot. *(repeated)*

Oh, now, they paved paradise and they put up a parking lot,
Hey, [they] steam rolled paradise and put up a parking lot.

Komposition und Text: Joni Mitchell

▶ W 10, 11

→ SKILLS

MEDIATION – A news story

1 A good news story about the environment
Read the article about Gina Gallant and then translate it into German.
» Zeitlimit in der Abschlussprüfung: 10 bis 12 Minuten. Schaffst du das?

Great idea for new roads
by Ella Huskisson

» You can use a dictionary to find the meaning of new words.

For many years cities have been trying[1] to re-use their rubbish and now a teenage girl in British Columbia, Canada, has invented[2] a material that recycles one of the most important waste products of all – plastic.

Gina Gallant worked for an oil company that treated asphalt for roads. Could some waste products, she wondered[3], also be used for road-building? She found that glass and rubber had already been tried[4] unsuccessfully. "Perhaps I could grind plastic?" she thought. After all, plastic and asphalt both come from oil.

It worked! Gina found that a mix of 6 % asphalt, 6 % ground[5] plastic and 88 % broken rock worked best. She then tried her new material on 500 metres of real road in Prince George, British Columbia. Now everybody is waiting in order to[6] see what happens when cars and lorries drive on it.

So far, it seems that Gina's material has fewer cracks than normal asphalt, and traffic apparently makes less noise on it than on other materials. If Gina can sell her idea to big road-building companies, her idea could recycle millions of tons of plastic in the world.

---

[1] *for + present perfect* = seit + Präsens auf Deutsch
[2] Du kennst *inventor* = Erfinder; also heißt *invented* wohl ...?
[3] word order!
[4] Passiv im *past perfect*: "... waren schon ausprobiert worden ..."
[5] Vorsicht bei der Suche im Wörterbuch: Gemeint ist nicht *ground n* = Boden, sondern *grind, ground, ground v* = mahlen.
[6] *in order to:* um zu

► W 12

Unit 5

WRITING – A picture-based story

1 You're a member of an environment group which produces a magazine. The magazine has reports and stories – and this month you decide to write the story.

a) Look at the photo and write a story of at least 120 words.

Tipps	• Erfinde einen Kontext: Wo ist das Wasser? Ist es z. B. in der Nähe deiner Stadt oder ganz woanders? Warum sind die Vögel gestorben? • Überlege dir eine Vorgeschichte: Hast du die Vögel entdeckt oder jemand anderes? Bei welcher Gelegenheit (z. B. zufällig bei einem Picknick oder …)? • Schildere die Folgen: Hast du die Behörden bzw. die Polizei alarmiert? Wurden die Verantwortlichen bestraft oder ist nichts passiert? • Beschreibe deine Gefühle: Warst du anfangs schockiert, wütend, …? Und am Ende fühltest du dich traurig, enttäuscht, …? • Denke dir erst eine Überschrift aus, wenn die Geschichte fertig ist.

b) OK, you've written your story. Can you now improve some sentences? For example, does your story have …
• **time phrases** (e. g. *two years, ago, during the summer holidays, an hour later* …)?
• **adverbs** (e. g. *suddenly, unfortunately,* …)?
• **words which connect** (e. g. *because, although,* …)?
• **a relative clause** (e. g. *the factory which* …)?
• **different words for** *said* (e. g. *answered,* …)?

c) Now work with a partner: Improve your partner's sentences.

» Think of the examples in b) above.

► W 13–15

LOOK AT LANGUAGE

STRUCTURES

Professor Clever gives a quick lesson in global warming.

2 • 40-43

Carbon dioxide is like a pullover around the earth – heat from the earth is caught in the gas and is not sent into space, but is sent back to the earth. When there is too much carbon dioxide, the pullover is too thick and too much heat is sent back to the earth. Most scientists agree that this is how global warming is caused.

1 There are nine phrases with *is* in the text above.
Copy the ones where *is* is part of the *simple present passive*.
Example: heat is caught, …

Till 2006 more greenhouse gases were produced by the USA than by any other country. In 2006 the USA was overtaken by China for the first time. But the amount of carbon dioxide that was produced per person in the USA was still much higher than in China.

2 Answer the questions in full sentences. Use the *simple past passive*.
1 Which country produced most greenhouse gases before 2006?   *Before 2006 most …*
2 In which year was the USA overtaken by China?   *The USA …*
3 What do you think: Why was the amount of carbon dioxide that was produced per person in the USA higher than in China?   *I think that … was higher because …*

3 Read and complete the revision box.

> **REVISION**
>
> **Mit dem Passiv sagst du, dass etwas mit einem Gegenstand oder einer Person gemacht wird bzw. wurde.**
> Beispiele: *Heat **is caught** by the greenhouse gases. Too many greenhouse gases **are produced**. More carbon dioxide **was produced** by the USA. The USA **was overtaken** by China in 2006.*
>
> **Simple present passive:** … or are + past participle
> **Simple past passive:** was or … + …
> Mit … zeigst du, von wem die Handlung ausgeführt wird bzw. wurde.

84
eighty-four

Unit 5

Fortunately some progress has been made. In many countries greenhouse gases have been cut since 1990. In Britain for example, carbon dioxide has been reduced by 15% since 1990. And more cuts have been agreed by countries which have signed the Kyoto Protocol.

4 **Look at the text. Then complete the sentences.** → has • have
1 Some progress … been made.
2 Greenhouse gases … been cut since 1990.
3 Carbon dioxide … been reduced since 1990.
4 More cuts … been agreed.

The question is, will global warming be stopped? If not, polar bears will be threatened with extinction, the USA will be hit by more hurricanes and more people will be killed by hot weather or floods. More dams will be built by countries which are afraid of water shortages and more wars will be fought for water.

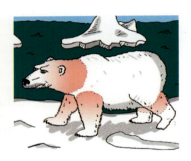

5 **Look at the text and write the sentences.**
1 Extinction will threaten polar bears.   *Polar bears will be …*
2 More hurricanes will hit the USA.   *The USA …*
3 Hot weather and floods will kill more people.   *More people …*
4 Countries which are afraid of water shortages will build more dams.   *More dams …*
5 People will fight more wars for water.   *More wars …*

6 **Read and complete the checkpoint.**

CHECKPOINT

Mit dem Passiv kannst du auch sagen, was gemacht worden ist bzw. was in der Zukunft gemacht werden wird.
Beispiele: *Some progress* **has been made**. *Greenhouse gases* **have been reduced**.
Polar bears **will be threatened** *with extinction. The USA* **will be hit** *by more hurricanes.*

Present perfect passive: *Carbon dioxide … … cut since 1990.*
Future tense passive: *More people … … killed by floods.*

Für alle Passivsätze gilt: Das Passiv wird mit einer Form von … und dem … des Verbs gebildet.

▶ W 16, 17

85
eighty-five

LOOK AT LANGUAGE

WORDPOWER

» Achtung: Kein Wörterbuch erlaubt (wie in der Prüfung)!

1 Global warming: Complete the network.

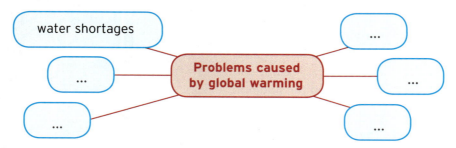

2 Sounds: Find the word which doesn't sound like the others and write a sentence with the word in it.

Example:
1 protective: Workers in nuclear power stations have to wear protective clothing.

1	div**i**de	protect**i**ve	carbon diox**i**de	d**i**ning room
2	r**a**ther	c**a**rbon	d**a**nger	h**a**lf
3	abr**oa**d	c**oa**st	downl**oa**d	m**oa**n
4	br**ea**the	thr**ea**ten	dis**ea**se	p**ea**ceful
5	de**s**ert	lun**g**s	ri**s**ing	ga**s**es
6	**g**overn	ar**g**ue	dama**g**e	be**g**in

3 The water cycle: Use the words and write sentences.

Example:
1 97 % of the world's water is in the oceans. When the sun shines, water ...

1
 • 97 % / water / oceans
 • sun / shine / water / rise / sky

2
 • water / form / clouds / atmosphere

3
 • water / fall / rain / snow
 • water / fill / rivers

4
 • rivers / bring / water / sea
 • some water / underground

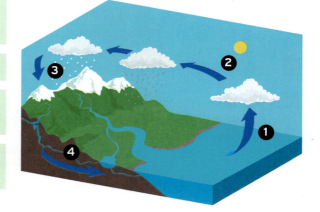

Unit 5

REVISION

» If you need help on this page, look at the *Summary Pages* (92–101).

4 Mumbai: Write the sentences in *reported speech*. Use different words for *said* in sentences 2, 3 and 4.

> Mumbai has grown fast in the last few years and is still growing. It's now one of the world's largest cities, although it was only the 12th largest city in 1975. In 2020 it will be the world's second largest city after Tokyo. Its population will then be nearly 22 million.

Professor Nair

1. Professor Nair said that Mumbai ... and ... growing.
2. She said that it ..., although it ...
3. She said that in 2020 ...
4. She said that its population ...

5 Beijing: Use the right form of the verbs.

» Achte auf Verben im Passiv!

Beijing's nearest desert is only 100 km away and it (still/come) closer. Every year China's capital city (disappear) in clouds of sand and the streets (often/cover) with tons of sand from the desert. In 2002 some sand from the Chinese deserts even (fall) in Japan.
In 1978 China (start) a new project which (call) "China's Great Green Wall". People (begin) to plant trees in the desert. Millions of trees (plant) since 1978 and now the people in Beijing are hoping that the trees (protect) the city from sand in the future.

6 What can *you* do? Use the right form of the verbs in these *if*-sentences.

1. If you travel 15,000 miles next year by car, you (produce) almost 500 kilos of carbon dioxide.
2. If you cycled more or (go) on foot, you (produce) much less!

7 Quick check

a) One world
1. Give an example for each problem:
   a) rising sea level   b) population explosion   c) water shortage
2. Explain what happened at Chernobyl in 1986 and what the place looks like now.

b) Write the sentences in the *passive*.
1. International companies have cut down parts of the Amazon forest.
   Parts of ...
2. They will destroy many more square miles of the forest in the next few years.
   Many more ...

▶ W 18–20

PARTNER PAGES

UNIT 3 (page 44)

2 Work again with two partners.

a) Partner B: You are Govind.
Partner C: You are Tobias.
Read the dialogue – Partner A will interpret your sentences.

GOVIND And what do you think of our weather in India?

PARTNER A ...

TOBIAS Ach, ich liebe das Wetter, weil es hier viel heißer und sonniger ist als in Deutschland.

PARTNER A ...

GOVIND Are there things which you don't like so much in India?

PARTNER A ...

TOBIAS Mit dem Zug fahren ist unbequem, weil die Züge oft zu voll sind.

PARTNER A ...

b) Partner A now reads Govind, Partner C reads Tobias.
Partner B listens and interprets.

GOVIND If you think the trains are full, you should see the buses – they're even fuller!

PARTNER B ...

TOBIAS Aber beim Reisen kommt man leicht mit anderen Menschen ins Gespräch.

PARTNER B ...

GOVIND Do you think Indians are friendly?

PARTNER B ...

TOBIAS Auf jeden Fall. Die Inder, die ich kennengelernt habe, sind fast alle sehr freundlich.

PARTNER B ...

c) Partner A now reads Govind, Partner B reads Tobias.
Partner C listens and interprets.

GOVIND What in your opinion is the biggest difference between India and Germany?

PARTNER C ...

TOBIAS Hier gibt es so viele Menschen – nicht nur in den Städten, auch auf dem Lande.

PARTNER C ...

GOVIND Do you like that?

PARTNER C ...

TOBIAS Ja und nein. Manchmal ist es toll, manchmal ist es mir zu viel.

PARTNER C ...

UNIT 3 (page 45)

2 When you're ready for your talk
Here are the questions for your partner.

1 **Geography of India**
   1 India has 15 % of the world's population, but only 2.4 % of the world's area.
     Is this a problem? Why (not)?
   2 If you could go on holiday in India, where would you go – and why?

2 **Work and industry in India**
   1 Why do some Indian parents want their children to earn money instead of going
     to school?
   2 Would you like to work in India when you leave school? Why (not)?

3 **Bollywood**
   1 Why do you think Bollywood films and shows weren't popular in Europe in the past?
     And why do you think they are so popular now?
   2 You have a good friend who wants to be an actor.
     Would you say he should try to work in Bollywood or not? Why?

UNIT 4 (page 62)

4 More partner work: Now work with two partners.

a) Partner B: You are Lena.
Partner C: You are Ben.
Read the dialogue – Partner A will interpret your sentences.

LENA Kannst du Auto fahren, Ben?
 BEN Well, I can't yet, but I'm taking driving lessons.
LENA Und wann machst du den Führerschein?
 BEN I'm not absolutely sure, but probably in June.
LENA Freust du dich darauf?
 BEN Oh, I'm really looking forward to being able to drive.
LENA Hast du dein eigenes Auto?
 BEN No, I haven't. Cars are expensive. And what's worse is the car insurance.
LENA Ja, die Autoversicherung ist auch in Deutschland sehr teuer.
 BEN Can you drive, Lena?
LENA Ja, ich fahre seit ein paar Monaten Auto.
 BEN Do you enjoy it?
LENA Oh ja. Es macht riesig Spaß.

b) Partner A now reads Lena, Partner C reads Ben. Partner B listens and interprets.

c) Partner A now reads Ben, Partner B reads Lena. Partner C listens and interprets.

PARTNER PAGES

UNIT 5 (page 76)

4 Interpreting: Ruby has come to Bavaria on a school exchange and is staying with you. Your mum doesn't speak English very well.
Work with two partners and interpret for them.

a) Partner B: You're Ruby.
Partner C: You're the mother.
Read the dialogue – partner A will interpret your sentences.

MOTHER   Hallo, Ruby. Freut mich, dich kennenzulernen. Hattest du eine gute Reise?

RUBY   Yes, thanks. The train was on time and very comfortable.

MOTHER   Du bist also nicht geflogen?

RUBY   No, I don't like flying. It's not good for the environment.

MOTHER   Du hast Recht. Aber Fliegen ist oft viel billiger als Zugfahren.

RUBY   Yes, but think of the cost to the environment!

MOTHER   Auf der anderen Seite fliegen doch jeden Tag so viele Maschinen, egal ob du selber in einem Flugzeug sitzt oder nicht.

RUBY   Yes, what each person can do has so little effect. But it's still worth doing what you can.

MOTHER   Denken viele Menschen in Großbritannien so wie du?

RUBY   Oh, I'm sure we're a minority. Lots of people talk a lot about the environment. But the number of people who really do something for the environment is much smaller.

MOTHER   Ja, so ist es hier in Deutschland auch.

b) Partner C now is Ruby, partner A is the mother.
Partner B listens and interprets.

MOTHER   Und du wohnst also in England, Ruby?

RUBY   No, I don't. I live in Scotland – in a little town in the west of Scotland.

MOTHER   Die Gegend ist sehr schön, nicht wahr?

RUBY   Yes, there are beautiful hills and islands with lots of sheep, and there's the sea, of course. But there's not really a lot to do for young people.

MOTHER   Ich habe gehört, das Meer soll warm sein, wegen des Golfstroms?

RUBY   Well, it's not really warm – not if you want to swim in it! But if we didn't have the Gulf Stream, we would have ice in winter.

MOTHER   Ich habe im Fernsehen gehört, dass der Golfstrom nun schwächer sei als früher.

RUBY   Yes, that's true. It's now 12% weaker than it was 12 years ago.

MOTHER   Und woran liegt das?

RUBY   Oh, there are probably several reasons. But one reason is that the Arctic ice is melting, and cold Arctic water is mixing with the warm water of the Gulf Stream.

MOTHER   Ach ja. Daran habe ich nicht gedacht.

c) Partner A now reads Ruby, partner B reads the mother.
Partner C listens and interprets.

RUBY   What are you doing in the summer holidays?

MOTHER Mein Mann und ich fliegen nach China. Ich freue mich darauf. Es wird unser erster Besuch in China sein.

RUBY   Are you going to travel around the country a bit?

MOTHER Ja, natürlich. Aber zunächst werden wir ein paar Tage in Peking verbringen.

RUBY   I've heard they have problems in Beijing because the desert is expanding.

MOTHER Ja, das habe ich auch gehört. An manchen Tagen gibt es anscheinend viel Sand in der Luft.

RUBY   That must be terrible!

MOTHER Danach werden wir in den Süden von China fliegen. Ach ja, Ruby: Ich weiß, für die Umwelt ist Fliegen nicht gut ...

RUBY   Well, every longer flight produces a few hundred tons of carbon dioxide!

MOTHER Das stimmt. Aber was kann man machen? Wir können doch nicht mit dem Zug nach China fahren, oder?

RUBY   Don't worry, I'm not really a crazy eco-freak! I came to Germany by train – but when I go back to Scotland, I'm flying!

UNIT 5 (page 77)

5 **A topic-based talk about a problem in the environment**

• **Show your partner one of the cards.**

1 **A problem in the environment**	2 **A problem in the environment**	3 **A problem in the environment**
• What are some of the causes of the problem which you have studied? • And what are some of the effects*? *effects = *Folgen*	• In what parts of the world is the topic which you have studied a problem? Give some examples. • What do you think people should do so that this problem does not get worse?	• Describe one important problem for the world environment. • Do you think that the problem which you studied is the biggest danger for the world or is another problem even more important?

• **Listen to your partner's talk and then ask two of the questions below.**

Why in your opinion do more and more countries suffer from water shortage?

Why is it a problem for the world if deserts are getting bigger?

Why is the Gulf Stream important for winter weather in Europe?

What are some of the problems if the sea level rises?

Why does Britain (population 60 million) have a bigger carbon footprint than, for example, Nigeria (population 133 million)?

Why are polar bears threatened with extinction?

SUMMARY

1 Verbs and tenses

1.1 Simple present

Mit der einfachen Gegenwart sagst du,
was manchmal, oft, immer wieder oder nie passiert.
I always **go** to school by bus.
My sister **doesn't eat** meat.
Do you live here? – Yes, I **do**. / No, I **don't**.

Typische Zeitangaben

always • never • sometimes • often • usually • every day every year • on Mondays • in the evening • at the weekend

1.2 Present progressive

Mit der Verlaufsform der Gegenwart sagst du,
was gerade geschieht.
What**'s** Tom **doing**? – He**'s listening** to music.
Is Tom **working** in his room? – No, he **isn't**.
Are your parents **travelling**? – No, they **aren't**.
I have a job, but I**'m** not **working** this weekend.
Where's Rachel? She **isn't watching** TV.

I'm falling!

Typische Zeitangaben

at the moment • just • today • this week • this summer

1.3 Simple past

Mit der einfachen Vergangenheit sagst du,
was zu einem bestimmten Zeitpunkt in der Vergangenheit geschah.
We visit**ed** Paris last year.   We **met** in town and **ate** a pizza.
Did you **see** the film yesterday?   We **didn't play** yesterday.

Regelmäßige Verben enden auf *-ed*; unregelmäßige Verben haben besondere Formen (vgl. S.180–181).

Typische Zeitangaben

yesterday • last night • last Wednesday • two days ago

1.4 Past progressive

Mit der Verlaufsform der Vergangenheit kannst du ausdrücken,
dass etwas zu einer bestimmten Zeit noch im Gange war.
I **was surfing** the Internet when the phone rang.
Was it **snowing** when you arrived?   – No, it wasn't. It **was raining** when we arrived.

1.5 Present perfect

Mit dem Perfekt sagst du, was zu einem unbestimmten Zeitpunkt (in der Vergangenheit), gerade, schon einmal, oft oder noch nie geschehen ist.
Titanic? Yes, I've **seen** it.   **Has** Grace just **arrived**?   – Yes, she has.
I've **been** to Scotland twice.   I've never **seen** a polar bear.

Signalwörter

> ever • never • already • often • once • twice • yet • before

Mit dem Perfekt sagst du auch, wie lange etwas schon andauert.
My mum **has worked** there for three years.   We've **lived** in Munich since 1999.

1.6 Present perfect progressive

Die Verlaufsform des Perfekt benutzt du, wenn eine schon begonnene Handlung oder ihre Folgen bis in die Gegenwart reicht.
I've **been doing** my homework for two hours.

1.7 Past perfect

Bei mehreren Ereignissen in der Vergangenheit kannst du mit der *past perfect*-Form, der Vorvergangenheit, anzeigen, welches Ereignis weiter zurücklag.
After I **had spoken** to Mark, I felt better.

Signalwörter

> after • before

1.8 Expressing future time

1.8.1 Going to-future

Mit dem *going to-future* kannst du sagen, was höchstwahrscheinlich geschehen wird oder was jemand plant oder vorhat.
Look, the film **is going to** begin.
Are you **going to** get on this bus?   – No, I'm **going to** wait for Joe.

1.8.2 Will-future

Mit dem *will-future* kannst du sagen, was voraussichtlich geschehen wird (Vorhersagen und Vermutungen).
Will getting a ticket for the match be easy?   – No, it **won't**!

Häufige Ausdrücke in Vorhersagen und Vermutungen

> I think • I'm sure • I suppose • I believe • I hope • probably • perhaps

Meist ist es egal, ob du das *going to-* oder das *will-future* benutzt.

SUMMARY

1.8.3 Simple present

Mit der *simple present*-Form kannst du über Ereignisse in der Zukunft sprechen, auf die du wenig Einfluss hast, weil sie durch einen Zeitplan, z.B. einen Kalender, einen Fahrplan oder ein Programm, festgelegt sind *(timetable future)*.

The next train from Cape Town **arrives** at five o'clock.

Der nächste Zug aus Kapstadt kommt um fünf Uhr.

1.8.4 Present progressive

Mit der *present progressive*-Form kannst du ausdrücken, dass etwas für die Zukunft fest geplant oder verabredet ist. Durch eine Zeitbestimmung der Zukunft (z.B. *this afternoon, on Saturday, tomorrow*) oder durch den Zusammenhang muss deutlich werden, dass es sich um etwas Zukünftiges handelt.

When **are** you **leaving** tomorrow?   – **I'm leaving** after lunch.

Wann fährst du morgen weg?   – Ich fahre nach dem Mittagessen.

1.9 The gerund

Mit dieser *ing*-Form, dem Gerundium, kannst du Tätigkeiten benennen.

- Sie kann Subjekt eines Satzes sein.   **Going** abroad is expensive.
- Sie folgt auf bestimmte Verben.   You should stop **smoking**.
- Sie wird häufig nach Ausdrücken   She's good at **dancing**.
  mit Präpositionen verwendet.

> **interested in ...** • **good/bad at ...** • **pleased about ...** •
> **instead of ...** • **tired of ...** • **worried about ...** • **look forward to ...** •
> **Thanks for ...** • **What about ...?**

2 Pronouns

2.1 mine, yours, ... (possessive pronouns without nouns)

Mit *mine, yours*, etc. sagst du, wem etwas gehört. Sie stehen allein, d.h. es folgt kein Nomen. Du verwendest sie oft, um ein bereits genanntes Nomen nicht zu wiederholen.

Don't eat that biscuit. It's **mine**!

I've found this book. Is it **yours**?

Vergleiche:

| It's | my / your / his/her / our / your / their | bike. | **Mit Nomen:**
It's my bike. | | It's | mine. / yours. / his/hers. / ours. / yours. / theirs. | **Ohne Nomen:**
It's mine. |

2.2 Reflexive pronouns

Du gebrauchst Reflexivpronomen mit bestimmten Verben (z. B. *hurt, enjoy, teach, buy*).
Sie zeigen an, dass sich die Handlung auf die ausführende Person zurückbezieht
(reflexiv – rückbezüglich).
We were enjoying **ourselves**, but then Hannah fell and hurt **herself**.

I – myself	we – ourselves
you – yourself	you – yourselves
he – himself	they – themselves
she – herself	
it – itself	

Lucy and Amy took a photo of **themselves**.

2.3 one, ones

Mit *one/ones* kannst du Wortwiederholungen vermeiden. Im Deutschen verzichtet man einfach auf die Wiederholung des Nomens. Im Englischen ersetzt man das Nomen durch *one* (Singular) bzw. *ones* (Plural).
Our car is a pretty small **one**.
The black horse is friendlier than the brown **ones**.

3 Adjectives

- Adjektive beschreiben eine Person oder eine Sache.
- Sie stehen oft unmittelbar vor einem Nomen.
- Mithilfe von Adverbien kann man ein Adjektiv verstärken.
- Sie können auch nach dem Verb *be* stehen.
- Adjektive können auch nach einigen anderen Verben stehen.

Diana is a **quiet** girl.
It's a **slow** car.
He's **totally mad**!
The cake is **fantastic**!

feel • **look** (= aussehen) • **sound** • **taste** • **become** • **get** • **seem**

I feel **terrible**.

3.1 Adjectives with (not) as ...as

Mit *as ... as* kannst du Personen oder Sachen miteinander vergleichen.
Mit *not as ... as* kann man auf Unterschiede hinweisen.
Peter is **as** old **as** Mike.
My computer **isn't as** modern **as** yours.

SUMMARY

3.2 Comparison of adjectives

Mit den Steigerungsformen der Adjektive kann man zwischen mehreren Dingen oder Personen unterscheiden und Vergleiche anstellen. Wie eine Steigerungsform gebildet wird, richtet sich nach der Wortlänge.
- Einsilbige Adjektive sowie zweisilbige Adjektive auf *-y* werden mit *-er* oder *-est* gesteigert.

Mr Smith is old.   Mr Johnson is **older**.   Mrs Ellis is the **oldest** person in our street.
- Das *-y* am Ende wird bei der Steigerungsform zu *-i*.

Max is friend**ly**. Daniel is friendl**ier**. And Sarah is the friendl**iest** student in my class.
- Alle Adjektive mit drei und mehr Silben und die meisten zweisilbigen Adjektive, die nicht auf *-y* enden, werden mit *more/most* gesteigert.

Maths is difficult. Art is **more difficult** than maths. Science is **the most difficult** lesson of all.
- Einige Adjektive haben besondere Steigerungsformen:

> **good – better – (the) best • bad – worse – (the) worst • little – less – (the) least**

4 Adverbs

Adverbien *(adverbs)* benutzt du, um zu beschreiben auf welche Art und Weise etwas geschieht.
Die meisten Adverbien bildest du, indem du *-ly* an das Adjektiv anhängst:
loud – loud**ly**
- Beachte die Rechtschreibung:

easy – eas**ily**, careful – careful**ly**, comfortable – comforta**bly**
Ausnahmen:
- fast – fast, hard – hard
- Das Adverb zu *good* ist *well*.

Meg is a **good** singer. She sings **well**.

5 Quantifiers

5.1 some, (not) any

- *some* und *any* werden meist mit zählbaren und nicht zählbaren Nomen gebraucht. Sie bezeichnen eine unbestimmte Anzahl (*some apples* = „einige Äpfel") oder eine unbestimmte Menge (*some butter* = „etwas Butter"). Im Deutschen wird „etwas" allerdings oft weggelassen.

There's **some** milk in the fridge.   Es ist (etwas) Milch im Kühlschrank.
- In verneinten Sätzen benutzt man *any* statt *some*. *Not any* entspricht dem deutschen „kein/keine".

We don't need **any** milk today.   Wir brauchen heute keine Milch.
- Statt *not any* wird gelegentlich auch *no* vor einem Nomen gebraucht; *no* ist aber weniger häufig.

There are **no** biscuits in the cupboard.   Es sind keine Kekse im Schrank.

5.2 *much, many*

Mit *much* und *many* sagst du, dass etwas vielfach oder in großer Menge vorhanden ist. Sie bedeuten dasselbe wie *a lot of*, werden aber weniger häufig gebraucht. Vor nicht zählbaren Nomen steht *much* (= „viel"), vor zählbaren Nomen in der Mehrzahl steht *many* (= „viele").

We don't have **much** time.   Wir haben nicht viel Zeit.
How **much** money do you have?   Wie viel Geld hast du?
How **many** pets do you have?   Wie viele Haustiere hast du?
I have **many** friends.   Ich habe viele Freunde.

5.3 Zusammensetzungen mit *some, any, no*

Durch die Zusammensetzung der Mengenbezeichnungen *some*, *any* und *no* mit *-body*, *-thing* und *-where* entstehen neue Wörter.
• Mit *some* bildest du diese Zusammensetzungen: *somebody, something, somewhere*
• In verneinten Sätzen verwendest du statt *somebody, something* und *somewhere* die entsprechenden Zusammensetzungen mit *any*.
I've eaten something. I have**n't** eaten **anything**.
• Mit *no* bildest du diese Zusammensetzungen: *nobody, nothing, nowhere*

Bei Personen	somebody	(not) anybody / nobody
-body	jemand	niemand
Bei Dingen	something	(not) anything / nothing
-thing	etwas	nichts
Bei Orten	somewhere	(not) anywhere / nowhere
-where	irgendwo(hin)	nirgendwo(hin) / nirgends

SUMMARY

6 Simple and complex sentences

6.1 Word order

In einem englischen Aussagesatz gilt die Reihenfolge: *subject – verb*.
Ist ein Objekt vorhanden, folgt es nach dem Verb.

subject	verb	object
I	play	tennis.

- Ortsangaben *(where?)* folgen nach dem Verb und Objekt (falls vorhanden).

subject	verb	object	(where?)
I	play	tennis	at school.

- Zeitangaben *(when?)* können ganz am Anfang oder ganz am Ende des Satzes stehen.

(when?)	subject	verb	object	(where?)	(when?)
	I	play	tennis	at school	every week.
Every week	I	play	tennis	at school.	

- Häufigkeitsangaben wie *often, sometimes, never, usually* stehen meist direkt vor dem Hauptverb.
It **often** rains in April.
Mum can **never** find her passport.

6.2 Sentences with conjunctions

Mit Konjunktionen (Bindewörter) wie *although, because, but, while, when, after, that* oder *so that* kannst du Sätze miteinander verknüpfen, zum Beispiel:
The dog barked. The cat ran away. ➜ The dog barked **and** the cat ran away.

Eine Konjunktion kann auch am Anfang eines komplexen Satzes stehen.
When you leave, switch the light off.

Anders als im Deutschen bleibt die Wortstellung in komplexen Sätzen unverändert.
Es gilt weiterhin die Reihenfolge: *subject – verb – object*
I have a job because I need the money.
Ich habe einen Job, weil ich das Geld brauche.

6.3 *Relative clauses* (Relativsätze)

Relativsätze mit *who, which* oder *that* geben zusätzliche Informationen über eine Person oder einen Gegenstand.
- Das Relativpronomen *who* verwendest du nur nach Personen.

This is **the girl who** I met yesterday.
Hier ist das Mädchen, das ich gestern kennengelernt habe.
- Das Relativpronomen *which* verwendest du nach Gegenständen.

It's not **the magazine which** I usually buy.
Es ist nicht die Zeitschrift, die ich normalerweise kaufe.
- Sowohl *who* als auch *which* werden manchmal durch *that* ersetzt.

They're **people that** I like very much. Es sind Menschen, die ich sehr mag.
Are these **the trousers that** you bought yesterday? Ist das die Hose, die du gestern gekauft hast?
- Durch einen Relativsatz kann man zwei einfache Sätze miteinander verbinden:

Kate has a camera. It takes great photos. ➔ Kate has a camera **which** takes great photos.
Laura has friends. They live in New York. ➔ Laura has friends **who** live in New York.

6.4 *if-sentences* (Bedingungssätze)

- Bedingungssätze mit *if* sagen aus, unter welchen Bedingungen etwas …

stattfindet *(type I)*. stattfinden würde *(type II)*. stattgefunden hätte *(type III)*.
- Bedingungssätze bestehen aus zwei Teilen:

einem Nebensatz mit *if*, der die Bedingung nennt, und einem Hauptsatz, der sagt, was sich aus dieser Bedingung ergibt.
If it rains, we'll get wet.
- Der *if*-Satz kann vor oder nach dem Hauptsatz stehen.

If you break that glass, **I'll be angry**. **I'll be angry** if you break that glass.

6.4.1 *if-sentences (type I)*

Bedingungssätze vom Typ I sagen aus, was unter bestimmten Bedingungen passieren wird. Es ist gut möglich, dass die Bedingung erfüllt wird.

Für die Sätze von diesem Typ gilt:
- der *if*-Satz steht in der Gegenwart,
- der Hauptsatz enthält eine Zukunftsform mit *will*.

Bedingung	Ergebnis
if + simple present	Zukunft mit *will*
If your train **is** late,	we**'ll meet** in town.

- Der Hauptsatz kann statt *will* auch ein modales Hilfsverb (z.B. *must, can, should*) enthalten.

If your train is late, we **can** meet in town.
If we want to get the bus, we **must** leave now.

SUMMARY

6.4.2 if-sentences (type II)

Bedingungssätze vom Typ II sagen aus, was unter bestimmten Bedingungen passieren würde. Es ist jedoch ziemlich unwahrscheinlich oder sogar unmöglich, dass die Bedingung erfüllt wird.

Für die Sätze von diesem Typ gilt:
- der *if*-Satz steht in der Vergangenheit,
- der Hauptsatz enthält *would* und einen Infinitiv.

Die Kurzform von *would* ist *'d*: I'd, you'd, he'd, she'd, we'd, they'd.

Bedingung	Ergebnis
if + Vergangenheit	*would* + Infinitiv
If I **had** my mobile,	I **would phone** Ella.

Beachte diese Sonderform:
if I were you: an deiner Stelle, wenn ich du wäre
if he were here: wenn er hier wäre

6.5 Reported speech

Mit *reported speech* (indirekter Rede) berichtest du darüber, was jemand sagt oder gesagt hat.
- Die indirekte Rede wird oft mit *tell* oder *say* eingeleitet. Diese Verben werden meistens zusammen mit dem Wort *that* gebraucht; manchmal entfällt das Wort *that*.

The hotel manager **says that** there are no rooms free. Ellen **said** she had no money.
- Fragen werden mit dem Verb *ask* oder einem ähnlichen Verb eingeleitet.

The boy **asks** if the cat will be OK.
- Wenn die indirekte Rede mit einem Verb in der einfachen Gegenwart eingeleitet wird (z. B. *says, tells*), bleibt die Zeitform des Gesagten unverändert.

"I **didn't enjoy** the film." → Tina **says** she **didn't enjoy** the film.
- Wird die indirekte Rede durch ein Verb in der einfachen Vergangenheit eingeleitet (z. B. *said, told*) wird das Gesagte gegenüber der direkten Rede meist zeitlich zurückversetzt.

direct speech		reported speech
"The motorbike **is** expensive."	→	Tom said that the motorbike **was** expensive.
"I **can** ride a motorbike."	→	Mrs Briggs said that she **could** ride a motorbike.
"I **saw** Ellie at the cinema."	→	Ben explained that he **had seen** Ellie at the cinema.
"We **have met** lots of interesting people."	→	Sue added that they **had met** lots of interesting people.
"We **will have** a good time."	→	Emma hoped that they **would have** a good time.

7 The passive

Die meisten Sätze sind Aktivsätze.
In einem Aktivsatz führt das Subjekt
eine Handlung aus.
Young people and old people read comics.
Junge und alte Menschen lesen Comics.

Ein Passivsatz sagt aus, dass etwas mit
einem Gegenstand oder einer Person
gemacht wird oder gemacht wurde.
Das Wort *by* zeigt an, von wem die
Handlung ausgeführt wird.
Comics are read by young people and old people.
Comics werden von jungen und alten Menschen gelesen.

7.1 *Tenses in the passive*

Einen Passivsatz in der Gegenwart bildest du mit *is/are* und dem *past participle*
eines Verbs.
Lots of Indian food **is eaten** in Britain.

Einen Passivsatz in der einfachen Vergangenheit bildest du mit *was/were* und dem
past participle eines Verbs.
Our school **was built** ten years ago.

Das Perfekt bildest du mit *have/has been* und dem *past participle* eines Verbs.
These cars **have been sold**.

Die Zukunftsform bildest du mit *will be* und dem *past participle* eines Verbs.
The film **will be shown** next week.

REVISION AND PRACTICE*

1 Ireland

» The information is on pages 8–11.

a) True or false? If false, write the right information.
1. The city of Dublin has a population of about half a million people.
2. The Irish language is spoken by a majority of the population.
3. Euros are used in the whole island of Ireland.
4. Northern Ireland and the Republic of Ireland play together in the same national rugby team.
5. Many Irish people starved in 1846.
6. Only people with Irish nationality work in Ireland.
7. In Northern Ireland there are more Catholics than Protestants.
8. 40% of all European cars are made in Ireland.

b) Find the information on the Internet and write your answers in English.
1. In what Irish province is the city of Cork?
2. What's the name of Cork's twin town in Germany?
3. Write one more piece of information about the city.

Tipp Suche im Internet z. B. unter "Cork city", "city of Cork" oder "Cork Ireland".

2 Sport in Ireland

a) Look at the two pictures below and prepare what you can say about them.
- Where are the people?
- What are they doing?
- How do they feel – and why?
- Do you like one of the sports? Why (not)?

You can make notes – but don't write complete sentences.

b) Now talk to your partner about the two pictures.
You can look at your notes while you speak. Can you talk for two minutes?

*Fakultativ: nach Unit 1 oder zu einem späteren Zeitpunkt

Unit 1

3 Irish music: Write the sentences with the verbs in the *past perfect*.
1. The Irish rock band U2 started in 1976. Before that Irish music (be) mostly folk music.
2. Before B*Witched split up in 2002, they (have) four singles at the top of the UK charts.
3. Boyzone toured the UK again in June 2008. Before that they (not tour) the UK for seven years.
4. Andrea Corr (sing) with her brother and sisters in The Corrs before she became a solo singer.
5. "I went to the *Riverdance* show last night. I (never see) it before, but I enjoyed it."

4 The harp, an Irish symbol: Translate into German.
The harp is Ireland's national musical instrument and one of the country's most important symbols. It isn't on the Irish flag, but it's on the Irish euro coin and on the president's flag and it's also the name of one of Ireland's most popular beers. In the past the harp was played at festivals and weddings in Irish castles. Later many players emigrated to Britain, Canada or the USA. However, the harp is still a popular instrument today.

5 Finish the story. Write at least 120 words.
Anna was sea kayaking in Ireland. She had often done this before in a group, but this was the first time she was alone. It was exciting because the waves were incredibly high. All went well till she made a stupid mistake: she put her paddle down for a moment and a big wave took it away! Now she was alone in her boat, without a paddle …

Ideas
- Did she have a mobile phone? Did it work?
- Did a tourist on the cliffs see her?
- What happened in the end?

→ REVISION AND PRACTICE*

1 South Africa » Look at the map at the back of the book and information in the unit.

a) Answer the questions.
1. Where in the country are Cape Town, Durban, Joburg and the Kruger Park?
2. What's the population of the country? Is the population bigger or smaller than Germany's?
3. What per cent of the population doesn't live in a real house or flat? How many people don't have a job?
4. What money is used in South Africa?
5. What are the colours in the South African flag?

b) You have three days in South Africa. You can visit one of the towns or the Kruger National Park. Which do you choose? Why?
Example: I'd like to … because I'm interested in …
On the other hand I don't really like …

2 A group of South Africans is on holiday in Bavaria. You're the guide. Explain the programme for next week. Use the information below or make a programme for the area where you live. You can make up the details (e.g. times).

Welcome to Bavaria!

Programme for six days in Munich (Mon–Sat)
◆ **Munich:** city centre, Olympic stadium, museums, shopping, etc.

Trips:
◆ **Tues:** *Starnberger See* (boat trip + beer garden)
◆ **Wed:** *Neuschwanstein* (castle + walk in mountains)
◆ **Fri:** *Zugspitze* (Bavaria's highest mountain with trip on mountain railway)

Example: This afternoon we have …   On Tuesday morning the bus leaves at …

3 And you? Write six sentences about your plans for one of the next weekends. Use the *present progressive* and remember to use time phrases.
1. On Saturday morning I'm meeting some friends and we're …
2. After that we're …   3. On Saturday evening I'm …   4. …   5. …   6. …

4 Problems

a) Write two emails and complain.
1. You have bought an MP3 player online from Paul Theron. The cable to the computer is missing.
2. You ordered a digital camera from the online shop *Flop* which still hasn't arrived.

Hi Paul! On March 6th I …

b) Write a letter to the manager of *Bing*.
On your way back from South Africa the airline *Bing* lost your rucksack. When it was found it was damaged and some things were missing.

Dear Sir or Madam, …

*Fakultativ: nach Unit 2 oder zu einem späteren Zeitpunkt

Unit 2

5 You're going to compare the two suburbs of Johannesburg.

a) **Plan it!** Look at the two pictures below and plan what you can say about them. Use your imagination and what you know about South Africa.

| Ideas | roads • houses • people • what they own • their jobs • lifestyles • … |

b) **Do it!** Write at least ten sentences about the two pictures.

c) **Check it!** Now check all your sentences.

Alexandra Township, Johannesburg

Sandton, Johannesburg

6 *Tsotsi*, a South African film
Write the adjectives in the right form.

» For help look at the *Summary Pages* (92–101).

Have you ever seen the film *Tsotsi*? It's one of (successful) films that South Africa has ever produced and it won the Oscar for the (good) foreign language film in 2006. The kwaito music in the film is performed by Zola, one of South Africa's (big) music stars. The film is about a gang in Soweto. When they steal a car they find a baby in it. For Tsotsi, the baby is the beginning of a (good) life than the one he had before.
Of course, life in the film is (dramatic) than real life for most people in Soweto. There's a lot of violence and one of the (bad) moments is when the gang kills a man on a train. It's an honest film with no easy answers.

7 At the cinema: Finish the story in at least 120 words.
It was the first time that Adam went to the cinema with his new girlfriend Grace. "It's *Tsotsi*," said Adam. "It's a great film. You'll like it." They walked to the cinema where they found that the film wasn't *Tsotsi* – it was a film for young children! And Adam found that he had left all his money at home. He felt really stupid …

| Ideas | • How did Grace feel? What did she say?
• What did Adam and Grace do?
• How did the evening end? |

REVISION AND PRACTICE*

1 India

**a) Be careful – there are ten mistakes about India in this text.
Copy the text and correct the wrong information.**

1. India is an enormous country and has a population of almost a billion people.
2. A majority of the population lives in the large cities, e.g. New Delhi, Chennai, Kolkata and Mumbai (the capital).
3. Indian parents usually arrange marriages for their children.
4. The children always have to agree with their parents' choice of husband or wife.
5. One problem in India is that in January and February monsoon winds can cause terrible floods.
6. The floods are in the country, not in towns.
7. There are many poor people in India and there is no middle class.
8. Many rich Indians work in sweatshops.
9. In India, children under 14 are still allowed to work in factories.
10. India has lots of beautiful buildings. One of the most famous ones is perhaps the Taj Mahal, which was built by a Hindu prince in 1648.

An Indian wedding

b) Look on the Internet and find two pieces of interesting information which are not in this unit. Write the information in English.

2 Some Indian students visited your school last week.
**Write an article for your school magazine and report what they said.
Use *reported speech* and use different words for 'said'.**

> Our Indian visitors arrived in Bavaria last Friday. We met them at the airport.
> Eswar complained that he was tired after the journey but he said …
> Rupa … that this was her …

Rupa: This is my first visit to Germany. I've never been outside India before.

Tuhina: My parents are proud that I've been able to come here. I'll tell them all about it when I get home.

Eswar: I'm tired after the journey, but I'm looking forward to my time in Germany.

Nirvan: I hope I'll be able to see a Bayern Munich football match. I've always wanted to see them.

*Fakultativ: nach Unit 3 oder zu einem späteren Zeitpunkt

Unit 3

3 Rupa told you about cricket which is a very popular sport in India. What did Rupa actually say? Write the sentences in direct speech.

When I chatted with Rupa, she explained that she was a real cricket fan. She said that she knew the names of all India's top players and she had watched many international matches. She told me that she was going to see the match between India and Pakistan next month and added that she hoped she would be able to stay in a hotel in Chennai. Rupa said that cricket matches could last three days, but were really exciting too. Well, perhaps – but I can't imagine it!

I'm a real cricket fan. I ...

4 You want to explain to your class how cricket is played. Translate the text into German.
» Use a dictionary to find the meaning of new words.

Tipp Zeitlimit: 10 bis 12 Minuten!

Two teams which each have eleven players play against each other. Only two players from Team A play at a time: they try to hit a small, very hard ball with their bats, which they hold in their hands. If they hit the ball far away, they can run between two sets of wooden sticks and score one point each time they run.
All eleven players in Team B are in the field. One of them throws the ball – the others try to catch the ball when the player from Team A has hit it. If they catch it, the player from Team A is "out" and a new player from Team A takes his place. When all the players in Team A are "out", the teams change places: Team A is in the field, Team B tries to hit the ball.
That's a *very* simplified explanation: the reality is even more complicated!

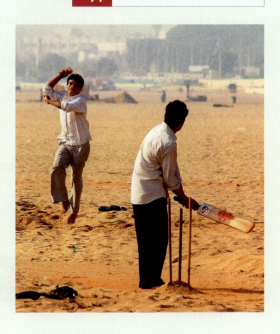

5 Rupa's hotel in Chennai was awful and now she wants to write a letter and complain. Write her letter (at least 120 words).

Ideas	• give dates • advert: "near stadium" / really: many kms • no bus • unfriendly (who?) • small room, dirty (what?), broken (what?) • noisy (why?) • wants her money back

107

one hundred and seven

REVISION AND PRACTICE*

1 Life for young people in Britain and where *you* live

a) Look at page 60 and make a list of all the problems that are talked about.
Poverty, knives, people who are addicted to designer clothes, ...

b) Look at page 62: What are the problems for young people who want to learn to drive?
Driving lessons are ..., ...

c) Look at your answers in a). Then write a short report about the area where you live. Say which of the problems you think exist in the area and which don't exist or aren't important. Write at least ten sentences.
*In our town there are some / aren't many/any young people who live in poverty.
I think / I don't think that many people carry knives.
...*

2 Picture-based conversation: Before you judge

a) Look at the picture and describe what each person is wearing.

b) Explain what people think when they see each person.
If you wear ... people often think that ...

c) The poster was made for people who are prejudiced against people in hoodies. What do *you* think: Is it a good poster? Explain your reasons.

| I think it's a good poster | because ... |
| I don't think it's a good poster | |

*Fakultativ: nach Unit 4 oder zu einem späteren Zeitpunkt

Unit 4

3 Work and dreams

**a) You receive this email from your British friend Kevin.
Translate it into German for a friend who can't speak English.**

» Aufgepasst bei *if*-Sätzen: *if we had more time* = wenn wir mehr Zeit hätten

> Hi,
>
> Sorry I haven't been in touch for so long, but I hope you're well.
>
> I'm having a pretty boring weekend because Charlotte (my girlfriend) is working in her department store today (Saturday) and tomorrow. But if she's not too tired, we'll go to a friend's party and we'll have a crazy time if his parents aren't at home.
>
> I wish Charlotte and I had more time together! If we had more time, we could travel abroad and see exotic places. But, of course, we would need money if we travelled!
>
> I suggested to Charlotte that we should buy a lottery ticket every week. Then, if we won, we could do what we wanted. But Charlotte said that it was a stupid idea. She said that we would never win.
>
> Kevin

b) What are *your* plans for next weekend?
1. If I'm not tired, …
2. If I don't have too much work for school, …
3. If I have time, …
4. If …

c) Dreams: Complete four of the six sentences.
1. If I won the lottery, …
2. If I were a celebrity, …
3. If I could choose where I lived, …
4. If I could have a really crazy party, …
5. If I could change one thing in the world, …
6. If …

4 A keyword story

Write a story for a teenage magazine competition about a party which went wrong.
- Choose at least six words from the box and include them in your story.
- Give your story a good title.
- Write at least 120 words.

• invite	• joke
• food	• alcohol
• loud	• angry
• happy	• floor
• atmosphere	• parents

REVISION AND PRACTICE*

1 Look at pages 74–75 and write eight sentences about the problems in the world's environment.

1 If the Gulf Stream becomes much weaker,
2 Polar bears will be threatened with extinction
3 If large parts of the rainforests are cut down,
4 If the ice melts in the Arctic Ocean,
5 The Gobi desert will reach Beijing
6 If people drove less,

a if the ice melts because of global warming.
b if it expands much more.
c they'd reduce their carbon footprint.
d they won't absorb so much carbon dioxide.
e winters in Europe will become colder.
f the sea level will rise.

2 Discussions

a) Holidays: Choose the right form of the verbs.

JACK I think people should (spend/spending) their holidays in their own country instead of (travel/travelling) abroad.
MARY That's easy (to say/saying), but it's totally unrealistic. Many people would rather (have/having) a holiday abroad. They want (to see/seeing) something a bit different.
JACK Well, it's no use (to complain/complaining) about global warming if you fly and pump carbon dioxide into the atmosphere!
MARY On the other hand you simply can't live without (to produce/producing) carbon dioxide.
JACK So what? It's worth (do/doing) what you can.

b) You and your friend are discussing one of the topics below. Write your own dialogue.
» Use words and phrases from the dialogue above.

- Eat exotic food or local food?
- Travel by car or by train?
- Use expensive eco-products or other cheap ones?
- Choose your own topic.

3 A disaster: Translate the text into German.
A huge explosion was heard in Prypiat in the morning of April 26th, 1986, but nobody knew that the Chernobyl nuclear power station had released radioactive gases into the air. Even the firefighters who were called to the power station had no idea of the danger and worked without protective clothing. The next day, however, buses suddenly appeared and everybody had to leave the city. In all about 130,000 people were evacuated from the area.

*Fakultativ: nach Unit 5

Unit 5

4 Sentences with the *passive*

a) Look at the texts on pages 74–75 of this unit and find one example of the ...

1 present tense passive
2 past tense passive
3 present perfect passive
4 future tense passive

b) In 2005 there were plans for a huge wind farm at Whinash, near the Lake District National Park in the north of England. People who were for and people who were against the wind farm both organised campaigns.
Complete the sentences in the campaign posters and use the same tenses as in a).

SAY YES TO THE WHINASH WIND FARM!
- More clean energy (need) in Britain.
- Wind farms aren't new – Britain's first wind farm (build) in 1991.
- Lots of wind farms (build) in other countries.
- Energy for 47,000 houses (produce) by this farm.

SAY NO TO THE WHINASH WIND FARM!
- No energy (produce) when there's no wind.
- The area (visit) by millions of tourists last year.
- Large protest marches (organise) against the wind farm.
- Beautiful views of hills and mountains (destroy) by the wind farm.

Note: In the end the "No" campaign was successful and the farm wasn't built.

c) What's your opinion about the advantages and disadvantages of wind farms? Write about what you think. Write 5–6 sentences.

Wind farms are good / better than ... because ...
The trouble is that ... • It's no use building ...
It's / It isn't worth building them because ...
If too many are built, ... • All in all I think that ...

5 You and your family would like to spend a few days in summer in the Lake District. Write a letter to the Skiddaw Hotel in Keswick.
- Book rooms (single/double). Tell them your dates.
- B&B or with meals?
- Ask for: cost? • deposit? • time for breakfast? • advice for activities in the Lake District?

Skiddaw Hotel

The Lake District National Park

EXAM PRACTICE*

LISTENING

2 ◉ 45–48

» You're not allowed to use a dictionary!

1 Listen to three answerphone messages in an office in Johannesburg and find out for each message:

| **Tipp** | Gib auch dann eine Antwort, wenn du nicht ganz sicher bist – keine Antwort, keine Punkte! |

a) **Who phoned?**
1 Message 1: ...
2 Message 2: ...
3 Message 3: ...

b) **At what time?**
1 Message 1: ...
2 Message 2: ...
3 Message 3: ...

c) **What's the message?**
1 Message 1: ...
2 Message 2: ...
3 Message 3: ...

2 South Africa's newest railway:
Listen and choose the right option.
1 The train will connect Johannesburg and Pretoria with
   a) Cape Town.   b) an airport.   c) Soweto.
2 Trains will travel up to
   a) 120   b) 140   c) 180   kilometres per hour.
3 The time from Johannesburg to Pretoria will be
   a) 14 minutes.   b) 24 minutes.   c) 40 minutes.
4 An advantage of the new train is
   a) new jobs.   b) cheap travel.   c) stations in poor townships.

3 An interview about kwaito music

a) **Listen: Are the sentences true or false?**
1 Kwaito music has both South African and American influences.
2 You can hear Zola's music in the South African film *Tsotsi*.
3 Zola is the name of a part of Soweto.
4 When kwaito began, people thought it was a bit dangerous.
5 There was no black South African music during the years of apartheid.
6 Kwaito lyrics can be about the problems and the good things in South Africa today.

b) **Listen again and complete the sentences with information from the interview.**
1 The name Zola is good for ...
2 Kwaito comes from the Afrikaans language, from a word which means ...
3 I would say kwaito is a voice from ...
4 In kwaito we, the young people of South Africa, are trying to say and to find out ...

4 A report about young people in South Africa on the radio news: Listen and take notes.
Then answer the questions.

| **Tipp** | Lies die Fragen, bevor du dir den Text anhörst. |

1 How many per cent of young South Africans are unemployed?
2 What are two disadvantages for black young people who are looking for work?
3 How do most young people in work find their jobs? Give two answers.
4 Why are young people especially important in South Africa? Give two reasons.

*Fakultativ

READING

» Use a dictionary to find the meaning of new words.

An angel for our times

1 Well, I've written in the past about why I admire celebrities, why I detest designer clothes, why I love box-office hits and why eco-freaks make me sick, but I never thought that I would use this blog in order to write about a work of art ...

2 But listen, guys: last weekend I was travelling with my parents north from London to Newcastle-Upon-Tyne in order to visit my brother who is now at college there. A few miles south of Newcastle I looked out of the car and suddenly I saw the Angel of the North for the first time. Have you ever heard of it? It's a huge statue of an angel who is standing with his legs together and spreading two enormous wings. It can be seen from miles around and because it is on a hill near the A1, the main London to Newcastle motorway, people say that it's seen by 90,000 people a day.

3 Now you'll know from my blogs that I'm not exactly an arty sort of person. For me, art is something that you see in museums and art galleries on school trips. And I walk past statues in town without even looking at them. But this statue is different: it's so large and strong and impressive that it gave me a real buzz – a feeling like when you see a great monument like the Eiffel Tower or the London Eye for the first time. It was great!

The Angel of the North from the A1

4 Why's the Angel so special? Well, it's very tall (it's 20 metres high) and it's incredibly wide – 54 metres wide, wider than a Boeing 767 or wider than the Statue of Liberty is tall. The wings seem wide enough to say "Hi!" to all the 90,000 people who travel past every day. And the wings are special because they aren't soft and beautiful, but hard and rectangular, like parts of a plane or a machine. They're the powerful wings of an angel from an industrial region where coal was once mined, where machines were once made and where people used to work in busy, noisy, dirty factories.

5 Personally, I really like the Angel's wings, but not everybody agrees with me. My mum said that she didn't think that the wings looked like angel's wings and my younger brother Tom said he had never seen such an ugly angel. But the moment we saw the Angel, we were all talking about it. And that's the most special thing about the Angel. Because it's not hidden in a museum, but is outside and very visible and because hundreds of thousands of people have seen it, everybody knows it and everybody has an opinion about it. You can't drive past the Angel of the North without arguing about it. And hey, I like that.

6 The area where the Angel now stands was very different thirty or forty years ago. My mum told me that she had visited Newcastle in the 1970s and she had found it a very depressing town. Apparently the old industries (e.g. coal and ships) had collapsed and there was massive unemployment. People had very little money, shops and cafés had closed and crime was a problem. My mum remembers that the whole area looked dirty, ugly and sad.

EXAM PRACTICE*

7 Well, today you can see that huge efforts have been made to regenerate the area. There are new houses, new factories, new parks and a new bridge for cyclists and pedestrians across the river Tyne. And art and music are playing a key role in the regeneration programme: an old factory in the middle of Newcastle has been re-opened as a gallery of modern art and next to it is a fantastic new concert hall. The Angel of the North is part of the regeneration programme too. Tourists who come to see it spend the day in Newcastle, have a meal and do some shopping. The money helps Newcastle to find a new role. So – like a "real" angel – the Angel is helping and protecting the people who live near it.

The Statue of Liberty – a work of art in a very public place

8 And here's why I'm writing this blog: do you agree with me that there should be many more works of art in public places? Not boring sculptures that you just walk past or works of art that don't mean anything to most people – but really impressive works of art like the Angel of the North or the Statue of Liberty in New York, statues or monuments that you can't help noticing and talking about. Most cities in Europe are now trying to improve the environment for their inhabitants with pedestrianised streets, street cafés, more trees and restored buildings. Perhaps good works of art could really help too?

Do you agree with me? Do you know any statues in public places which have given you a buzz? Or do you think I have become an art freak and works of art are a waste of time and money? Please write what you think!

Grace

For more info about the Angel of the North, key in "Angel of the North" on Wikipedia.

Comments

Works of art in our cities? You must be joking, Grace! They cost a lot of money and most people never even notice them. I think it would be better to spend the money on useful buildings, e.g. bridges, bus stations or even more public toilets.   Gavin

I had never really thought much about statues or works of art before I read your article, Grace – but after I read it I found pictures of the Angel of the North on the Internet and I see what you mean. I think I'll start looking at statues in town from now on! So thanks for your article, Grace.   Starstream

1 Find a title for each paragraph 1–8. You won't need two titles.
Example: Paragraph 1: D

- **A** More works of art in public places, please!
- **B** When Grace first saw the Angel of the North
- **C** Information about the artist
- **D** What Grace has written about before
- **E** How the area has improved
- **F** What people said when the Angel was built
- **G** The size of the Angel
- **H** Grace's usual reaction to art
- **I** A short history of the area
- **J** Everybody who sees the Angel talks about it.

*Fakultativ

2 **Now answer the questions in full sentences.**

Tipp Vorsicht, Pronomenwechsel!
Im Text heißt es **my**, aber in deiner Antwort wird daraus ...

1 What does Grace think of eco-freaks?
2 Why did Grace travel to Newcastle?
3 Why is it surprising that Grace was so impressed by a work of art?
4 Why do so many people in Britain know the Angel of the North?
5 What was the area around Newcastle like thirty or forty years ago?
6 How are art and music important for the regeneration of Newcastle?
   Give three examples.

3 **What's the correct option?**

1 Grace   **a)** often   **b)** usually never   **c)** sometimes
   writes about art in her blogs.
2 Tom thought that the Angel's wings were
   a) beautiful.   **b)** much too big.   **c)** not very beautiful.
3 The new bridge in Newcastle is for
   a) bikes and people on foot.   **b)** cars and bikes.   **c)** buses and cars.
4 Gavin thinks that works of art in public places are
   a) funny.   **b)** worth the money.   **c)** a waste of money.
5 Starstream says he/she will
   a) become an artist when she's older.
   b) try not to walk past works of art without noticing them.
   c) find out more about works of art in her town.

4 **Explain the words according to their meaning in the text.**
Write complete sentences.

1 statue *(n)* *(line 8)*   2 motorway *(n)* *(line 10)*   3 ugly *(adj)* *(line 31)*
4 visible *(adj)* *(line 33)*   5 collapse *(v)* *(line 38)*   6 regenerate *(v)* *(line 42)*

5 **Mediation: Translate paragraph 8 into German.**

6 **What did Grace's mother and younger brother actually say about the Angel?**
Write their words in direct speech.

1 Grace's mother said, "I ... "
2 Grace's brother Tom said, "I ... "

7 **Write your own answer to Grace. Write 3–4 sentences.**

Ideas Do you know any statues or public works of art which you really like?
Should there be more public works of art in your town or village?
Or are they a waste of money?

→ EXAM PRACTICE*

TEXT PRODUCTION

» Use a dictionary to find the meaning of new words.

1 An open-ended story
Finish the story. Write at least 120 words.

Paul had just bought himself a new laptop computer. He came out of the shopping centre and he was thinking about what computer games he would buy as he walked home. Suddenly Paul realised that he was in a street with very few people in it. And in front of him were four young people with hoodies on. They were slowly walking towards him.
Paul felt a bit frightened …

2 Letter writing: A summer camp in Croatia

European Youth Project

Split, Croatia

"Helping others & having fun"

- Summer camp on the Croatian coast for young people from all over Europe
- Mornings: work together, prepare the land and build a home for children who have lost their parents
- Afternoons and evenings: relax, swim, explore the city of Split, make new friends
- Working language: English
- More information from:
  Mrs Marion Thomas, EYP, 32 Howard Street, London SW23 4RJ

Du hast diese Anzeige in einer Zeitschrift gefunden und hättest Lust an dem Camp teilzunehmen. Doch vorher willst du noch weitere Informationen einholen und schreibst deshalb einen Brief an Marion Thomas.

Dein Brief sollte folgende Punkte enthalten:
– Fundstelle der Anzeige und Grund deines Interesses
– Zeitpunkt und Dauer des Camps
– Hinfahrt: Wie? Wohin? Abholmöglichkeiten?
– Unterkunft und Verpflegung
– Ausflüge?
– Reisekosten und Art und Weise der Bezahlung

Use a separate sheet of paper for your letter and write at least 120 words.

*Fakultativ

USE OF ENGLISH

» You're not allowed to use a dictionary!

1 The Mozart of Madras*
Write the right form of the verb.
When the British film *Slumdog Millionaire* (win) a *Golden Globe Award* for best film music in January 2009, few people in Britain (ever/hear) of A. R. Rahman, the man behind the music. But the award (not/come) as a surprise to his fans in India, where for many years A. R. Rahman (be) one of the most popular names in Indian music.
Born in Chennai in 1966, A.R. Rahman (found) his own rock band, *Nemesis Avenue*, when he was still a boy. He (able/begin) work in his own studio in 1991. As early as 1992 he (ask) to write the music for the Indian film *Roja*. Although he (never/write) music for a film before, his music for the film was a great success. Since 1992 A. R. Rahman (write) the music for many more films. He has an original style which usually (mix) classical Indian music with western music and traditional instruments with electronic technology. In February 2009 A. R. Rahman (win) two Oscars for *Slumdog Millionaire*: one for the best film music and one for the best song.

* Madras is a city which is now called Chennai.

2 Bollywood stars

a) Use the right form of the adjectives.
1 Male stars are often (popular) than female stars in India.
2 Amitabh Bachchan is perhaps the (successful) Bollywood star of all.
3 He was probably India's (good) actor in the 1970s and is still (famous) today.
4 Of the younger actors, Shah Rukh Khan is one of the (big) names in Bollywood.
5 He works successfully in films and on TV and is one of the (rich) actors in the world.
6 In 2008 *Newsweek* magazine called him one of the 50 (powerful) people in the world.

b) Write the missing words.
1 Female stars in Bollywood don't earn ... much ... male stars.
2 Top female stars often get less ... half the money earned by male stars.

c) Write the correct form of the verb in these *if*-sentences.
1 I think it would be fairer if male and female stars both (earn) the same.
2 If male stars were paid less money than female stars, I'm sure they (protest)!

Aishwarya Rai

d) Write the sentences in indirect speech.
1 **SOPHIE** My favourite female star is Aishwarya Rai.   *My sister Sophie said that ...*
2 **SOPHIE** I've seen four of her films.   *She added that ...*

EXAM PRACTICE*

3 Vocabulary

a) Write the corresponding verb or adjective.

noun	verb
1 speech	???
2 choice	???
3 argument	???
4 decision	???
5 explosion	???

noun	adjective
6 freedom	???
7 music	???
8 violence	???
9 electricity	???
10 poverty	???

b) Write two nouns from the list which have the following sounds:
1 [i]   2 [iː]   3 [ju]

ORAL EXAM

» Use a dictionary to find the meaning of new words.

1 Picture-based conversation: The perfect hotel?

a) Look at the two pictures below and compare them.
Describe what you can see and make notes (if you want to).

Ideas building? • weather? • atmosphere? • noise? • clean and tidy? • many people?

The hotel brochure

What the hotel is really like

b) Now talk to your partner about the two pictures.

c) What would you do if you had booked this hotel and arrived there for a holiday?

*Fakultativ

2 Interpreting

You and your friend Claudia are chatting with a British teenager, Mark, who is spending a week at your school in Bavaria. Mark doesn't speak German and Claudia doesn't speak English very well. Work with two partners and interpret for them.

a) Partners B and C:
Look at page 120 and read part a) of Mark and Claudia's dialogue.
Partner A: Listen to Mark and Claudia and interpret for them.

b) Now change roles.
Partners A and C: Read part b) of Mark and Claudia's dialogue on page 120.
Partner B: Listen and interpret.

c) Change roles again.
Partners A and B: Read part c) of Mark and Claudia's dialogue on page 121.
Partner C: Listen and interpret.

3 A topic-based talk

a) Choose a topic for your topic-based talk.

The tourist industry in Ireland	South Africa – the rainbow nation	India – a modern giant

Young women in the modern world	The two most urgent problems for the world's environment

b) Find information about your topic and prepare your talk.
- Divide your topic into different parts and find examples for each part.
- Say what *you* think about each topic. *Your* opinion is important!

c) Now look at the card for your topic.

"Ireland is very pretty, but it doesn't have much for young people."
- Do you agree or disagree? Give examples which support your opinion.
- What's very pretty in Ireland?

"South Africa shows that different peoples can live together in peace."
- Give examples which support the sentence above.
- Describe some problems in modern South Africa too.

"The future belongs to India."
- How has life improved for many Indians?
- What problems does the country still have?

"British women who work full-time earn 13 % less than men." (Report in 2006)
- What sort of low-paid jobs do many women work in? Why?
- Has the role of women improved in the last few years? Give examples.

"In the next few years, wars will be fought for water."
- Why won't there soon be enough drinking water in the world?
- How can people in Europe best help the environment?

d) Now work with a partner.
- Give your talk and include answers to the questions on the cards.
- Your partner then asks two questions on page 121.
  Listen and give full, interesting answers.
- Then change roles: Your partner gives his/her talk and you ask the questions on page 121.

→ EXAM PRACTICE

ORAL EXAM (page 118)

2 Interpreting

a) Partners B and C

MARC   Hi, Claudia. Nice to see you again. What are you doing?

CLAUDIA   Ich mache meine Hausaufgaben. Ich lese einen Text über Südafrika. Warst du mal da?

MARC   Yes, I went to South Africa two years ago. I have an uncle there.

CLAUDIA   Wie war es?

MARC   I really liked it. I thought Cape Town was great.

CLAUDIA   Warst du auch im Krüger Nationalpark?

MARC   No, I was in the south of South Africa and the Kruger National Park is at the other end of the country.

CLAUDIA   Ich würde gerne mal Tiere wie Löwen und Nilpferde in freier Wildbahn sehen.

b) Partners A and C

MARC   Have you ever been to Ireland?

CLAUDIA   Ich nicht, aber eine Freundin von mir war letztes Jahr dort. Ihr hat es sehr gefallen.

MARC   Do you know where in Ireland she was?

CLAUDIA   Ich weiß, dass sie nach Dublin geflogen ist. Ich glaube, sie war ein paar Tage in Dublin.

MARC   I think Dublin's a great city. There are so many people there from all over the world.

CLAUDIA   Meine Freundin war mit ihren Eltern unterwegs und ich glaube, sie haben ein Auto gemietet.

MARC   Did they travel to the west of Ireland? It's not the part I like best, but it's where most tourists want to go.

CLAUDIA   Sie hat von Bergen und Klippen geredet. Das war wohl im Westen.

c) Partners B and A

MARC Which country would you like to visit if you could choose?

CLAUDIA Ich würde, glaube ich, nach Indien fahren. Das Land ist so groß – es muss faszinierend sein.

MARC I have a good friend from Mumbai. He's shown me lots of photos of the north of India and it looks great.

CLAUDIA Ich würde auch am liebsten nach Mumbai fahren und mir Bollywood anschauen.

MARC I'd like to see the cities too, although I think I would be a bit frightened of them sometimes.

CLAUDIA Warum hättest du Angst?

MARC Well, they're so huge that I would be afraid of getting lost. And I think I would sometimes find the big crowds in the streets a bit frightening.

CLAUDIA Du hast recht. Aber andererseits muss das Leben in den Städten auch sehr interessant sein!

ORAL EXAM (page 119)

3 **Topic-based talk**

d) Listen to your partner's talk and then ask two of the questions below.

Ireland
• Why were there many years of fighting in Northern Ireland?
• Would you like to visit Ireland? Why (not)?

South Africa
• What was apartheid?
• What has Nelson Mandela done for his country?

India
• Can you describe one of India's modern industries?
• Why are there still many Indians who are very poor?

Young women in the modern world
• Is life for young women in Europe more difficult than for young men?
• Tell me something about a famous woman who you admire.

Two urgent problems for the environment
• Why are "expanding deserts" a problem? Give an example.
• Are you for or against nuclear power stations? Why?

VOCABULARY

Schlüssel zu den Einträgen

Ein Lerntipp
steht am Anfang jeder Unit.

Die Seitenzahl
gibt an, auf welcher Seite in der Unit das neue Wort zum ersten Mal vorkommt.

Wortschatz
Die fett gedruckten Wörter sollst du verstehen und benutzen können. Normal gedruckte Wörter sollst du verstehen.

Pfeile
verweisen auf die Kästen rechts.

Die Lautschrift
zeigt dir die richtige Aussprache.

Wortschatz
Schräg gedruckte Wörter kommen z. B. in Liedern vor.

VOCABULARY

Unit 2

TIPP Lernen mit Gleichem oder Gegensätzlichem
Zu zweit lernt es sich leichter! Du kannst mit einem Partner / einer Partnerin Spiele zum Vokabellernen machen. Verwende auch die Hinweise auf Wortgruppen, ähnliche Wörter oder Gegensätze hier aus der Vokabelliste.

- **Odd one out:** Jede/r schreibt vier bis sechs Wörter auf, von denen immer ein Wort nicht zu den anderen passt. Der Partner / die Partnerin muss diesen „Außenseiter" finden.
  Beispiele:
  1 *lion – leopard – fish – elephant – buffalo*
  2 *worried – confident – scared – afraid*

- **Fourth word:** Drei von vier Wörtern werden vorgegeben, gesucht wird das vierte.
  Beispiele:
  3 *armed • unarmed – dependent • ???* (hier geht es um Gegensätze!)
  4 *country: the Netherlands – language: ???* (die Sprache in dem Land ...?)

1 lion – leopard – FISH – elephant – buffalo
2 worried – CONFIDENT – scared – afraid
3 armed – unarmed, dependent – INDEPENDENT
4 country – the Netherlands, language – DUTCH

South Africa

24 **railway** [ˈreɪlweɪ]	Eisenbahn	
wealthy [ˈwelθi]	reich, wohlhabend →	
running water	fließendes Wasser	
World Cup	Weltmeisterschaft (hier: Fußball)	
rhinoceros, rhinoceroses [raɪˈnɒsərəs]	Nashorn	
leopard [ˈlepəd]	Leopard	
elephant [ˈelɪfənt]	Elefant	
buffalo, buffaloes [ˈbʌfələʊ]	Büffel	
lion [ˈlaɪən]	Löwe	
25 **rainbow nation** [ˈreɪnbəʊ neɪʃn]	„Regenbogennation" (Name für Südafrika aufgrund seiner ethnischen Vielfalt)	
the Whites [waɪts]	die Weißen	
Afrikaans [æfrɪˈkɑːns]	Afrikaans (Sprache in Südafrika) →	
Dutch [dʌtʃ]	Niederländisch	
the Coloureds [ˈkʌlədz]	die „Farbigen" (Menschen, die sowohl schwarze als auch weiße Vorfahren haben)	
no wonder that [ˈwʌndə]	kein Wunder, dass	
united	vereint	
strive for [straɪv]	streben nach	
freedom [ˈfriːdəm]	Freiheit	

→ The *railway* system is very good. You can go everywhere by train.

→ *wealthy • rich*

→ A *rhinoceros* has one or two horns on its nose.
[ˈlepəd]
[ˈelɪfənt]

→ Afrikaans entstand um 1770 aus dem Niederländischen, hat aber eine stark vereinfachte Grammatik.

→ England – English
   the Netherlands – Dutch

→ You practise every day?
   No wonder that you're so good!

Die rechte Spalte enthält
Anwendungsbeispiele sowie
Kästen mit zusätzlichen Informationen:
Rot = Schwerpunkt Grammatik
Blau = Schwerpunkt Sprache
Gelb = Schwerpunkt kulturelle Besonderheiten

A world language | Unit 1

A world language

6 widely-spoken ['waɪdli spəʊkən]	weit verbreitet, viel gesprochen	→ What's the most *widely-spoken* language in the world?
7 English-speaking	englischsprachig	→ understand
Celtic ['keltɪk]	keltisch	I understood [ʌndə'stʊd]
majority [mə'dʒɒrəti]	Mehrheit	I've understood [ʌndə'stʊd]
understand: it is understood [ʌndə'stʊd]	verstehen: es wird verstanden →	
minority [maɪ'nɒrəti]	Minderheit →	→ majority – minority
South Africa [saʊθ 'æfrɪkə]	Südafrika	→ speak • speaker
speaker ['spiːkə]	Sprecher/in →	
South African [saʊθ 'æfrɪkən]	südafrikanisch; Südafrikaner/in	→ the *South African* flag

Unit 1

> **TIPP Wörter bauen**
>
> Manche Wörter setzen sich aus zwei anderen zusammen.
>
> **Nomen + Nomen = neues Nomen**
>
>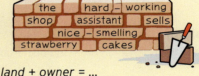
>
> home + town = hometown • race + horse = racehorse • land + owner = …
>
> Achte auf die Schreibweise! Manchmal sind es auch zwei Wörter mit oder ohne Bindestrich: *ice skating, ski resort, flower-bed, sleeping-bag*
>
> **Adjektiv/Adverb + Verb = neues Adjektiv, immer mit Bindestrich.**
>
> good + looking = good-looking • English + speaking = …
> well + paid = well-paid • widely + spoken = …
>
> Ob ein so gebautes Wort wirklich existiert und wie es richtig geschrieben wird, solltest du im Zweifelsfall im Wörterbuch nachschauen.

Ireland

8 at the bottom ['bɒtəm] (of the photo)	unten (auf dem Foto)	→ "Click on the link at the *bottom* of this page."
9 republic [rɪ'pʌblɪk]	Republik	→ ❗ [rɪ'pʌblɪk]
spire ['spaɪə]	Turm; Kirchturmspitze	
tower ['taʊə]	Turm	
multinational [mʌlti'næʃnəl]	multinational, aus vielen Nationen	
tourist industry	Tourismusindustrie	
coast [kəʊst]	Küste	
wide [waɪd]	breit →	→ wide – narrow
sandy ['sændi]	sandig, Sand-	

Ireland – past and present

10 county ['kaʊnti]	Grafschaft (Verwaltungsbezirk)	→ ❗ one county, two counties
disease [dɪ'ziːz]	Krankheit	→ AIDS is a serious *disease*.
starve [stɑːv]	verhungern	→ What's for lunch? I'm *starving*!

VOCABULARY

ruined house ['ruːɪnd]	verfallenes Haus	
leave behind:	zurücklassen:	→ leave behind [liːv bɪ'haɪnd] I left behind [left] I've left behind [left]
they left behind	sie ließen zurück →	
Protestant ['prɒtɪstənt]	Protestant/in; protestantisch	→ ❗ ['prɒtɪstənt]
Catholic ['kæθlɪk]	Katholik/in; katholisch	→ ❗ ['kæθlɪk]
both Catholics and Protestants	sowohl Katholiken als auch Protestanten	
peace [piːs]	Friede(n) →	→ peace • peaceful
bomb [bɒm]	Bombe	→ ❗ [bɒm]

Why not work in Ireland?

→ England – English
Poland – Polish

11 Polish ['pəʊlɪʃ]	Pole/Polin; polnisch; Polnisch	
Poland ['pəʊlənd]	Polen →	
any ['eni]	irgendein/e; jede/r/s →	→ any I don't have any time. kein/e She's nicer than any other girl in my class. jede/r/s
European Union [jʊərəpiːən 'juːniən]	Europäische Union	
the only company	die einzige Firma →	→ only It's only 7.30. There's only one bike. It's the only bike.
doughnut ['dəʊnʌt]	Doughnut (ringförmiges Hefegebäck); Berliner, Krapfen	

Speaking

13 it's your turn	du bist dran	→ I'm at the front of the queue, so it's my turn now.
tourist poster	Touristenposter	
brief(ly) [briːf, 'briːfli]	kurz	

Reading

14 celebrity [sə'lebrəti]	Berühmtheit, berühmte Person →	→ In den Medien siehst du oft nur die Kurzform celeb [sə'leb].
post [pəʊst]	schicken (per Post oder E-Mail)	
selfish ['selfɪʃ]	egoistisch	→ You're thinking of yourself all the time: you're very selfish!
spend money on	Geld ausgeben für →	→ spend money on – spent – spent
luxury yacht ['lʌkʃəri jɒt]	Luxusjacht	
in order to help	um zu helfen	
form	gründen	
sixth out of 200	Sechste/r von 200	→ Three out of ten, that's thirty per cent.
gang [gæŋ]	Clique, (Jugend-)Bande	
Latin ['lætɪn]	Latein	
nickname ['nɪkneɪm]	Spitzname	
poverty ['pɒvəti]	Armut →	→ poverty ['pɒvəti] • poor [pʊə]
take part in: he took part in	teilnehmen an: er nahm teil an →	→ take part in [teɪk 'pɑːt ɪn] I took part in [tʊk] I've taken part in ['teɪkən]
aid [eɪd]	Hilfe, Unterstützung	
Ethiopia [iːθi'əʊpiə]	Äthiopien	
raise [reɪz]	(Spendengelder) sammeln; (Kinder) großziehen	→ How much money did you raise? She raised four kids.
15 injustice [ɪn'dʒʌstɪs]	Ungerechtigkeit	
HIV [eɪtʃ aɪ 'viː]	Virus, das Aids verursacht	
president ['prezɪdənt]	Präsident/in	→ ❗ ['prezɪdənt]
criticise ['krɪtɪsaɪz]	kritisieren	→ ❗ ['krɪtɪsaɪz]

Unit 1

the Netherlands ['neðələndz]	die Niederlande	→	**cause** Smoking can *cause* heart disease. Live Aid – that's music for a good *cause*!
tax [tæks]	Steuer(n)		
for good causes ['kɔːziz]	für gute/wohltätige Zwecke →		
poll [pəʊl]	Umfrage		
comment ['kɒment]	Kommentar	→	The president said, "No *comment*."
idealistic [aɪdɪə'lɪstɪk]	idealistisch		
naive [naɪ'iːv]	naiv	→	❗ [naɪ'iːv]
hometown ['həʊmtaʊn]	Heimatstadt		
Colombia [kə'lʌmbɪə]	Kolumbien		
16 **musician** [mjuː'zɪʃn]	Musiker/in		

Listening

17 **giant** ['dʒaɪənt]	Riese/Riesin	→	Many basketball players are real *giants*.
ha'penny ['heɪpni]	= halfpenny *(ehem. kleinste britische Münze)*	→	❗ ['heɪpni]

Writing

19 **wake up: he woke up** [wəʊk]	aufwachen: er wachte auf →	→	**wake up** [weɪk 'ʌp] I woke up [wəʊk] I've woken up ['wəʊkən]
racehorse ['reɪs hɔːs]	Rennpferd		

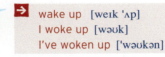

Look at language

20 **ancestor** ['ænsestə]	Vorfahre/Vorfahrin	→	**pick** *Pick* a number between 1 and 10. We can *pick* these apples now.
landowner ['lændəʊnə]	Grundbesitzer/in		
pick [pɪk]	*hier:* ernten →		
smell [smel]	Geruch	→	What an awful *smell*! It smells like old socks!
rent [rent]	Miete, Pacht(gebühr)	→	When you rent a flat, you have to pay *rent*.
workhouse ['wɜːkhaʊs]	Arbeitshaus →		**Arbeitshaus** Hier konnten arme Menschen wohnen und arbeiten, aber es ging ziemlich rau zu.
separate ['sepəreɪt]	trennen		
surprising [sə'praɪzɪŋ]	überraschend, verwunderlich		
wash [wɒʃ]	sich waschen		
dining room ['daɪnɪŋ ruːm]	Esszimmer →	→	**dining room** living room • kitchen bathroom • bedroom
reception [rɪ'sepʃn]	Rezeption, Empfang *(Hotel)*		
receptionist [rɪ'sepʃənɪst]	Empfangsmitarbeiter/in *(Hotel)*		
21 **chambermaid** ['tʃeɪmbəmeɪd]	Zimmermädchen		
Bosnia ['bɒznɪə]	Bosnien		
marry ['mæri]	heiraten	→	My sister *married* my best friend.
23 **ban** [bæn]	verbieten →	→	**it is banned** • **it is not allowed**

125

one hundred and twenty-five

VOCABULARY

Unit 2

TIPP **Lernen mit Gleichem oder Gegensätzlichem**

Zu zweit lernt es sich leichter! Du kannst mit einem Partner / einer Partnerin Spiele zum Vokabellernen machen. Verwende auch die Hinweise auf Wortgruppen, ähnliche Wörter oder Gegensätze hier aus der Vokabelliste.

- **Odd one out:** Jede/r schreibt vier bis sechs Wörter auf, von denen immer ein Wort <u>nicht</u> zu den anderen passt. Der Partner / die Partnerin muss diesen „Außenseiter" finden.
  Beispiele:
  1 *lion – leopard – fish – elephant – buffalo*
  2 *worried – confident – scared – afraid*

- **Fourth word:** Drei von vier Wörtern werden vorgegeben, gesucht wird das vierte.
  Beispiele:
  3 *armed • <u>un</u>armed – dependent • ???*   (hier geht es um Gegensätze!)
  4 *country: the Netherlands – language: ???*   (die Sprache in dem Land …?)

1 lion – leopard – FISH – elephant – buffalo
2 worried – CONFIDENT – scared – afraid
3 armed – unarmed, dependent – INDEPENDENT
4 country – the Netherlands, language – DUTCH

South Africa

24	**railway** ['reɪlweɪ]	Eisenbahn
	wealthy ['welθi]	reich, wohlhabend →
	running water	fließendes Wasser
	World Cup	Weltmeisterschaft (hier: Fußball)
	rhinoceros, rhinoceroses [raɪ'nɒsərəs]	Nashorn
	leopard ['lepəd]	Leopard
	elephant ['elɪfənt]	Elefant
	buffalo, buffaloes ['bʌfələʊ]	Büffel
	lion [laɪən]	Löwe
25	**rainbow nation** ['reɪnbəʊ neɪʃn]	„Regenbogennation" (Name für Südafrika aufgrund seiner ethnischen Vielfalt)
	the Whites [waɪts]	die Weißen
	Afrikaans [æfrɪ'kɑːns]	Afrikaans (Sprache in Südafrika) →
	Dutch [dʌtʃ]	Niederländisch →
	the Coloureds ['kʌlədz]	die „Farbigen" (Menschen, die sowohl schwarze als auch weiße Vorfahren haben)
	no wonder that ['wʌndə]	kein Wunder, dass
	united	vereint
	strive for [straɪv]	streben nach
	freedom ['friːdəm]	Freiheit

→ The *railway* system is very good. You can go everywhere by train.

→ *wealthy • rich*

→ A *rhinoceros* has one or two horns on its nose.

→ ! ['lepəd]
→ ! ['elɪfənt]

Afrikaans entstand um 1770 aus dem Niederländischen, hat aber eine stark vereinfachte Grammatik.

→ England – English
  the Netherlands – Dutch

→ You practise every day? *No wonder that* you're so good!

Unit 2

go up	zunehmen, steigen		Everything costs more now. Prices *have gone up*.
go down	abnehmen, sinken ➡	➡ go up – go down	
electric [ɪˈlektrɪk]	elektrisch		
disagree with [dɪsəˈgriː]	nicht übereinstimmen mit ➡	➡ agree – disagree	

Apartheid and after

26
apartheid [əˈpɑːtaɪt]	Apartheid *(früheres System der Trennung zwischen Weißen und Schwarzen)*		
the Blacks [blæks]	die Schwarzen ➡	➡ Blacks • Whites • Coloureds	
govern [ˈgʌvn]	regieren ➡	➡ govern • government	
back then	damals		
township [ˈtaʊnʃɪp]	Township *(von Schwarzen und Farbigen bewohnte Siedlung)*		
badly-paid [ˈbædli peɪd]	schlecht bezahlt ➡	➡ badly-paid – well-paid	
sex [seks]	Sex		
fire at [ˈfaɪr ət]	schießen auf		I certainly didn't *fire at* anybody …
unarmed [ʌnˈɑːmd]	unbewaffnet		… I was *unarmed*!
injure [ˈɪndʒə]	verletzen ➡	➡ injure • hurt	
more and more	immer mehr		
free [friː]	befreien		Let's *free* that poor bird. It should be free!
disadvantage [dɪsədˈvɑːntɪdʒ]	Nachteil		
education [edʒuˈkeɪʃn]	(Schul-)Bildung		A good *education* is important if you want to be successful.
rate (of HIV/AIDS) [reɪt]	(HIV/Aids-)Quote		

Young South Africans

27
kwaito [ˈkweɪtəʊ]	Kwaito *(südafrikanische Musikstilrichtung)*		
sort of [ˈsɔːt əv]	Art (von)		What *sort of* music do you like?
hip-hop [ˈhɪp hɒp]	Hiphop		
dress	sich kleiden		You're cool. I like the way you *dress*.
braai [braɪ]	Grillfest *(südafrikanisch)*		
ostrich [ˈɒstrɪtʃ]	Strauß *(Vogel)*		
taste [teɪst]	schmecken		Wow! This *tastes* good!
security [sɪˈkjʊərəti]	Sicherheit		
be afraid of [əˈfreɪd]	Angst haben vor		
thief, thieves [θiːf, θiːvz]	Dieb/in		*Thieves* steal things from people.
chill out [tʃɪl ˈaʊt]	sich entspannen, „chillen"		
huge [hjuːdʒ]	riesig		What a *huge* building!
lawyer [ˈlɔːjə]	Rechtsanwalt/-anwältin		
diamond [ˈdaɪəmənd]	Diamant		❗ [ˈdaɪəmənd]

Speaking

28
Cape Town [ˈkeɪp taʊn]	Kapstadt		
rand [rænd]	Rand *(südafr. Währung)*		One euro is about 13 *rand* = R13.
altogether [ɔːltəˈgeðə]	insgesamt, im Ganzen	➡ entrance – exit	
bone [bəʊn]	Knochen		
guided tour [gaɪdɪd ˈtʊə]	Führung		We went on a *guided tour* of the museum.
exit [ˈeksɪt]	Ausgang ➡		
guide [gaɪd]	(Museums-)Führer/in		A *guide* led us through the old castle.

VOCABULARY

	penguin [ˈpeŋgwɪn]	Pinguin	
29	**divide into** [dɪˈvaɪd]	einteilen in	→ Let's *divide* the cake *into* 16 pieces.
	size [saɪz]	Größe	
	detailed [ˈdiːteɪld]	detailliert	

Reading

30	**heavy** [ˈhevi]	schwer *(Gewicht)* →	→ a **heavy** bag/box
	bucket [ˈbʌkɪt]	Eimer	a **difficult** job/exercise
	exist [ɪgˈzɪst]	existieren	
	get into trouble [ˈtrʌbl]	in Schwierigkeiten geraten, Probleme bekommen	→ Don't *get into trouble* with the police!
	kids stuff [ˈkɪdz ˈstʌf]	Kinderkram	
	traditional [trəˈdɪʃənl]	traditionell	→ ❗ [trəˈdɪʃənl]
	fast-food restaurant [fɑːst fuːd ˈrestrɒnt]	Fastfoodrestaurant, Schnellrestaurant	
	cycle [ˈsaɪkl]	Rad fahren	→ I like riding my bike. I *cycle* to school every day.
	anything **else** [els]	irgendetwas anderes, sonst noch irgendetwas	
	course [kɔːs]	Kurs(us); Lehrgang	→ I want to do a *course* in photography.
	positive [ˈpɒzətɪv]	positiv	
	disappointed [dɪsəˈpɔɪntɪd]	enttäuscht	→ We were very *disappointed* when our team lost.
	useless [ˈjuːsləs]	nutzlos →	→ useful – useless
	Mozambique [məʊzæmˈbiːk]	Mosambik	
	Zimbabwe [zɪmˈbɑːbwi]	Simbabwe	
31	the **very** first day	der allererste Tag	→ I got to the station at the *very* last minute!
	welcome [ˈwelkəm]	willkommen heißen	→ We *welcomed* the new guests to our hotel.
	training [ˈtreɪnɪŋ]	Ausbildung →	→ I did some *training*. I did a *training course*.
	natural catastrophe [nætʃrəl kəˈtæstrəfi]	Naturkatastrophe	
	flood [flʌd]	Überschwemmung	
	hippo, hippos [ˈhɪpəʊ]	Nilpferd	
	zebra [ˈzebrə]	Zebra	
	break the rules [ruːlz]	gegen die Regeln verstoßen	
	put the animals **in danger**	die Tiere in Gefahr bringen	→ Be careful when you ride your bike. Don't *put* yourself *in danger*.
	monkey [ˈmʌŋki]	Affe	
	aggressive [əˈgresɪv]	aggressiv, angriffslustig	
	colleague [ˈkɒliːg]	Kollege, Kollegin	→ ❗ [ˈkɒliːg]
	the tourists' **fault** [fɔːlt]	die Schuld der Touristen	→ I'm sorry! It's all my *fault*!
	outer fence [aʊtə ˈfens]	Außenzaun	
	human [ˈhjuːmən]	Mensch →	→ humans • people

Listening

33	**halfway** up [hɑːfweɪ ˈʌp]	halb oben, auf halber Höhe	→ We were only *halfway* up the mountain, but we were already getting tired.
	HIV positive [eɪtʃ aɪ viː ˈpɒzətɪv]	HIV-positiv	

Mediation

34	**translate** [trænsˈleɪt]	übersetzen	→ Can you *translate* this text from Spanish into English?

128 one hundred and twenty-eight

Unit 2|3

Writing

35	**catalogue** ['kætəlɒg]	Katalog	→ ❗ ['kætəlɒg]
	screen [skri:n]	Bildschirm	
	miss [mɪs]	fehlen	→ Something is *missing* here!
	return [rɪ'tɜ:n]	zurückschicken	
	replacement [rɪ'pleɪsmənt]	Ersatz(gerät)	
	receive [rɪ'si:v]	erhalten →	→ send a letter – receive a letter
	ASAP (= as soon as possible) [eɪ es eɪ 'pi:]	so bald wie möglich	→ Please send us your application *ASAP*.
	stay [steɪ]	Aufenthalt	→ We stayed at the Oasis Hotel. We really enjoyed our *stay*.
	television ['telɪvɪʒn]	Fernsehen, Fernsehgerät	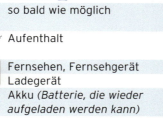
	charger ['tʃɑ:dʒə]	Ladegerät	
	rechargeable battery [ri:'tʃɑ:dʒɪbl]	Akku (*Batterie, die wieder aufgeladen werden kann*)	

Look at language

36	**ladies and gentlemen** ['dʒentlmən]	meine Damen und Herren	→ Good evening, *ladies and gentlemen*, and welcome to our programme.
38	**dependent** [dɪ'pendənt]	abhängig →	→ dependent – independent
	armed [ɑ:md]	bewaffnet →	→ armed – unarmed

Unit 3

> **TIPP** Umschreiben
>
> Kennst du das? Du willst was auf Englisch sagen, aber dir fällt das Wort einfach nicht ein. Damit du aber nicht mitten im Satz ganz verstummst, gibt's ein paar Tricks, mit denen du das fehlende Wort umschreiben kannst.
>
> - Du kennst ein Wort, das ungefähr dasselbe bedeutet.
>   Umschreibe z. B. mit „it's like",
>   „it's almost the same as" oder „it looks like",
>   „*It's like a big meeting with lots of important people.*" (conference)
> - Du kennst das genaue Gegenteil, „the opposite of".
>   „*The house was … well, the opposite of clean.*" (dirty)
> - Du kennst ein allgemeines Wort oder einen Oberbegriff und kannst das gesuchte Wort beschreiben (z. B. Aussehen oder Verwendung).
>   „*It's an animal, big, four legs, with a horn on its nose.*" (rhinoceros)
>   „*It's an area where animals in danger can live and where they are protected.*" (reserve)
> - Relativsätze können dir helfen.
>   „*It's somebody who steals things.*" (thief)
>   „*It's something that farmers do to get vegetables from their fields.*" (grow crops)
> - Manchmal führt auch das Aufzählen von Beispielen zum Ziel.
>   „*It's your family, but also aunts, uncles, grandparents, cousins …*" (relatives)

→ VOCABULARY

India

40	**introduction** [ɪntrə'dʌkʃn]	Einführung	→ This book is a good *introduction to* photography.
	come to mind [maɪnd]	in den Sinn kommen, einfallen	
	religion [rɪ'lɪdʒən]	Religion	→ ❗ [rɪ'lɪdʒən]
	New Delhi [nju: 'deli]	Neu-Delhi	
	northwest [nɔːθ'west]	Nordwesten, Nordwest-	
	Russia ['rʌʃə]	Russland	
	Muslim ['mʊzlɪm, 'mʌzlɪm]	Moslem/in; moslemisch	
	prince [prɪns]	Prinz	→ The son of a king or queen is a *prince*.
	Hindu ['hɪndu:]~	Hindu; hinduistisch	
	tiger ['taɪɡə]	Tiger	
	extinct [ɪk'stɪŋkt]	ausgestorben	
	protect [prə'tekt]	(be)schützen	
	reserve [rɪ'zɜːv]	Reservat, Schutzgebiet	
41	one **billion** people ['bɪljən]	eine Milliarde Menschen	→ = 1 000 000 000 people
	department store [dɪ'pɑːtmənt stɔː]	Kaufhaus	
	rupee [ruː'piː]	Rupie *(indische Währung)*	→ ❗ [ruː'piː]
	crop [krɒp]	(Feld-)Frucht, Ernte	
	grow crops	Feldfrüchte anbauen ➡	➡ grow crops – grew – grown
	monsoon wind [mɒn'suːn]	Monsunwind	

Different faces of India

42	**face** [feɪs]	Gesicht	→ a smiling *face*
	Bollywood ['bɒliwʊd]	Bollywood *(indische Film-industrie; **Bo**mbay + Ho**llywood**)*	
	career [kə'rɪə]	Karriere	
	box-office hit ['bɒks ɒfɪs]	Kassenschlager	
	romantic [rəʊ'mæntɪk]	romantisch	
	good **looks**	gutes Aussehen	
	illegal [ɪ'liːɡl]	illegal	→ ❗ [ɪ'liːɡl]
	condition [kən'dɪʃn]	Bedingung; Zustand	
	they said that they would ...	sie sagten, sie würden ...	→ He *said that he'd* be here at 6.30 ...
	child **labour** ['leɪbə]	Kinderarbeit	
	United Nations, UN [junaɪtɪd 'neɪʃnz, juː 'en]	Vereinte Nationen	
	according to the UN [ə'kɔːdɪŋ tʊ]	nach/gemäß Aussagen der UN	→ *According to* this report more and more people are finding new jobs.
	millionaire [mɪljə'neə]	Millionär/in	
43	**arrange** [ə'reɪndʒ]	arrangieren	→ I'd like to *arrange* a meeting for next week.
	marriage ['mærɪdʒ]	Hochzeit; Ehe ➡	➡ marry · marriage
	horoscope ['hɒrəskəʊp]	Horoskop	
	choice [tʃɔɪs]	(Aus-)Wahl ➡	➡ you choose = you make a choice
	height [haɪt]	Höhe; Körpergröße ➡	➡ high · height
	centimetre, cm ['sentɪmiːtə]	Zentimeter (cm)	
	mother language ['mʌðə læŋɡwɪdʒ]	Muttersprache	
	Hindi ['hɪndi]	Hindi *(Amtssprache in Indien)*	
	smoker ['sməʊkə]	Raucher/in	
	eating **habit** ['hæbɪt]	Essgewohnheit	→ Smoking is a bad *habit*.
	dress style	Kleidungsstil	

Unit 3

ethnic clothes [ˈeθnɪk]	landestypische Kleidung	
ghost town [ˈgəʊst taʊn]	Geisterstadt	
cholera [ˈkɒlərə]	Cholera *(ansteckende Magen-Darm-Erkrankung)*	

Reading

46	**matter to you** [ˈmætə]	dir wichtig sein, dich betreffen	→ Do what you want. It doesn't *matter to me*.
	consider [kənˈsɪdə]	sich überlegen, nachdenken über	→ Let's *consider* what to do next.
	middle class [mɪdl ˈklɑːs]	Mittelschicht	
	event [ɪˈvent]	Veranstaltung, Ereignis	
	pump [pʌmp]	pumpen	
	motor industry [ˈməʊtə ɪndəstri]	Autoindustrie	
	result [rɪˈzʌlt]	Ergebnis	→ Many African children lose their parents as a *result* of AIDS.
	maker [ˈmeɪkə]	Hersteller/in, Produzent/in	
	steel [stiːl]	Stahl	
	businessman [ˈbɪznəsmæn]	Geschäftsmann	→ ❗ a businessman, two businessmen
	steel **plant** [plɑːnt]	Stahlfabrik	→ a garden *plant* — a steel *plant*
	steel-making [ˈstiːl meɪkɪŋ]	Stahlproduktion(s-)	
	they **used to** be British [ˈjuːst tə]	sie waren (früher) britisch	→ ❗ I used [juːst] to drive used [juːzd] cars.
47	**influence** [ˈɪnfluəns]	Einfluss	
	entertainment [entəˈteɪnmənt]	Unterhaltung	
	emotion [ɪˈməʊʃn]	Gefühl	
	happy ending [hæpi ˈendɪŋ]	Happy End	→ Does the film have a sad or a *happy ending*?
	extra terrestrial [ekstrə təˈrestriəl]	außerirdisch	
	gold medal [gəʊld ˈmedl]	Goldmedaille	→ an Olympic *gold medal*
	Commonwealth Games [ˈkɒmənwelθ geɪmz]	Commonwealth Games *(Sportereignis der Länder des ehem. Commonwealth)*	
	Formula One Grand Prix [fɔːmjələ wʌn grɑː ˈpriː]	Grand Prix der Formel Eins	→ **stumme Buchstaben** doubt • answer • island • Christmas • know • autumn • honest
	no doubt [daʊt]	kein Zweifel →	→ ❗ [daʊt]
	from now on	ab jetzt	
	world sport	(der) Weltsport	
	dominate [ˈdɒmɪneɪt]	dominieren	
	the other way round	anders herum	→ Do we have English first and then maths, or is it *the other way round*?
	salary [ˈsæləri]	Gehalt	
48	**spread** [spred]	sich ausbreiten →	→ spread – it spread [spred] it has spread [spred]

Listening

49	**chicken tikka masala** [tʃɪkɪn tɪkə məˈsɑːlə]	Hähnchen Tikka Massala *(indisches Gericht aus gegrilltem Hähnchen in würziger Tomatensauce)*	
	menu [ˈmenjuː]	Speisekarte	
	use [juːs]	Gebrauch, Anwendung →	→ use (Verb) [juːz] – use (Nomen) [juːs]

one hundred and thirty-one

VOCABULARY

	film **director** [dəˈrektə]	Filmregisseur	
	origin [ˈɒrɪdʒɪn]	Herkunft	

Look at language

52	**conference** [ˈkɒnfərəns]	Konferenz	
	everywhere they go	überall, wo sie hingehen	→ My dog follows me *everywhere I go*.
	add [æd]	hinzufügen	
53	**contrast** [ˈkɒntrɑːst]	Gegensatz	→ ❗ [ˈkɒntrɑːst]
	replace … with [rɪˈpleɪs]	… ersetzen durch	→ Let's *replace* this old door *with* a new one.
	brackets [ˈbrækɪts]	(runde) Klammern	
	report [rɪˈpɔːt]	berichten	
54	**be educated** [ˈedʒukeɪtɪd]	zur Schule gehen	

Unit 4

> ### TIPP Notizen
>
> Wenn du einen längeren Text hörst oder liest, wärst du in der Lage, dir das Wichtigste daraus zu notieren? Das kann nützlich sein: Du kannst die Notizen später z. B. als Ausgangsmaterial für ein Referat verwenden. Hier sind ein paar Tipps.
>
> - **About the text**
>   Damit du später noch weißt, woher das Material stammt: Titel und Autor des gelesenen oder gehörten Textes aufschreiben, bei Texten aus dem Internet die Internet-Adresse, Datum der Aufzeichnungen.
> - **Important or not?**
>   Versuche, schon beim Hören/Lesen Wichtiges von Unwichtigem zu unterscheiden. Fakten sind wichtig, erläuternde Beispiele oder Meinungsäußerungen eher nicht.
> - **Be brief**
>   Schreibe nicht zu viel auf! Achte auf wichtige „Schlüsselwörter", die häufiger vorkommen. Kürzere eigene Formulierungen, Abkürzungen und Symbole sind gut, du brauchst keine ganzen Sätze.
> - **For your eyes only**
>   Deine Notizen benotet niemand! Nur du musst deine Aufzeichnungen später noch verstehen. Schreibfehler sind verzeihlich, nicht aber unleserliche Schrift. Lass etwas Platz für eventuelle spätere Ergänzungen.
>   Nutze optische Hilfen wie unterschiedliche Farben, Unterstreichen oder Großbuchstaben für besonders Wichtiges. Manchmal macht es auch Sinn, Informationen in einer Grafik festzuhalten.
>   Wieder gilt: Du musst es hinterher noch durchschauen!
> - **Later …**
>   Schau deine Notizen recht bald noch mal durch und vervollständige sie eventuell. Dann kannst du dir das Gehörte/Gelesene besser merken.

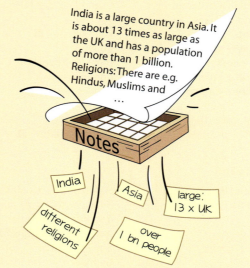

Unit 4

Young adults

60	Internet forum ['fɔːrəm]	Internetforum	
	apparently [ə'pærəntli]	anscheinend	→ I don't know what happened, but *apparently* it was quite funny.
	teenage girl ['tiːneɪdʒ]	Mädchen im Teenager-Alter	
	have a baby	ein Kind bekommen	→ Kate is going to *have a baby* soon, ...
	pregnant ['pregnənt]	schwanger	→ ... she's eight months *pregnant*.
	get drunk [drʌŋk]	sich betrinken	
	row [raʊ]	Streit →	→ row [rəʊ] = Reihe – row [raʊ] = Streit
	argue ['ɑːgjuː]	(sich) streiten	
	pretty well ['prɪti]	ziemlich gut	→ I've been *pretty* busy all day.
	mug [mʌg]	überfallen und ausrauben	→ ❗ I was mugged
	commit a crime [kə'mɪt]	ein Verbrechen begehen	→ ❗ they committed crimes
	kind of ['kaɪnd əv]	Art (von) →	→ sort of • kind of
	voluntary work ['vɒləntri]	ehrenamtliche Arbeit	
	instead of reporting ...	statt ... zu berichten	→ In poor countries many children have to work *instead of* going to school.
	for once [fə 'wʌns]	ausnahmsweise (ein)mal	
	stress [stres]	Stress	
	addicted to [ə'dɪktɪd]	süchtig nach	→ I think he's *addicted to* the Internet.
	be prejudiced against ['predʒədɪst]	Vorurteile haben gegen, voreingenommen sein gegen	→ Are you *prejudiced against* people on motorbikes?
	portray [pɔː'treɪ]	darstellen, porträtieren	
	chav [tʃæv]	(GB) Jugendliche/r, der/die durch bestimmte Kleidung auffällt und zu störendem Verhalten neigt	
	driving test	Fahrprüfung	
	take a test	eine Prüfung machen	
	unless [ən'les]	außer, wenn ... nicht	→ I don't go by car *unless* I really have to.
61	aged 11 [eɪdʒd]	im Alter von 11	
	several ['sevrəl]	mehrere, verschiedene →	→ many / some / several / a few / no
	aspect ['æspekt]	Aspekt	
	outsider [aʊt'saɪdə]	Außenseiter/in	
	cannabis ['kænəbɪs]	Cannabis, Haschisch	
	rank [ræŋk]	einstufen, (ein)ordnen	

Speaking

62	Wish me luck!	Wünsch mir Glück!	
	oh, right ...	ah ja, ach so	
	driving lesson	Fahrstunde	
	pass a test [pɑːs]	eine Prüfung bestehen →	→ take a test • pass a test
	even if	selbst/sogar wenn	→ I'll walk there *even if* it takes a bit longer.
	motorway ['məʊtəweɪ]	Autobahn	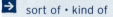
	not ... either ['aɪðə]	auch nicht	→ I don't eat meat, and I don't like fish *either*.
	it's no use being ... [juːz]	es hat keinen Sinn, ... zu sein	→ *It's no use* being sad, we can't do anything about it.
	I'll cross my fingers for you.	*etwa:* Ich drück dir die Daumen.	
	expression [ɪk'spreʃn]	Ausdruck	
63	whereas [weər'æz]	während, wohingegen	
	remind you of ... [rɪ'maɪnd]	dich an ... erinnern →	→ I *remember* my holiday in Italy. This photo *reminds me of* Italy.

133

one hundred and thirty-three

VOCABULARY

Reading

64	**best-selling** book [best 'selɪŋ]	Erfolgsbuch, Bestselle	→	! [best 'selɪŋ]
	make it into a film	einen Film daraus machen		
	move from ... to	(um)ziehen von ... nach	→	„Being" + Adjektiv beschreibt ein momentanes Verhalten.
	Are you being funny?	(etwa) Machst du Witze? / Soll das lustig sein? →		
	whether ['weðə]	ob	→	! weather = Wetter – whether = ob
	perfectly ['pɜːfɪktli]	vollkommen, absolut		
	sensible ['sensəbl]	vernünftig	→	while I'm waiting • it takes a *while*
	while	Weile, Zeit →		
	shake: he had shaken [ʃeɪk, 'ʃeɪkən]	schütteln: er hatte geschüttelt →	→	shake [ʃeɪk] I shook [ʃʊk] I've shaken ['ʃeɪkən]
	it looks to me like ...	für mich sieht es aus, als ob ...		
	make sure	sichergehen		
	he's gone [gɒn]	er ist weg		
	get used to [juːst]	sich gewöhnen an →	→	I used [juːst] to go I got *used* [juːst] to it I used [juːzd] Jo's pen
	business	Sache, Problem; *hier:* Zustand		
	he didn't **mind**	es machte ihm nichts aus		
	weird [wɪəd]	seltsam		
	pee [piː]	pinkeln	→	! I p**ee**d
	someone ['sʌmwʌn]	(irgend)jemand		
	you ought to ['ɔːt tə]	du solltest (eigentlich)	→	You really *ought to* wear your helmet!
	keep in touch with	in Kontakt bleiben mit		
	somehow ['sʌmhaʊ]	irgendwie		
	argument ['ɑːgjumənt]	Streit		
	pepperoni [pepə'rəʊni]	(scharfe) Salami →	→	Englisch | Deutsch pepperoni | Salami chilli(es) | Peperoni
	pick the pepperoni **off**	die Salami (von der Pizza) runternehmen		
	right now	gerade jetzt		
65	**miss the point**	nicht verstehen, worum es geht		
	course not	= of course not		
	you've been good about it	(etwa) du bist gut damit umgegangen		
	considering [kən'sɪdərɪŋ]	wenn man berücksichtigt, dass	→	She's very fit, *considering* she's 85!
	messy ['mesi]	chaotisch, durcheinander	→	! messier, messiest
	he wasn't **bothered** ['bɒðəd]	es störte ihn nicht		
	so far ['səʊ fɑː]	bisher	→	*So far* my holiday has been great.
	he had been to see ...	er war ... anschauen gegangen		
	they had been to have a look at ...	sie waren ... anschauen gegangen		
	horrible ['hɒrəbl]	schrecklich →	→	awful • terrible • horrible
	straight out of the box	direkt aus der Verpackung		
	soggy ['sɒgi]	matschig, durchgeweicht	→	! soggier, soggiest
	optimistic [ɒptɪ'mɪstɪk]	optimistisch		
	remote control [rɪməʊt kən'trəʊl]	Fernbedienung		
	sofa ['səʊfə]	Sofa		
	down the back of the sofa	in der hintersten Ecke des Sofas		
	zap through the channels [zæp]	durch die Programme „zappen" (schnell durchschalten, um zu sehen, was läuft)	→	! I za**pp**ed through the channels.

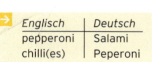

Unit 4

Listening

67	exchange [ɪksˈtʃeɪndʒ]	austauschen	→ During the meeting we *exchanged* ideas and information.
	audio message [ˈɔːdiəʊ mesɪdʒ]	Audio-Message *(gesprochene Nachricht)*	
	hoody [ˈhʊdi]	Kapuzenpullover	→ ❗ one hoody, two hood<u>ies</u>
	mosquito [məˈskiːtəʊ]	Mücke; *hier:* Gerät, das Ultraschall-Störgeräusche produziert	→ ❗ one mosquito, many mosquit<u>oes</u>

Writing

69	scheme [skiːm]	Projekt, Programm	→ They've started a *scheme* to make our town greener.
	available [əˈveɪləbl]	erhältlich; *(Hotelzimmer)* frei	→ This bag is *available* in different colours.
	double room [ˈdʌbl ruːm]	Doppelzimmer	
	half board [hɑːf ˈbɔːd]	*(Hotel)* Halbpension	
	deposit [dɪˈpɒzɪt]	Anzahlung	
	recommend [rekəˈmend]	empfehlen	
	B&B (= bed and breakfast)	Übernachtung mit Frühstück, Frühstückspension	
	cost	Kosten; Preis →	
	youth camp	Zeltlager für Jugendliche	

       …

→ The *cost* isn't too high. It costs less than £50.

→ „Agony" ist das englische Wort für schlimme Schmerzen oder Qualen.

Look at language

70	agony aunt [ˈægəni ɑːnt]	„Kummerkastentante" →	
	advice [ədˈvaɪs]	Rat, Ratschläge	→ ❗ no plural! I gave him <u>some</u> *advice*.
	secret [ˈsiːkrət]	heimlich	→ They had to meet *secretly*.
	sixteen-year-old [sɪksˈtiːn jɪər əʊld]	Sechzehnjährige/r	→ ❗ [sɪksˈ<u>tiː</u>n jɪər əʊld] • five-year-olds [ˈfaɪv jɪər əʊldz]
71	hit the roof [hɪt]	an die Decke gehen →	→ hit – I hit – I've hit
72	appropriate [əˈprəʊpriət]	passend, richtig	
73	discussion [dɪˈskʌʃn]	Diskussion →	→ discuss • discussion
	kind [kaɪnd]	nett, freundlich →	→ What kind of boy is Tom? – He's good-looking and *kind*.
	strict [strɪkt]	streng	
	private school [praɪvət ˈskuːl]	Privatschule	
	writer [ˈraɪtə]	Autor/in →	→ author • writer

one hundred and thirty-five

VOCABULARY

Unit 5

TIPP Arbeiten mit dem Wörterbuch

Wenn du im deutsch-englischen Wörterbuch ein Wort nachschaust, findest du oft mehrere Übersetzungen. Welche ist denn nun die richtige?
Beispiel: Du brauchst ein neues Schloss für dein Fahrrad und suchst das englische Wort dafür.

1. Gute Wörterbücher geben dir schon bei den Übersetzungen Hinweise. Lies deswegen den Eintrag genau durch, auch Angaben in Klammern oder Beispielsätze, selbst wenn du in Eile bist!

   > **Schloss** 1 *(Burg)* castle; *(Palast)* palace; 2 *(an Türen, Fahrzeugen etc.)* lock

2. In manchen Wörterbüchern fehlen leider jegliche Zusatzangaben.

   > **Schloss** 1 castle; palace; 2 lock

3. Handelt es sich um ein zweisprachiges Wörterbuch für beide Richtungen, also Deutsch-Englisch *und* Englisch-Deutsch, kannst du erst mal für die gefundenen Wörter im englisch-deutschen Teil die „Gegenprobe" machen. Für *castle* findest du dann vielleicht etwas, das dir sagt: dieses Schloss ist nicht fürs Fahrrad!

   > **castle** [ˈkɑːsl] *Nomen* 1 Schloss, Burg; 2 *(Schach)* Turm

4. Manchmal hilft dir das aber nicht weiter, weil im englisch-deutschen Wörterbuch auch wieder nur das eine Wort steht, also *castle = Schloss*. Nicht aufgeben!
   Such dir noch ein anderes Wörterbuch, am besten ein einsprachiges englisches. Dort findest du für die Wörter englische Definitionen. Solche Wörterbücher haben meist Beispielsätze oder Bilder.

   > **castle** [ˈkɑːsl] *noun* a big strong building with thick walls, built long ago to keep the people inside safe

   > **lock¹** [lɒk] *noun* 1 thing that keeps a door etc. closed so that you cannot open it; 2 thing with a key that stops other people from using a machine or a vehicle *a bicycle lock*
   > **lock²** [lɒk] *verb* close something with a key

5. Jetzt hast du dein Wort – *lock*! Noch schnell nachsehen, ob irgendwas daran unregelmäßig ist, was du beim Benutzen beachten solltest. Bei Nomen kann das die Pluralform sein, bei Verben z. B. *simple past* und *past participle* oder bei Adjektiven die Steigerungsformen.

Unit 5

One world

74	global warming [gləʊbl 'wɔːmɪŋ]	globale Erwärmung	
	greenhouse gas ['griːnhaʊs gæs]	Treibhausgas	→ a *greenhouse*
	Arctic Ocean [ɑːktɪk 'əʊʃn]	Arktischer Ozean	
	ocean ['əʊʃn]	Ozean	
	continue [kən'tɪnjuː]	weitergehen/weitermachen, (sich) fortsetzen	→ I'll stop now and *continue* my work later.
	threaten ['θretn]	(be)drohen	
	extinction [ɪk'stɪŋkʃn]	Ausrottung, Aussterben	
	Gulf Stream ['gʌlf striːm]	Golfstrom	
	across [ə'krɒs]	(quer) über, durch	→ Birds can fly *across* the ocean.
	Atlantic Ocean [ətlæntɪk 'əʊʃn]	Atlantik, atlantischer Ozean	
	shortage ['ʃɔːtɪdʒ]	Mangel	→ a water *shortage* = a *shortage* of water
	expand [ɪk'spænd]	sich ausdehnen	
	deforestation [diːfɒrɪ'steɪʃn]	Entwaldung *(Zerstörung großer Waldflächen)*	
	Amazon ['æməzən]	Amazonas	
	rainforest ['reɪnfɒrɪst]	Regenwald	
	lung [lʌŋ]	Lunge	→ Smoking is bad for your *lungs*.
	absorb [əb'sɔːb]	aufnehmen, absorbieren	
	release [rɪ'liːs]	abgeben, freisetzen	
	oxygen ['ɒksɪdʒən]	Sauerstoff	
	cut down trees	Bäume fällen	
	carbon footprint [kɑːbən 'fʊtprɪnt]	CO_2-Bilanz	
	carbon ['kɑːbən]	Kohlenstoff	
	footprint ['fʊtprɪnt]	Fußabdruck	
	Syria ['sɪriə]	Syrien	
	the Maldives ['mɔːldiːvz]	die Malediven	
75	population explosion [ɪk'spləʊʒn]	Bevölkerungsexplosion →	→ explode • explosion
	rise [raɪz]	wachsen, (an)steigen →	→ rise – it rose [rəʊz] it has risen ['rɪzn]
	sand [sænd]	Sand	
	Beijing [beɪ'dʒɪŋ]	Peking	
	the Middle East [mɪdl 'iːst]	der Nahe Osten	
	dam [dæm]	(Stau-)Damm	
	amount (of water) [ə'maʊnt]	(Wasser-)Menge →	→ a large <u>number</u> of cars a large <u>amount</u> of water
	pass through	gehen/fahren/fließen durch	
	reduce [rɪ'djuːs]	reduzieren, verringern	
	sea level ['siː levl]	Meeresspiegel	→ Our village is 950 metres above *sea level*.
	disappear [dɪsə'pɪə]	verschwinden	
	save money	Geld sparen	→ I've already *saved* £250 for a new bike.

Speaking

76	Oh, come on!	Ach, komm schon!	
	total ['təʊtl]	total, ganz	→ My sister is *totally* crazy about football.
	unrealistic [ʌnrɪə'lɪstɪk]	unrealistisch	
	they would rather have ... ['rɑːðə]	sie hätten lieber ...	→ I'd *rather* stay here than go to work.

VOCABULARY

kilo, kilogram ['kiːləʊ, 'kɪləgræm]	Kilo(gramm)	
frightening ['fraɪtnɪŋ]	beängstigend →	→ scary • frightening
without producing ...	ohne ... zu produzieren	
excuse for not trying ...	Ausrede, um nicht ... zu versuchen	
the trouble is that ...	das Problem ist, dass ...	
effect [ɪ'fekt]	Effekt, Auswirkung	→ Learn more about climate change and its *effects* on your life.
So what?	Na und?	
it's worth doing ...	es lohnt sich, ... zu tun	This show is great. It's well *worth seeing*.
school exchange	Schüleraustausch	
77 sand storm	Sandsturm	

Reading

78 sky [skaɪ]	Himmel	→ We saw lots of stars in the night *sky*.
balcony ['bælkəni]	Balkon	
apartment block [ə'pɑːtmənt blɒk]	Wohnblock, Mehrfamilienhaus	→ an *apartment block* with *balconies*
pretty	hübsch →	
bush [bʊʃ]	Busch	→ it's pretty good – the flowers are *pretty*
abandon [ə'bændən]	verlassen	
square [skweə]	Platz *(in einer Stadt)*	→ Times *Square* in New York is very famous.
buildings are being built	Gebäude werden gebaut	
fun park	Freizeitpark	
bumper car ['bʌmpə kɑː]	Autoskooter *(Fahrzeug)*	
big wheel	Riesenrad	
silent ['saɪlənt]	still, ruhig	→ First read this text *silently*, then we'll read it aloud.
Ukraine [juː'kreɪn]	Ukraine	
Soviet Union [səʊviət 'juːnɪən]	Sowjetunion	
cloud [klaʊd]	Wolke	→ There are some *clouds* in the sky.
radioactivity [reɪdɪəʊæk'tɪvəti]	Radioaktivität	
protective clothing [prətektɪv 'kləʊðɪŋ]	Schutzkleidung	
safety equipment ['seɪfti]	Sicherheitsausrüstung	→ For your own *safety*, please drive carefully.
Sweden ['swiːdn]	Schweden	
Switzerland ['swɪtsələnd]	die Schweiz	
Norway ['nɔːweɪ]	Norwegen	
they stopped eating ...	sie hörten auf, ... zu essen	
fresh [freʃ]	frisch	→ I love *fresh* rolls for breakfast.
in case	für den Fall, dass	→ Take some water *in case* you get thirsty.
contaminate [kən'tæmɪneɪt]	verseuchen	
tinned vegetables [tɪnd]	Dosengemüse	
indoors [ɪn'dɔːz]	drinnen, im Haus	
playground ['pleɪgraʊnd]	Spielplatz	
radioactive level [reɪdɪəʊ'æktɪv]	Wert/Menge an Radioaktivität →	→ radioactive • radioactivity
79 dramatically [drə'mætɪkli]	dramatisch →	→ dramatic changes • things changed *dramatically*
appear [ə'pɪə]	erscheinen, auftauchen →	
evacuate [ɪ'vækjueɪt]	evakuieren	→ appear – disappear
zone [zəʊn]	Zone	
thick [θɪk]	dick	

138

one hundred and thirty-eight

Unit 5

	concrete ['kɒnkri:t]	Beton, Beton-	→ a *concrete* building
	reactor [ri'æktə]	Reaktor	
	crack [kræk]	Riss	
	collapse [kə'læps]	einstürzen	→ The building threatened to *collapse*.
	expert ['ekspɜ:t]	Experte/Expertin	
	cancer ['kɑ:nsə]	Krebs(erkrankung)	
	leukaemia [lu:'ki:miə]	Leukämie *(Blutkrebs)*	→ ❗ [lu:'ki:miə]
	future **generation** [dʒenə'reɪʃn]	zukünftige Generation	
	uninhabitable [ʌnɪn'hæbɪtəbl]	unbewohnbar	→ This ruined house is totally *uninhabitable*.
	macabre [mə'kɑ:brə]	makaber	
	attraction [ə'trækʃn]	Attraktion	
80	**advantage** [əd'vɑ:ntɪdʒ]	Vorteil →	→ *advantage* – *disadvantage*

Listening

81	**version** ['vɜ:ʃn]	Version	
	pave [peɪv]	pflastern *(mit Pflastersteinen)*	→ a *paved* street
	paradise ['pærədaɪs]	Paradies	
	put up	(auf)bauen	
	parking lot	*(AE)* Parkplatz →	→ car park (BE) • parking lot (AE)
	swinging hot spot ['swɪŋɪŋ]	*(infml)* „heißer Schuppen" (Club/Disko, wo viel los ist)	
	'em [əm]	= them	
	charge people [tʃɑ:dʒ]	Leuten Geld abnehmen	→ What? They *charge* you for using the toilet?
	buck [bʌk]	*(infml)* Dollar	
	DDT	Name eines gefährlichen Pflanzenschutzmittels	
	spot [spɒt]	Fleck	
	bee [bi:]	Biene	
	screen door	zusätzliche Außentür zum Schutz vor Insekten	
	my old man	*(infml)* mein „Alter" (Ehemann oder Vater)	
	steam roll ['sti:m rəʊl]	glatt walzen	

Look at language

84	**heat** [hi:t]	Wärme, Hitze	→ **catch** [kætʃ] I caught [kɔ:t] I've caught [kɔ:t]
	catch: it is caught [kɔ:t]	fangen: es wird gefangen →	
	overtake [əʊvə'teɪk]	überholen →	
85	**progress** ['prəʊgres]	Fortschritt(e)	→ ❗ no plural! We've made *some* progress.
	cut [kʌt]	hier: verringern; Verringerung	→ **overtake** [əʊvə'teɪk] I overtook [əʊvə'tʊk] I've overtaken [əʊvə'teɪkən]
	Kyoto Protocol [kiəʊtəʊ 'prəʊtəkɒl]	Kyoto-Protokoll	
86	**cycle** ['saɪkl]	Kreislauf, Zyklus	
87	**tons of ...** ['tʌnz əv]	Tonnen ..., tonnenweise ...	→ I have to carry *tons of* books to school!

VOCABULARY

Revision and practice 1

103	folk music ['fəʊk mjuːzɪk]	Folk (auf englischsprachiger Volksmusik basierende Popmusik)
	split up: they split up [splɪt 'ʌp]	sich trennen: sie trennten sich →
	solo singer ['səʊləʊ sɪŋə]	Solo-Sänger/in
	harp [hɑːp]	Harfe
	symbol ['sɪmbl]	Symbol
	coin [kɔɪn]	Münze
	beer [bɪə]	Bier
	sea kayaking ['siː kaɪækɪŋ]	Seekajak fahren
	wave [weɪv]	Welle
	paddle ['pædl]	Paddel

→ split up [splɪt 'ʌp]
we split up [splɪt]
we've split up [splɪt]

→ A heart is a *symbol* of love.

→ Let's go *sea kayaking* ...
→ ... the *waves* are great!

Revision and practice 2

104	airline ['eəlaɪn]	Fluggesellschaft
105	imagination [ɪmædʒɪ'neɪʃn]	Fantasie
	Oscar ['ɒskə]	Oscar (amerikanischer Filmpreis)
	perform [pə'fɔːm]	spielen, aufführen →

→ You don't know the answer? Well, use your *imagination*!

→ perform • act

Revision and Practice 3

107	bat [bæt]	Schläger
	set [set]	Satz
	wooden ['wʊdn]	hölzern, aus Holz →
	stick [stɪk]	Stock
	simplified ['sɪmplɪfaɪd]	vereinfacht
	explanation [eksplə'neɪʃn]	Erklärung →
	reality [rɪ'æləti]	Wirklichkeit
	complicated ['kɒmplɪkeɪtɪd]	kompliziert

→ it's *wooden* = it's made of wood

→ explain • explanation

Revision and practice 4

108	judge [dʒʌdʒ]	ein Urteil fällen (über), (be)urteilen
109	suggest [sə'dʒest]	vorschlagen
	lottery ticket ['lɒtəri tɪkɪt]	Lotterieschein, Lottoschein
	keyword ['kiːwɜːd]	Stichwort, Schlüsselwort

→ Don't *judge* people by the colour of their skin!

140
one hundred and forty

IN ENGLISH

ALPHABET

a	[eɪ]
b	[biː]
c	[siː]
d	[diː]
e	[iː]
f	[ef]
g	[dʒiː]
h	[eɪtʃ]
i	[aɪ]
j	[dʒeɪ]
k	[keɪ]
l	[el]
m	[em]
n	[en]
o	[əʊ]
p	[piː]
q	[kjuː]
r	[aː]
s	[es]
t	[tiː]
u	[juː]
v	[viː]
w	['dʌbljuː]
x	[eks]
y	[waɪ]
z	[zed]

SOUNDS

[iː]	m**ee**t, t**ea**m, h**e**
[ɑː]	**a**nswer, cl**a**ss, c**a**r
[ɔː]	**or**, b**a**ll, d**oo**r
[uː]	r**u**ler, bl**ue**, t**oo**
[ɜː]	g**ir**l, w**or**d, h**er**
[i]	rad**io**, vide**o**, sorr**y**
[u]	J**u**ly, Febr**u**ary
[ɪ]	**i**n, m**i**lk, b**i**g
[e]	**e**mpty, y**e**s, b**e**d
[æ]	c**a**t, bl**a**ck
[ʌ]	b**u**s, c**o**me
[ɒ]	**o**n, d**o**g, wh**a**t
[ʊ]	p**u**t, g**oo**d, w**o**man
[ə]	**a**gain, t**o**day, sist**er**

[eɪ]	**eigh**t, n**a**me, pl**ay**
[aɪ]	**I**, t**i**me, m**y**
[ɔɪ]	b**oy**, t**oi**let
[əʊ]	**o**ld, n**o**, r**oa**d
[aʊ]	h**ou**se, n**ow**
[ɪə]	n**ear**, **here**, we'**re**
[eə]	th**ere**, ch**air**
[ʊə]	you'**re**, s**ure**

[b]	**b**ike, ho**bb**y, jo**b**
[p]	**p**en, **p**u**p**il, sho**p**
[d]	**d**ay, win**d**ow, goo**d**
[t]	**t**en, foo**t**ball, a**t**
[k]	**c**ar, lu**ck**y, boo**k**
[g]	**g**o, a**g**ain, ba**g**
[ŋ]	fi**ng**er, wro**ng**, ba**nk**
[l]	**l**ike, o**l**d, sma**ll**
[r]	**r**uler, f**r**iend, bi**r**o
[v]	**v**ery, se**v**en, ha**ve**
[w]	**w**e, **wh**ere, s**w**im, q**u**iz
[s]	**s**ix, po**s**ter, ye**s**
[z]	**z**oo, vi**s**it, hi**s**, plea**se**
[ʃ]	**sh**e, ac**ti**on, Engli**sh**
[tʃ]	**ch**ild, tea**ch**er, ma**tch**
[dʒ]	**j**eans, **G**erman, ba**dge**
[ʒ]	u**s**ually, gara**ge**
[j]	**y**es, **y**ou, **y**oung
[θ]	**th**ing, ma**th**s, mon**th**
[ð]	**th**e, fa**th**er, wi**th**

ORDINAL NUMBERS

1st	first	[fɜːst]
2nd	second	['sekənd]
3rd	third	[θɜːd]
4th	fourth	[fɔːθ]
5th	fifth	[fɪfθ]
6th	sixth	[sɪksθ]
7th	seventh	['sevnθ]
8th	eighth	[eɪtθ]
9th	ninth	[naɪnθ]
10th	tenth	[tenθ]
11th	eleventh	[ɪ'levnθ]
12th	twelfth	[twelfθ]
13th	thirteenth	[θɜː'tiːnθ]
14th	fourteenth	[fɔː'tiːnθ]
15th	fifteenth	[fɪf'tiːnθ]
16th	sixteenth	[sɪks'tiːnθ]
17th	seventeenth	[sevn'tiːnθ]
18th	eighteenth	[eɪ'tiːnθ]
19th	nineteenth	[naɪn'tiːnθ]
20th	twentieth	['twentiəθ]
21st	twenty-first	[twenti'fɜːst]
22nd	twenty-second	[twenti'sekənd]
23rd	twenty-third	[twenti'θɜːd]
24th	twenty-fourth	[twenti'fɔːθ]
25th	twenty-fifth	[twenti'fɪfθ]
26th	twenty-sixth	[twenti'sɪksθ]
27th	twenty-seventh	[twenti'sevnθ]
28th	twenty-eighth	[twenti'eɪtθ]
29th	twenty-ninth	[twenti'naɪnθ]
30th	thirtieth	['θɜːtiəθ]

141

one hundred and forty-one

→ DICTIONARY

Alphabetische Liste der Wörter aus den Bänden 1–6 (Englisch – Deutsch)

Die Angaben nach den Einträgen verweisen auf ihr erstes Vorkommen.

Abkürzungen: Intro = Introduction; RP = Revision and Practice; U = Unit

Fundstellen aus früheren Bänden geht der Hinweis (Band) 1/2/3/4/5 › voraus.

Der Schriftstil zeigt den Lernstatus eines Wortes an:
U2: 32 = **produktives Wort** (in Unit 2 auf Seite 32), U3: 54 = rezeptives Wort, *U5: 93 = fakultatives Wort*

Der Zusatz (AE) heißt, dass dieses Wort überwiegend im amerikanischen Englisch gebraucht wird.

Der Pfeil (→) verweist auf die Grundform eines Wortes.

A

a [ə] ein/eine **1›Intro:** 10; **seven lessons a day** sieben Stunden am/pro Tag **2›U1:** 14

abandon [ə'bændən] verlassen **U5:** 78

able ['eɪbl]: **I'm able to swim** ich kann schwimmen **4›U2:** 30

Aboriginal [æbə'rɪdʒnl] eingeboren **5›U3:** 45; **Aboriginal Australian** australische/r Ureinwohner/in, eingeborene/r Australier/in **5›U3:** 45

about [ə'baʊt] 1 über **1›U2:** 49; 2 ungefähr **2›U1:** 15; 3 wegen **4›U2:** 36; **What about you?** Und du? **4›U3:** 56; **What about…?** Wie wäre es mit…? **1›U3:** 54

above [ə'bʌv] über **1›Intro:** 18

abroad [ə'brɔːd] im/ins Ausland **4›U5:** 91; **from abroad** aus dem Ausland **3›U1:** 9

abseiling ['æbseɪlɪŋ] Abseilen 3›U2: 31

absolutely ['æbsəluːtli] absolut, völlig **5›U2:** 32

absorb [əb'sɔːb] aufnehmen, absorbieren **U5:** 74

accent ['æksent] Akzent **2›U1:** 18

accident ['æksɪdənt] Unfall **2›U2:** 30

according to the UN [ə'kɔːdɪŋ tʊ] nach/gemäß Aussagen der UN **U3:** 42

account [ə'kaʊnt] Konto **5›U4:** 76; (1›U6: 115); **account holder** Kontoinhaber/in **5›U4:** 76; **account number** Kontonummer **5›U4:** 76

across [ə'krɒs] (quer) über, durch **U5:** 74

act [ækt] spielen (in einem Film/ Theaterstück), nachspielen 3›U3: 57

action ['ækʃn] Action **2›U2:** 28; **in action** aktiv **4›U2:** 28

activity [æk'tɪvəti] Aktivität **1›U4:** 69

actor ['æktə] Schauspieler/ Schauspielerin **5›U1:** 13

actually ['æktʃuəli] eigentlich **4›U1:** 14

add [æd] hinzufügen **U3:** 52

addicted to [ə'dɪktɪd] süchtig nach **U4:** 60

address [ə'dres] Adresse, Anschrift **2›U5:** 85

admire (in) [əd'maɪə] bewundern (an) **4›U3:** 53

adult ['ædʌlt] Erwachsene/r **2›U1:** 18

advance [əd'vɑːns]: **in advance** im Voraus **4›U5:** 94

advantage [əd'vɑːntɪdʒ] Vorteil **U5:** 80

adventure [əd'ventʃə] Abenteuer **4›U2:** 34

advert ['ædvɜːt] Anzeige **2›U6:** 93

advice [əd'vaɪs] Rat, Ratschläge **U4:** 70

afraid [ə'freɪd]: **be afraid of** Angst haben vor **U2:** 27; **I'm afraid …** Leider … 3›U2: 36

Africa ['æfrɪkə] Afrika **4›U1:** 8

Afrikaans [æfrɪ'kɑːns] Afrikaans *(Sprache in Südafrika)* **U2:** 25

after ['ɑːftə] 1 nach *(zeitlich)* **1›U3:** 59; 2 nachdem **5›U3:** 46; **after that** danach 3›U1: 10

after all ['ɑːftər ɔːl]: **he went after all** er ging doch **4›U1:** 14

afternoon [ɑːftə'nuːn] Nachmittag **2›U1:** 25

again [ə'gen] noch einmal, (schon) wieder **2›U1:** 18

against [ə'geɪnst] gegen **1›U5:** 92; **for or against** dafür oder dagegen **5›U2:** 32

age [eɪdʒ] Alter **4›U1:** 8; **ages** eine Ewigkeit **5›U5:** 88; **What's your age?** Wie alt bist du? **4›U1:** 8

aged 11 [eɪdʒd] im Alter von 11 **U4:** 61

aggressive [ə'gresɪv] aggressiv, angriffslustig **U2:** 31

ago [ə'gəʊ]: **two years ago** vor zwei Jahren **2›U3:** 48

agony aunt ['ægəni ɑːnt] Kummerkastentante **U4:** 70

agree (with) [ə'griː] zustimmen, übereinstimmen (mit), einer Meinung sein (mit) **4›U3:** 56

ahead [ə'hed] voraus 3›U2: 34

aid [eɪd] Hilfe, Unterstützung **U1:** 14

AIDS [eɪdz] Aids *(gefährliche Infektionskrankheit)* **U1:** 15

air [eə] Luft **4›U2:** 28

air-conditioning ['eə kəndɪʃnɪŋ] Klimatisierung, Klimaanlage **2›U6:** 94

airline ['eəlaɪn] Fluggesellschaft *U2:* 104

airport ['eəpɔːt] Flughafen **4›U1:** 16

aisle [aɪl] Gang **4›U1:** 16

alarm clock [ə'lɑːm klɒk] Wecker **2›U1:** 15

album ['ælbəm] Album **4›U3:** 56

alcohol ['ælkəhɒl] Alkohol **5›U2:** 30

alcoholism ['ælkəhɒlɪzəm] Alkoholismus 5›U3: 54

alien ['eɪliən] Außerirdische/r **2›U2:** 37

all [ɔːl] der/die/das ganze; alle **2›Intro:** 7; **(That's) All for now.** Das war's erst einmal. **3›U4:** 74; **"All work and no play makes Jack a dull boy."** „Arbeit allein macht nicht glücklich." 3›U5: 91; **all in all** insgesamt **5›U2:** 32;

142
one hundred and forty-two

all over überall **2>U3:** 48;
all the time die ganze Zeit
3>U5: 90; **from all over the**
world aus der ganzen Welt
3>U1: 8; **it wasn't all fun** es
bestand nicht nur aus Spaß
5>U3: 54

all right [ɔːl ˈraɪt] in Ordnung, okay
5>U3: 52

allowed [əˈlaʊd] erlaubt **4>U1:** 16;
I'm allowed to go ich darf gehen
4>U2: 30

almost [ˈɔːlməʊst] fast, beinahe
2>U1: 18

alone [əˈləʊn] allein **1>U6:** 107

along [əˈlɒŋ]: **go along** entlang-
gehen **2>U3:** 52

aloud [əˈlaʊd]: **Read them aloud to**
your partner. Lies sie deinem
Partner / deiner Partnerin laut
vor. **4>U2:** 41

alphabet [ˈælfəbet] Alphabet
4>U3: 59

alphabetical [ælfəˈbetɪkl] alpha-
betisch **2>U1:** 23

already [ɔːlˈredi] schon **3>U2:** 32

also [ˈɔːlsəʊ] auch **2>U4:** 62

although [ɔːlˈðəʊ] obwohl
4>U3: 48

altogether [ɔːltəˈgeðə] insgesamt,
im Ganzen **U2:** 26

always [ˈɔːlweɪz] immer **1>U2:**
40

a.m. [eɪ ˈem] morgens, vormittags
3>U1: 17

am [æm] bin **1>Intro:** 17

amazing [əˈmeɪzɪŋ] erstaunlich
4>U3: 55

Amazon [ˈæməzən] Amazonas
U5: 74

ambulance [ˈæmbjələns] Kranken-
wagen **5>U4:** 73; **ambulance**
service [ˈæmbjələns sɜːvɪs]
„Krankenwagendienst",
Rettungsleitstelle **5>U1:** 8

America [əˈmerɪkə] Amerika
1>U5: 96

American [əˈmerɪkən] amerika-
nisch; Amerikaner/in **2>U5:** 81

amount [əˈmaʊnt] Betrag
5>U4: 76; **amount (of water)**
(Wasser-)Menge **U5:** 75

an [æn] ein/eine **1>U2:** 38

ancestor [ˈænsestə] Vorfahre/
Vorfahrin **U1:** 20

and [ænd] und **1>Intro:** 10

angry (with) [ˈæŋgri] böse, wütend
(auf) **1>U3:** 57

animal [ˈænɪml] Tier **1>U4:** 72

announcement [əˈnaʊnsmənt]
Durchsage **4>U1:** 21

anorak [ˈænəræk] Anorak
5>U2: 26

another [əˈnʌðə] ein anderer/s,
eine andere; noch ein/e/s
4>U1: 8

answer [ˈɑːnsə] **1** antworten;
beantworten **2>U3:** 50;
answer the phone ans Telefon
gehen **3>U2:** 37; **2** Antwort
2>U1: 16

any [ˈeni] irgendein/e; jede/r/s
U1: 11; **not ... any** kein/keine
3>U4: 73

anybody [ˈenibɒdi]: **not ... anybody**
niemand **4>U4:** 72

anything [ˈeniθɪŋ]: **Anything else?**
Sonst noch etwas? **1>U4:** 75;
not ... anything nichts
4>U4: 72

anyway [ˈeniweɪ] jedenfalls,
wenigstens **4>U3:** 51;
Anyway, ... Wie auch immer, ...
4>U1: 14

anywhere [ˈeniweə]: **not ...**
anywhere nirgendwo(hin)
3>U5: 88

apart from [əˈpɑːt] außer,
abgesehen von **2>U3:** 47

apartheid [əˈpɑːtaɪt] Apartheid
(früheres System der Trennung
zwischen Weißen und Schwar-
zen) **U2:** 26

apartment [əˈpɑːtmənt] Ferien-
wohnung **5>U5:** 88

apparently [əˈpærəntli]
anscheinend **U4:** 60

appear [əˈpɪə] erscheinen,
auftauchen **U5:** 79

apple [ˈæpl] Apfel **1>U3:** 53;
apple pie [æpl ˈpaɪ] gedeckter
Apfelkuchen **3>U4:** 76

application form [æplɪˈkeɪʃn fɔːm]
Bewerbungsformular, -bogen
5>U4: 68

apply (for/to) [əˈplaɪ] sich bewer-
ben (um/bei) **4>U5:** 90

appropriate [əˈprəʊpriət] passend,
richtig **U4:** 72

April [ˈeɪprəl] April **1>U5:** 98

aquarium [əˈkweəriəm] Aquarium
3>U1: 14

Arctic Ocean [ɑːktɪk ˈəʊʃn]
Arktischer Ozean **U5:** 74

are [ɑː] bist, seid, sind **1>U1:** 22;
How are you? Wie geht es dir/
euch/Ihnen? **1>U6:** 114; **they're**
killed sie werden getötet
5>U2: 34

area [ˈeəriə] Gebiet, Gegend
5>U5: 82; **area of population**
bewohntes Gebiet **5>U5:** 82

aren't (= are not) [ˈɑːnt] bist nicht,
seid nicht, sind nicht **1>U2:** 39;
..., aren't I? ..., nicht wahr?
5>U5: 84

argue [ˈɑːgjuː] (sich) streiten
U4: 60

argument [ˈɑːgjumənt] Streit
U4: 64

armed [ɑːmd] bewaffnet **U2:** 38

around [əˈraʊnd] (in/um ...) herum
3>U3: 51; **look around** sich
umschauen, umherschauen
3>U2: 30; **show her around**
Sydney sie in Sydney herum-
führen **5>U3:** 48

arrange [əˈreɪndʒ] arrangieren
U3: 43

arrive [əˈraɪv] ankommen,
eintreffen **2>U1:** 15

arrow [ˈærəʊ] Pfeil
2>A Legend: 108

art [ɑːt] Kunst **2>U1:** 20; **art**
gallery Kunstgalerie **2>U3:** 50

article [ˈɑːtɪkl] Artikel **3>U3:** 50

artist [ˈɑːtɪst] Künstler/in
3>U5: 107

as [əz] wie **1>U4:** 75; **as a**
tourist als Tourist/in **3>U1:** 14;
as high as so hoch wie
3>U2: 34; **as soon as** sobald
5>U1: 10; **not as good as that**
nicht so gut **4>U5:** 88

ASAP (= as soon as possible)
[eɪ es eɪ ˈpiː] so bald wie möglich
U2: 35

Asia [ˈeɪʃə] Asien **5>U3:** 46

Asian [ˈeɪʃn] asiatisch; Asiat/in
5>U3: 48

ask [ɑːsk] bitten **4>U2:** 37;
ask (about) fragen (nach)
2>U2: 31; **ask for** verlangen,
fragen nach **3>U2:** 37; **ask**
questions Fragen stellen
2>U1: 16

aspect [ˈæspekt] Aspekt **U4:** 61

assistant [əˈsɪstənt] Mitarbeiter/
Mitarbeiterin **3>U4:** 76;
shop assistant Verkäufer/
Verkäuferin **4>U5:** 89;
vet's assistant Tierarzthelfer/
Tierarzthelferin **4>U5:** 89;
X-ray assistant [ˈeks reɪ
əsɪstənt] Röntgenassistent/
Röntgenassistentin **4>U5:** 99

astronaut [ˈæstrənɔːt] Astronaut/
Astronautin **3>U4:** 72

→ DICTIONARY

at [æt] an, in; bei **1 › Intro:** 19;
zu **3 › U1:** 14; **at ... o'clock**
um ... Uhr **1 › U3:** 64; **at church**
in der Kirche **3 › U5:** 102;
at home zu Hause, daheim
1 › U2: 36; **at last** [ət 'lɑːst]
endlich, schließlich **5 › U5:** 91;
at least [ət 'liːst] zumindest;
wenigstens; mindestens
4 › U4: 71; **at night** nachts,
in der Nacht **5 › U1:** 13; **at once**
sofort **4 › U2:** 31; **at school**
in der Schule **1 › Intro:** 10;
at the back/front of the bus
hinten/vorne im Bus **5 › U4:** 73;
at the seaside am Meer
1 › U5: 86; **at the weekend**
am Wochenende **1 › U5:** 84;
at work bei der Arbeit
2 › U2: 33; **not at all** überhaupt
nicht **4 › U2:** 34
ate [et] (→ eat): **I ate** ich aß,
ich habe gegessen **3 › U1:** 11
Atlantic Ocean [ətlæntɪk 'əʊʃn]
Atlantik, atlantischer Ozean
U5: 74
atmosphere ['ætməsfɪə]
Atmosphäre, Stimmung
5 › U1: 11
attraction [ə'trækʃn] Attraktion
U5: 79
attractive [ə'træktɪv] attraktiv,
ansprechend **5 › U4:** 64
audio message ['ɔːdɪəʊ mesɪdʒ]
Audio-Message (gesprochene
Nachricht) **U4:** 67
audition [ɔː'dɪʃn] Vorsprechen,
Vorsingen **5 › U4:** 68
August ['ɔːgəst] August
1 › U5: 98
aunt [ɑːnt] Tante **1 › U3:** 60
Australia [ɒ'streɪlɪə] Australien
3 › U5: 107
Australian [ɒ'streɪlɪən] austra-
lisch; Australier/in(nen)
5 › U3: 44
Austria ['ɒstrɪə] Österreich
2 › Intro: 11
autumn ['ɔːtəm] Herbst **1 › U5:** 99
available [ə'veɪləbl] erhältlich;
(Hotelzimmer) frei **U4:** 69
average ['ævərɪdʒ] durchschnitt-
lich, Durchschnitts- **5 › U1:** 7
award [ə'wɔːd] Preis, Auszeich-
nung **3 › U5:** 107
away [ə'weɪ] weg; verreist
2 › Intro: 7; **away match**
[ə'weɪ mætʃ] Auswärtsspiel
4 › U4: 74; **go away** verreisen **1 › U5:** 87

awesome ['ɔːsəm] (AE) irre, toll
4 › U3: 54
awful ['ɔːfl] furchtbar, schrecklich
3 › U5: 90

B

B&B (= bed and breakfast)
[biː ən 'biː] Übernachtung mit
Frühstück, Frühstückspension
U4: 69
baby ['beɪbi] Baby **4 › U5:** 106;
have a baby ein Kind bekommen **U4:** 60; **when I was a
baby** als ich klein war **5 › U1:** 12
babysat ['beɪbisæt] (→ babysit):
I babysat ich passte auf kleine
Kinder auf **4 › U5:** 92; **I've
babysat** ich habe auf kleine
Kinder aufgepasst **4 › U5:** 92
babysit ['beɪbisɪt] (I babysat, I've
babysat) babysitten (auf kleine
Kinder aufpassen) **4 › U5:** 92
babysitter ['beɪbisɪtə] Babysitter/
Babysitterin **4 › U5:** 99
back [bæk] zurück **1 › U6:** 109;
at the back of the bus hinten
im Bus **5 › U4:** 73; **back home**
daheim **3 › U3:** 53; **back then**
damals **U2:** 26; **down the back
of the sofa** in der hintersten
Ecke des Sofas **U4:** 65
backcountry ['bækʌntri] „Hinter-
land" (unerschlossenes Gelände)
4 › U2: 30
background ['bækgraʊnd] Hintergrund **3 › U1:** 8; Herkunft
5 › U1: 8
backpack ['bækpæk] (AE)
Rucksack **4 › U2:** 34
bacon ['beɪkən] Speck **3 › U4:** 76
bad [bæd] schlecht, schlimm
2 › U1: 18; **I'm not bad at
dancing** ich bin ganz gut im
Tanzen **3 › U4:** 71; **not bad**
nicht schlecht, es geht/ging so
2 › Intro: 11
badge [bædʒ] Abzeichen, Button
1 › U1: 23
badly-paid ['bædli peɪd] schlecht
bezahlt **U2:** 26
badminton ['bædmɪntən]
Badminton, Federball(spiel)
3 › U1: 13
bag [bæg] (Schul-)Tasche
1 › Intro: 11; Beutel, Tüte, Sack
2 › U4: 63
bagel ['beɪgl] Bagel (eine Art
ringförmiges, festes Brötchen)
3 › U4: 76

bagpipes ['bægpaɪps] Dudelsack
3 › U3: 53
baked [beɪkt]: **baked beans**
gebackene Bohnen (in Tomaten-
soße) **2 › U5:** 82; **baked potato**
gebackene Kartoffel **2 › U4:** 62
balcony ['bælkəni] Balkon **U5:** 78
ball [bɔːl] Ball **2 › U2:** 29
ban [bæn] verbieten **U1:** 23
banana [bə'nɑːnə] Banane
1 › U3: 53
band [bænd] Band, (Musik-)Gruppe
2 › U1: 17
banjo ['bændʒəʊ] Banjo
3 › U5: 107
bank [bæŋk] Bank, Sparkasse
2 › U3: 52
bar [bɑː] Riegel **3 › U5:** 107;
bar chart ['bɑː tʃɑːt]
Säulendiagramm **4 › U1:** 11
barb [bɑːb] (mit Widerhaken
versehener) Stachel **5 › U3:** 54
barbecue ['bɑːbɪkjuː] Grillparty
2 › U6: 97
barbie ['bɑːbi] kurz für „barbecue"
5 › U3: 49
bark [bɑːk] bellen **SUM:** 98
baseball ['beɪsbɔːl] Baseball
3 › U4: 68
basketball ['bɑːskɪtbɔːl] Basketball
1 › U6: 105; **basketball court**
['bɑːskɪtbɔːl kɔːt] Basketball-
Spielfeld **3 › U1:** 13
bass guitar [beɪs gɪ'tɑː] Bass-
gitarre **3 › U5:** 88
bat [bæt] Schläger **U3:** 107
bathroom ['bɑːθruːm]
Badezimmer **1 › U2:** 37
battery ['bætəri] Batterie
1 › U5: 96
Bavaria [bə'veərɪə] Bayern
1 › U2: 49
Bavarian [bə'veərɪən] bayerisch
4 › U2: 28
bay [beɪ] Bucht **2 › A Legend:** 111
BBC [biː biː 'siː] BBC (British
Broadcasting Corporation)
1 › U4: 74
be [biː] (I/he was, you were;
I've been) sein **2 › U5:** 90
beach [biːtʃ] Strand **2 › U5:** 78
bean [biːn] Bohne **1 › U3:** 53
bear [beə] Bär **4 › U2:** 28; **teddy
bear** Teddybär **1 › U4:** 73
beautiful ['bjuːtɪfl] schön, wunder-
schön **4 › U2:** 28
became [bɪ'keɪm] (→ become):
I became ich wurde, ich bin
geworden **3 › U4:** 68
because [bɪ'kɒz] weil **1 › U5:** 85;
because of wegen **5 › U2:** 26

become [bɪˈkʌm] (I became, I've become) werden **3 › U4:** 68; **he becomes friendly with her** er freundet sich mit ihr an **4 › U5:** 95; **I've become** ich bin geworden **3 › U4:** 68

bed [bed] Bett **1 › U3:** 62; **bed and breakfast** [bed ən ˈbrekfəst] einfaches Frühstückshotel, Pension **5 › U5:** 82

bedroom [ˈbedruːm] Schlafzimmer **1 › U2:** 37

bee [biː] Biene *U5: 81*

been [biːn, bɪn] (→ be): **I've been** ich bin gewesen **3 › U3:** 51; **he had been to see ...** er war ... anschauen gegangen **U4:** 65; **it has been training** es hat ausgebildet **5 › U3:** 51; **they had been to have a look at ...** sie waren ... anschauen gegangen **U4:** 65

beer [bɪə] Bier *U1: 103*

before [bɪˈfɔː] **1** vor **1 › U5:** 92; **2** bevor **2 › U3:** 50; **3** schon einmal, vorher **3 › U2:** 32; **People before seals!** Erst die Menschen, dann die Seehunde! **5 › U2:** 35; **the day before** am Tag zuvor **5 › U1:** 17

began [bɪˈgæn] (→ begin): **I began** ich begann, ich habe begonnen **4 › U3:** 48

begin [bɪˈgɪn] (I began, I've begun) beginnen, anfangen **4 › U3:** 48

beginner [bɪˈgɪnə] Anfänger/in **5 › U1:** 10

beginning [bɪˈgɪnɪŋ] Anfang, Beginn **4 › U3:** 48; **from the beginning of September** von Anfang September **4 › U3:** 48

begun [bɪˈgʌn] (→ begin): **I've begun** ich habe begonnen **4 › U3:** 48

behind [bɪˈhaɪnd] hinter **2 › A Legend:** 110

Beijing [beɪˈdʒɪŋ] Peking **U5:** 75

being [ˈbiːɪŋ]: **Are you being funny?** *etwa:* Machst du Witze? / Soll das lustig sein? **U4:** 64; **buildings are being built** Gebäude werden gebaut **U5:** 78

Belgium [ˈbeldʒəm] Belgien **5 › U5:** 84

believe [bɪˈliːv] glauben **4 › U3:** 51

belong (to) [bɪˈlɒŋ] gehören (zu) **2 › U2:** 29

below [bɪˈləʊ] unter, unterhalb (von); unten **2 › U6:** 104

bench [bentʃ] Bank *(zum Sitzen)* **4 › U1:** 14

best [best] beste/r/s **1 › U4:** 74; **Best wishes, ...** Viele Grüße ... **3 › U4:** 74

best-selling book [best ˈselɪŋ] Erfolgsbuch, Bestseller **U4:** 64

bet [bet] (I bet, I've bet) wetten **5 › U4:** 71; **I bet** ich wettete, ich habe gewettet **5 › U4:** 71; **I've bet** ich habe gewettet **5 › U4:** 71

better [ˈbetə] besser **1 › U3:** 58

between [bɪˈtwiːn] zwischen **4 › U1:** 9

big [bɪg] groß **1 › U1:** 24; **big wheel** Riesenrad **U5:** 78; **the sixth biggest** der/die/das sechstgrößte **5 › U3:** 44

bike [baɪk] Fahrrad **1 › Intro:** 10

billion [ˈbɪljən]: **one billion people** eine Milliarde Menschen **U3:** 41

biography [baɪˈɒgrəfi] Biografie **4 › U3:** 62

biology [baɪˈɒlədʒi] Biologie **4 › U4:** 68

bird [bɜːd] Vogel **2 › U2:** 33

biro [ˈbaɪrəʊ] Kugelschreiber **1 › U1:** 32

birth [bɜːθ]: **place/date of birth** Geburtsort/-datum **4 › U3:** 62

birthday [ˈbɜːθdeɪ] Geburtstag **1 › U3:** 62; **Happy birthday (to you)!** Herzlichen Glückwunsch (zum Geburtstag)! **3 › U3:** 56

biscuit [ˈbɪskɪt] Keks **1 › U4:** 74

bison [ˈbaɪsn] Bison, Bisons **4 › U2:** 28

bit [bɪt]: **a bit** ein bisschen, ein wenig **3 › U4:** 68

black [blæk] schwarz **1 › Intro:** 14

Blacks [blæks]: **the Blacks** die Schwarzen **U2:** 26

blind [blaɪnd] blind **4 › U5:** 93

block [blɒk] blockieren **5 › U1:** 17; **apartment block** [əˈpɑːtmənt blɒk] Wohnblock, Mehrfamilienhaus **U5:** 78; **block subject** Blockfach, Blockunterricht **4 › U3:** 50

blog [blɒg] Blog *(von Weblog; hier eine Art Online-Tagebuch)* **4 › U4:** 80

blow up [bləʊ ˈʌp] (I blew up, I've blown up) sprengen **2 › U4:** 62

BLT (= bacon, lettuce, tomato) [biː el ˈtiː] Brot mit Speck, Salat und Tomate **3 › U4:** 76

blue [bluː] blau **1 › Intro:** 10

blues [bluːz] Blues **3 › U5:** 102

board [bɔːd] **1** Tafel **1 › Intro:** 11; **2** Brett; Skateboard **1 › U6:** 110

boarding [ˈbɔːdɪŋ] Einsteigen **4 › U1:** 16; **boarding pass** [ˈbɔːdɪŋ pɑːs] Bordkarte **4 › U1:** 16

boat [bəʊt] Boot, Schiff **2 › A Legend:** 110

Bollywood [ˈbɒliwʊd] Bollywood *(indische Filmindustrie; Bombay + Hollywood)* **U3:** 42

bomb [bɒm] Bombe **U1:** 10

bone [bəʊn] Knochen **U2:** 28

book [bʊk] **1** buchen, reservieren **2 › U4:** 64; **2** Buch **1 › U1:** 26

boomerang [ˈbuːməræŋ] Bumerang **5 › U3:** 51

boot [buːt] Stiefel **3 › U2:** 33

border [ˈbɔːdə] Grenze **5 › U1:** 6

bored [bɔːd]: **I'm bored** ich langweile mich **1 › U6:** 106

boring [ˈbɔːrɪŋ] langweilig **2 › Intro:** 7

born [bɔːn]: **I was born in 1994.** Ich bin 1994 geboren. **2 › U2:** 40; **When were you born?** Wann bist du geboren? **2 › U2:** 40

Bosnia [ˈbɒzniə] Bosnien **U1:** 21

boss [bɒs] Boss **5 › U1:** 13

both [bəʊθ] beide **3 › U5:** 88; **both Catholics and Protestants** sowohl Katholiken als auch Protestanten **U1:** 10

bothered [ˈbɒðəd]: **he wasn't bothered** es störte ihn nicht **U4:** 65

bottle [ˈbɒtl] Flasche **1 › U3:** 55

bottom [ˈbɒtəm]: **at the bottom (of the photo)** unten (auf dem Foto) **U1:** 8; **the bottom of the sea** der Meeresgrund **5 › U2:** 31

bought [bɔːt] (→ buy): **I bought** ich kaufte, ich habe gekauft **2 › U3:** 51; **I've bought** ich habe gekauft **3 › U3:** 53

boutique [buːˈtiːk] Boutique *U5: 81*

bow [bəʊ] Bogen **2 › A Legend:** 108

bowling [ˈbəʊlɪŋ] Bowling **3 › U5:** 107

box [bɒks] Kiste; „Fernsehkiste"; Kasten **5 › U2:** 41; (**2 › U1:** 18)

box-office hit [ˈbɒks ɒfɪs] Kassenschlager **U3:** 42

boy [bɔɪ] Junge **1 › Intro:** 10; **Boy, was I scared!** Mann, hatte ich Angst! **5 › U5:** 87

boyfriend [ˈbɔɪfrend] (fester) Freund **4 › U5:** 90

→ DICTIONARY

braai [braɪ] Grillfest *(südafrikanisch)* U2: 27

brackets ['brækɪts] (runde) Klammern U3: 53

brand [brænd] Marke, Sorte **2 ▸ U4:** 68; **brand name** Markenzeichen, -name **1 ▸ U6:** 108

bread [bred] Brot **1 ▸ U3:** 54

break [breɪk] (I broke, I've broken) (zer)brechen, kaputtmachen **1 ▸ U4:** 78; kaputtgehen **5 ▸ U2:** 28; **break in** einbrechen **5 ▸ U2:** 30; **break the rules** gegen die Regeln verstoßen **U2:** 31

breakfast ['brekfəst] Frühstück **2 ▸ U1:** 15; **have breakfast** frühstücken **1 ▸ U4:** 80

breathe [briːð] atmen **5 ▸ U5:** 85

bridge [brɪdʒ] Brücke **4 ▸ U2:** 34

brief [briːf] kurz **U1:** 13

brilliant ['brɪliənt] toll, glänzend, großartig **3 ▸ U1:** 8

bring [brɪŋ] (I brought, I've brought) bringen, mitbringen **1 ▸ U6:** 102

Britain ['brɪtn] Großbritannien **1 ▸ U4:** 74

British ['brɪtɪʃ] britisch; Brite/Britin **2 ▸ U1:** 13

broccoli ['brɒkəli] Brokkoli **1 ▸ U3:** 53

brochure ['brəʊʃə] Prospekt, Broschüre **2 ▸ U1:** 14

broke [brəʊk] (→ break): **I broke** ich zerbrach, ich habe zerbrochen **5 ▸ U2:** 28

broken ['brəʊkən] kaputt, defekt **1 ▸ U2:** 42

broken ['brəʊkən] (→ break): **I've broken** ich habe zerbrochen **5 ▸ U2:** 28; **families broken by unemployment** von Arbeitslosigkeit zerstörte Familien **5 ▸ U3:** 54

brolga bird ['brɒlgə bɜːd] Brolgakranich **5 ▸ U5:** 86

brother ['brʌðə] Bruder **1 ▸ U2:** 39; **brothers or sisters** Geschwister **4 ▸ U1:** 8

brought [brɔːt] (→ bring): **I brought** ich brachte, ich habe gebracht **2 ▸ U5:** 87; **I've brought** ich habe gebracht **3 ▸ U3:** 54

brown [braʊn] braun **1 ▸ Intro:** 14

brush [brʌʃ] bürsten; putzen **2 ▸ U2:** 32

buck [bʌk] *(infml)* Dollar **U5:** 81

bucket ['bʌkɪt] Eimer **U2:** 30

buddy ['bʌdi]: **learning buddy** Lernpate/Lernpatin **4 ▸ U3:** 51

buffalo, buffaloes ['bʌfələʊ] Büffel **U2:** 24

build [bɪld] (I built, I've built) bauen **4 ▸ U4:** 68

building ['bɪldɪŋ] Gebäude **2 ▸ U3:** 50

built [bɪlt]: **I built** ich baute, ich habe gebaut **4 ▸ U4:** 68; **I've built** ich habe gebaut **4 ▸ U4:** 68

bumper car ['bʌmpə kɑː] Autoskooter *(Fahrzeug)* U5: 78

bunch spear grass ['bʌntʃ spɪə grɑːs] *austral.* Grasart **5 ▸ U5:** 86

burger ['bɜːgə] Hamburger **1 ▸ U3:** 54

burn [bɜːn] (I burnt, I've burnt) brennen; verbrennen **4 ▸ U4:** 69

burnt [bɜːnt]: **I burnt** ich verbrannte, ich habe verbrannt **4 ▸ U4:** 69; **I've burnt** ich habe verbrannt **4 ▸ U4:** 69

bury ['beri] beerdigen; vergraben **5 ▸ U5:** 90

bus [bʌs] Bus **1 ▸ U1:** 21; **bus driver** Busfahrer/in **2 ▸ U3:** 54; **bus station** Bushof, Busbahnhof **4 ▸ U4:** 76; **bus stop** Bushaltestelle **1 ▸ U5:** 88; **bus tour** Bus(rund)reise **1 ▸ U6:** 102

bush [bʊʃ] Busch **U5:** 78; **the bush** der (australische) Busch **5 ▸ U5:** 87

bushfire ['bʊʃfaɪə] Buschfeuer **5 ▸ U5:** 86

business ['bɪznəs] Geschäft, Betrieb **4 ▸ U5:** 94; Sache, Problem; Zustand **U4:** 64

businessman, businessmen ['bɪznəsmæn] Geschäftsmann **U3:** 46

busk [bʌsk] Straßenmusik machen **4 ▸ U5:** 92

busy ['bɪzi] beschäftigt **1 ▸ U2:** 40; hektisch, belebt **4 ▸ U2:** 33; **busy shop** gut besuchter Laden **1 ▸ U2:** 40

but [bʌt] **1** aber **1 ▸ U1:** 27; **2** sondern **5 ▸ U1:** 8

buy [baɪ] (I bought, I've bought) kaufen **1 ▸ U4:** 68

buzz [bʌz]: **a city with a buzz** eine Stadt voller Energie **4 ▸ U4:** 68

by [baɪ] von; durch **5 ▸ U3:** 51; **by 2070** bis 2070 **5 ▸ U5:** 86; **by bike/bus/car/...** mit dem Rad/Bus/Auto/... **2 ▸ Intro:** 8; **by the way** übrigens **4 ▸ U2:** 34; **learn/say by heart** auswendig lernen/sprechen **4 ▸ U2:** 37; **one by one** einer/eins nach dem anderen, eine nach der anderen **5 ▸ U4:** 75; **pay by card** mit (Kredit-)Karte bezahlen **4 ▸ U2:** 36

Bye./Bye-bye. [baɪ, bə 'baɪ] Tschüs. **1 ▸ U1:** 28

C

cable ['keɪbl] Kabel, Kabel- **5 ▸ U3:** 55

café ['kæfeɪ] Café **2 ▸ U3:** 51

cafeteria [kæfə'tɪəriə] Kantine, Mensa **4 ▸ U3:** 48

cage [keɪdʒ] Käfig **2 ▸ U2:** 34

cake [keɪk] Kuchen **1 ▸ U3:** 59

calculator ['kælkjuleɪtə] Taschenrechner **2 ▸ U5:** 88

calendar ['kælɪndə] Kalender **2 ▸ U4:** 72

California [kælə'fɔːniə] Kalifornien **3 ▸ U5:** 96

call [kɔːl] **1** anrufen; (herbei) rufen **5 ▸ U1:** 13; **call out** in die Klasse rufen **1 ▸ Intro:** 13; **2** nennen **3 ▸ U1:** 14; **it's called** es (er/sie) heißt **3 ▸ U2:** 33

call centre worker ['kɔːl sentə wɜːkə] Callcenter-Mitarbeiter/in **4 ▸ U5:** 89

came [keɪm] (→ come): **I came** ich kam, ich bin gekommen **1 ▸ U3:** 59

camel ['kæml] Kamel **5 ▸ U5:** 82

camera ['kæmərə] Kamera; Fotoapparat **2 ▸ U3:** 51

camp [kæmp] **1** Lager **5 ▸ U5:** 90; **2** zelten **4 ▸ U2:** 30; **make a camp** ein Lager aufschlagen **5 ▸ U5:** 90

campaign [kæm'peɪn] Aktion; Kampagne **2 ▸ U1:** 18

camper ['kæmpə] Camper/Camperin **4 ▸ U2:** 34

campfire ['kæmpfaɪə] Lagerfeuer **4 ▸ U2:** 34

campground ['kæmpgraʊnd] (AE) Campingplatz **4 ▸ U2:** 30

camping ['kæmpɪŋ] Camping **3 ▸ U3:** 66

campsite ['kæmpsaɪt] Camping-platz **2 > Intro:** 8

can [kæn] **1** können **1 > Intro:** 10; **2** Dose, Büchse **2 > U4:** 63

can't [kɑːnt] nicht können **1 > U5:** 91

Canada ['kænədə] Kanada **5 > U1:** 6

Canadian [kə'neɪdiən] kanadisch; Kanadier/in **5 > U1:** 6

canal [kə'næl] Kanal **4 > U4:** 68

cancer ['kɑːnsə] Krebs(erkran-kung) **U5:** 79

candidate ['kændɪdət] Kandidat/Kandidatin **4 > U5:** 103

cannabis ['kænəbɪs] Cannabis, Haschisch **U4:** 61

canoe [kə'nuː] Kanu **3 > U2:** 126

canoeing [kə'nuːɪŋ] Kanufahren, Paddeln **3 > U2:** 31

canyon ['kænjən] Cañon **4 > U2:** 28

cap [kæp] Kappe **4 > U1:** 12

Cape Town ['keɪp taʊn] Kapstadt **U2:** 28

capital ['kæpɪtl] Hauptstadt **3 > U1:** 9

capital letter [kæpɪtl 'letə] Großbuchstabe **5 > U1:** 21

car [kɑː] Auto **1 > Intro:** 10; **car park** Parkhaus, Parkplatz **1 > U6:** 107; **car-boot sale** (eine Art) Trödelmarkt **1 > U4:** 68

caravan ['kærəvæn] Wohnwagen, Caravan **2 > Intro:** 9; **caravan park** Campingplatz für Wohn-wagen **2 > Intro:** 9

carbon ['kɑːbən] Kohlenstoff **U5:** 74; **carbon dioxide** [kɑːbən daɪ'ɒksaɪd] Kohlendioxid **4 > U4:** 71; **carbon footprint** [kɑːbən 'fʊtprɪnt] CO2-Bilanz **U5:** 74

card [kɑːd] (Spiel-)Karte **1 > U5:** 95; Karteikarte **2 > U1:** 21; **pay by card** mit (Kredit-)Karte bezahlen **4 > U2:** 36

care home ['keə həʊm] Pflegeheim **5 > U4:** 66; **care worker** ['keə wɜːkə] Pfleger/Pflegerin **4 > U5:** 89; **we don't care** [keə] es ist uns egal **2 > U3:** 57

career [kə'rɪə] Karriere **U3:** 42

careful ['keəfl] vorsichtig, sorg-fältig **1 > U6:** 107

Caribbean [kærə'biːən] **1** Karibik; **2** karibisch **4 > U1:** 8

carnival ['kɑːnɪvl] Karneval **5 > U5:** 89

carrot ['kærət] Karotte, Möhre **1 > U3:** 53

carry ['kæri] tragen; befördern **3 > U1:** 15

carton ['kɑːtn] Karton, Packung **1 > U3:** 55

cartoon [kɑː'tuːn] Cartoon, Karikatur **5 > U3:** 50

case [keɪs]: **in case** für den Fall, dass **U5:** 78

cash desk ['kæʃ desk] Kasse, Kassentisch **5 > U3:** 52; **cash machine** ['kæʃ məʃiːn] Geldautomat **4 > U1:** 17; **pay cash** [kæʃ] bar bezahlen **4 > U2:** 36

castle ['kɑːsl] Burg, Schloss **2 > U5:** 80

cat [kæt] Katze, Kater **1 > U1:** 21

catalogue ['kætəlɒg] Katalog **U2:** 35

catastrophe [kə'tæstrəfi]: **natural catastrophe** Naturkatastrophe **U2:** 31

catch [kætʃ] (I caught, I've caught) fangen, erwischen **2 > A Legend:** 108

category ['kætəgəri] Kategorie **4 > U3:** 59

Catholic ['kæθlɪk] Katholik/in; katholisch **U5:** 10

cattle ['kætl] Vieh, Rinder **5 > U5:** 84

caught [kɔːt] (→ catch): **it is caught** es wird gefangen **U5:** 84

cause [kɔːz] verursachen **4 > U4:** 69; **for good causes** ['kɔːziz] für gute/wohltätige Zwecke **U1:** 15

CD [siː 'diː] CD **1 > U2:** 47; **CD player** CD-Player **1 > U3:** 62

celebrity [sə'lebrəti] Berühmtheit, berühmte Person **U1:** 14

cello ['tʃeləʊ] Cello **3 > U5:** 88

cellphone ['selfəʊn] (AE) Mobil-telefon, Handy **4 > U1:** 12

Celtic ['keltɪk] keltisch **Intro:** 7

cent [sent] Cent **2 > U5:** 88

centimetre, cm ['sentimiːtə] Zentimeter (cm) **U3:** 43

central ['sentrəl] zentral, Zentral- **3 > U1:** 8

centre ['sentə] Zentrum, Mittel-punkt **2 > U3:** 48

century ['sentʃəri] Jahrhundert **4 > U1:** 10

certainly ['sɜːtnli] sicher, bestimmt **5 > U4:** 67

certificate [sə'tɪfɪkət] Bescheinigung **4 > U5:** 96

chair [tʃeə] Stuhl **1 > Intro:** 10

chambermaid ['tʃeɪmbəmeɪd] Zimmermädchen **U1:** 21

change [tʃeɪndʒ] **1** (sich) (ver)ändern **4 > U4:** 74; **2** wechseln, tauschen **4 > U1:** 17; **3** umstei-gen **3 > U1:** 14; **4** Veränderung **4 > U5:** 95; **get changed** sich umziehen **4 > U5:** 92

channel ['tʃænl] Programm, Sender, Kanal **3 > U5:** 95

character ['kærəktə] **1** Figur, Person; **2** Charakter **5 > U4:** 64

charge [tʃɑːdʒ]: **charge people** Leuten Geld abnehmen **U5:** 81

charger ['tʃɑːdʒə] Ladegerät **U2:** 35

charts [tʃɑːts]: **the US charts** die amerikanische Hitparade **3 > U5:** 102

chat [tʃæt] sich unterhalten, plaudern **3 > U4:** 70

chav [tʃæv] (GB) Jugendliche/r, der/die durch bestimmte Kleidung auffällt und zu stören-dem Verhalten neigt **U4:** 60

cheap [tʃiːp] billig **1 > U4:** 69; **the cheapest** am billigsten **1 > U6:** 107

check [tʃek] (über)prüfen, kontrollieren **1 > U6:** 110; **check in** [tʃek 'ɪn] einchecken; aufgeben **4 > U1:** 16

cheer [tʃɪə] (zu)jubeln, hurra rufen **4 > U4:** 74

cheerful ['tʃɪəfl] gut gelaunt, vergnügt; heiter **4 > U5:** 92

cheerleader ['tʃɪəliːdə] Person, die das Publikum bei einem Wettkampf zum Beifall anfeuert **3 > U4:** 68

cheerleading ['tʃɪəliːdɪŋ] Anfeuern des Publikums zum Beifall bei einem Wettkampf **3 > U4:** 71

Cheers! [tʃɪəz] Tschüs! **1 > U6:** 115

cheese [tʃiːz] Käse **1 > U3:** 54

cheeseburger ['tʃiːzbɜːgə] Cheeseburger **1 > U3:** 54

cheesecake ['tʃiːzkeɪk] Käse-kuchen **3 > U4:** 76

chewing gum ['tʃuːɪŋ gʌm] Kaugummi **2 > U3:** 51

chicken ['tʃɪkɪn] Huhn **1 > U5:** 90; **chicken tikka masala** [tʃɪkɪn tɪkə mə'sɑːlə] Hähnchen Tikka Massala (indisches Gericht aus gegrilltem Hähnchen in würziger Tomatensauce) **U3:** 49

DICTIONARY

child, children [tʃaɪld, 'tʃɪldrən] Kind, Kinder **1 › U3:** 60

chill out [tʃɪl 'aʊt] sich entspannen, „chillen" **U2:** 27; **Chill out!** Bleib(t) cool! **1 › U5:** 90

China ['tʃaɪnə] China **4 › U1:** 8

Chinese [tʃaɪ'niːz] chinesisch; Chinesisch; Chinese/Chinesin **4 › U1:** 9

chips [tʃɪps] Pommes frites **3 › U1:** 15

chip shop ['tʃɪp ʃɒp] Pommes-frites-Bude, Imbissbude **1 › U3:** 59

chocolate ['tʃɒklət] Schokolade **1 › U3:** 56

choice [tʃɔɪs] (Aus-)Wahl **U3:** 43

cholera ['kɒlərə] Cholera *(ansteckende Magen-Darm-Erkrankung)* **U3:** 43

choose [tʃuːz] (I chose, I've chosen) aussuchen, auswählen, wählen **4 › U2:** 42

chose [tʃəʊz] (→ choose): **I chose** ich wählte aus, ich habe ausgewählt **4 › U2:** 42

chosen ['tʃəʊzn] (→ choose): **I've chosen** ich habe ausgewählt **4 › U2:** 42

Christmas ['krɪsməs] Weihnachten **3 › U3:** 56; **Christmas Day** der 1. Weihnachtstag **1 › U5:** 98; **the Christmas sales** der Weihnachtsausverkauf **5 › U3:** 49

church [tʃɜːtʃ] Kirche **3 › U5:** 102; **at church** in der Kirche **3 › U5:** 102

cinema ['sɪnəmə] Kino **1 › U6:** 104

circuit [sɜːkɪt] Gerichtsbezirk **5 › U4:** 64

circus ['sɜːkəs] Zirkus **1 › U6:** 115

city ['sɪti] Stadt, Großstadt **2 › U1:** 22

class [klɑːs] **1** (Schul-)Klasse **1 › U1:** 24; **2** Unterricht, Unterrichtsstunde **4 › U3:** 48

classical ['klæsɪkl] klassisch **3 › U5:** 89

classroom ['klɑːsruːm] Klassenzimmer **1 › Intro:** 11

clean [kliːn] **1** putzen **1 › U4:** 80; **clean up** gründlich reinigen, sauber machen **4 › U4:** 68; **2** sauber **5 › U2:** 31

cleaning ['kliːnɪŋ] Saubermachen **2 › U2:** 35; **cleaning product** ['kliːnɪŋ prɒdʌkt] Reinigungsmittel **5 › U4:** 72

clever ['klevə] schlau, klug **1 › U6:** 109

click [klɪk] (an-, hin-)klicken **2 › U5:** 77

cliff [klɪf] Klippe, Felsen **5 › U5:** 82

climate change ['klaɪmət tʃeɪndʒ] Klimawandel **4 › U4:** 69

climb [klaɪm] klettern, steigen (auf) **3 › U2:** 33

clock [klɒk] Uhr **1 › U6:** 102; **alarm clock** Wecker **2 › U1:** 15

close 1 [kləʊz] schließen, zumachen **2 › U2:** 34; **2** [kləʊs] nahe, dicht **5 › U3:** 49

closed [kləʊzd] geschlossen, zu **2 › U2:** 31

clothes [kləʊðz] Kleidung, Kleider **1 › U4:** 69

cloud [klaʊd] Wolke **U5:** 78

cloudy ['klaʊdi] bewölkt, wolkig **2 › U6:** 104

club [klʌb] Club, Arbeitsgemeinschaft **2 › U1:** 17; Verein **4 › U4:** 68

cluck [klʌk] gack **1 › U5:** 90

coach [kəʊtʃ] Reisebus **5 › U5:** 88

coal [kəʊl] Kohle **4 › U4:** 69

coast [kəʊst] Küste **U1:** 9

coat [kəʊt] Mantel, Jacke **5 › U2:** 26

coffee ['kɒfi] Kaffee **3 › U4:** 76; **coffee pot** ['kɒfi pɒt] Kaffeekanne **4 › U5:** 94

coin [kɔɪn] Münze *U1: 103*

cola ['kəʊlə] Cola **1 › U4:** 70

cold [kəʊld] kalt **2 › U4:** 62; **I'm cold.** Mir ist kalt./Ich friere. **3 › U2:** 34

collapse [kə'læps] einstürzen **U5:** 79

colleague ['kɒliːg] Kollege, Kollegin **U2:** 31

collect [kə'lekt] (ein)sammeln **1 › U4:** 74

college ['kɒlɪdʒ] Berufsschule, Fach(hoch)schule **4 › U5:** 88

Colombia [kə'lʌmbiə] Kolumbien *U1: 15*

colony ['kɒləni] Kolonie **5 › U1:** 7

colour ['kʌlə] Farbe **1 › Intro:** 14

Coloureds ['kʌlədz]: **the Coloureds** die „Farbigen" *(Menschen, die sowohl schwarze als auch weiße Vorfahren haben)* **U2:** 25

come [kʌm] (I came, I've come) kommen **1 › U3:** 58; **come and see me** komm zu mir **5 › U1:** 14; **come in** [kʌm 'ɪn] hereinkommen **3 › U3:** 62; **I've come** ich bin gekommen **3 › U3:** 131; **Oh, come on!** Ach, komm schon! **U5:** 76

comedy ['kɒmədi] Komödie, Comedy(show) **1 › U2:** 45

comfortable ['kʌmftəbl] komfortabel, bequem **3 › U5:** 92

comic ['kɒmɪk] Comic(heft) **1 › U3:** 55

comment ['kɒment] Kommentar **U1:** 15

commit [kə'mɪt]: **commit a crime** ein Verbrechen begehen **U4:** 60

Commonwealth Games ['kɒmənwelθ geɪmz] Commonwealth Games *(Sportereignis der Länder des ehem. Commonwealth)* **U3:** 47

community [kə'mjuːnəti] Gemeinschaft, Bevölkerungsgruppe **5 › U3:** 50

compact [kəm'pækt] kompakt **3 › U5:** 92

company ['kʌmpəni] Firma, Unternehmen **2 › U6:** 94

compare [kəm'peə] vergleichen **2 › U5:** 79

competition [kɒmpə'tɪʃn] Wettbewerb **3 › U4:** 70; **be in a competition** an einem Wettbewerb teilnehmen **3 › U4:** 70

complain [kəm'pleɪn] sich beschweren **4 › U5:** 91

complete [kəm'pliːt] vervollständigen **3 › U3:** 66; **complete an application form** ein Bewerbungsformular ausfüllen **5 › U4:** 68

completely [kəm'pliːtli] völlig **5 › U2:** 31

complicated ['kɒmplɪkeɪtɪd] kompliziert *U3: 107*

comprehensive school [kɒmprɪ'hensɪv skuːl] Gesamtschule **4 › U5:** 88

compulsory [kəm'pʌlsəri] Pflicht- **4 › U3:** 50

computer [kəm'pjuːtə] Computer **1 › Intro:** 10

concert ['kɒnsət] Konzert **3 › U1:** 13

concrete ['kɒŋkriːt] Beton, Beton- **U5:** 79

148
one hundred and forty-eight

condition [kənˈdɪʃn] Bedingung; Zustand **U3:** 42

conference [ˈkɒnfərəns] Konferenz **U3:** 52

confident [ˈkɒnfɪdənt] zuversichtlich, selbstsicher **5>U4:** 67

Congratulations! [kəngrætʃʊˈleɪʃnz] Herzlichen Glückwunsch! **3>U3:** 55

connect [kəˈnekt] verbunden sein **5>U4:** 72; **it connected them to their land** es verband sie mit ihrem Land **5>U5:** 82

consider [kənˈsɪdə] sich überlegen, nachdenken über **U3:** 46

considering [kənˈsɪdərɪŋ] wenn man berücksichtigt, dass **U4:** 65

console [ˈkɒnsəʊl]: **games console** Spielkonsole **2>U2:** 29

consumer [kənˈsjuːmə]: **family and consumer science** Hauswirtschaft **4>U3:** 50

contact [ˈkɒntækt] **1** sich in Verbindung setzen mit **2>U6:** 94; **2** Kontakt, Verbindung **5>U2:** 31

contaminate [kənˈtæmɪneɪt] verseuchen **U5:** 78

continent [ˈkɒntɪnənt] Kontinent **5>U3:** 45

continue [kənˈtɪnjuː] weitergehen/ weitermachen, (sich) fortsetzen **U5:** 74

contrast [ˈkɒntrɑːst] Gegensatz **U3:** 53

convention [kənˈvenʃn] Tagung **3>U5:** 94

convict [ˈkɒnvɪkt] Sträfling, Strafgefangene/r **5>U3:** 46

cook [kʊk] kochen **1>U3:** 58

cookie [ˈkʊki] (AE) Keks **3>U5:** 96; **cookies and cream** [ˌkʊkiz ənd ˈkriːm] „Cookies and cream" (Kekse und Sahne; eine Eissorte) **3>U5:** 96

cooking [ˈkʊkɪŋ] Kochen **2>U5:** 82

cool [kuːl] cool, scharf, stark **2>U1:** 18

copy [ˈkɒpi] **1** abschreiben; kopieren **3>U3:** 66; **2** Exemplar **5>U3:** 55

core [kɔː]: **core subject** Kernfach, Hauptfach **4>U3:** 50

cornflakes [ˈkɔːnfleɪks] Cornflakes **1>U3:** 61

correct [kəˈrekt] verbessern **5>U5:** 96; (**1>U6:** 109)

cosmetics [kɒzˈmetɪks] Kosmetik (produkte) **5>U4:** 77

cosmopolitan [ˌkɒzməˈpɒlɪtən] weltoffen, kosmopolitisch **4>U1:** 8

cost [kɒst] **1** (it cost, it has cost) kosten **1>U4:** 73; **2** Kosten; Preis **U4:** 69

cotton [ˈkɒtn] Baumwolle **2>U3:** 50

could [kʊd] **1** konnte/n **2>U5:** 81; **2** könnte/n **4>U1:** 8

couldn't [ˈkʊdnt] konnte/n nicht **2>U5:** 81

council [ˈkaʊnsl] (Stadt-) Verwaltung **3>U1:** 13

count [kaʊnt] zählen **1>U4:** 80

country [ˈkʌntri] Land **2>U1:** 13; **country (music)** Countrymusik **3>U5:** 88; **country and western music** (**3>U5:** 89); **king and country** König und Vaterland **5>U1:** 17

county [ˈkaʊnti] Grafschaft (Verwaltungsbezirk) **U1:** 10

course [kɔːs] Kurs(us); Lehrgang **U2:** 30; **course not** = of course not **U4:** 65

court [kɔːt] Gericht **5>U3:** 55; **basketball court** Basketball-Spielfeld **3>U1:** 13; **go to court** vor Gericht gehen **5>U3:** 55

cousin [ˈkʌzn] Cousin, Cousine **1>U5:** 89

cover [ˈkʌvə] bedecken; verhüllen **5>U1:** 8

cow [kaʊ] Kuh **1>U3:** 58

cowboy [ˈkaʊbɔɪ] Cowboy **3>U3:** 52

cozzie (= swimming costume) [ˈkɒzi] Badeanzug **5>U3:** 49

crack [kræk] Riss **U5:** 79

cracker [ˈkrækə] Cracker (salziger Keks) **3>U4:** 73

crash (into) [kræʃ] einen Unfall haben (mit), zusammenstoßen (mit) **5>U5:** 85

crazy (about) [ˈkreɪzi] verrückt (nach) **3>U4:** 68

cream [kriːm] Sahne **3>U4:** 76; **cream cheese** [kriːm ˈtʃiːz] Frischkäse **3>U4:** 76

cricket [ˈkrɪkɪt] Kricket **5>U3:** 45; (**2>Intro:** 9)

crime [kraɪm] Verbrechen, Kriminalität **3>U1:** 8

criminal [ˈkrɪmɪnl] **1** Verbrecher/ in, Kriminelle/r **5>U3:** 46; **2** kriminell **5>U3:** 54

crisps [krɪsps] Kartoffelchips **1>U3:** 56

criticise [ˈkrɪtɪsaɪz] kritisieren **U1:** 15

Croatia [krəʊˈeɪʃə] Kroatien **5>U4:** 70

Croatian [krəʊˈeɪʃən] kroatisch; Kroatisch; Kroate/Kroatin **5>U4:** 70

crocodile [ˈkrɒkədaɪl] Krokodil **5>U4:** 54

crop [krɒp] (Feld-)Frucht, Ernte **U3:** 41; **grow crops** Feldfrüchte anbauen **U3:** 41

cross [krɒs] überqueren, kreuzen **2>U3:** 46; **Fingers crossed!** Ich drücke die Daumen! **3>U3:** 56; **I'll cross my fingers for you.** etwa: Ich drück dir die Daumen. **U4:** 62

cross-country skiing [krɒs kʌntri ˈskiːɪŋ] Skilanglauf **5>U1:** 10

crowd [kraʊd] (Menschen-)Menge **4>U4:** 74

Crown Jewels [kraʊn ˈdʒuːəlz] Kronjuwelen **3>U1:** 10

cruel [ˈkruːəl] grausam, gefühllos **5>U2:** 31

cry [kraɪ] weinen **3>U2:** 34

culture [ˈkʌltʃə] Kultur **5>U2:** 34

cup [kʌp] Tasse **3>U4:** 76; **a cup of coffee** eine Tasse Kaffee **3>U4:** 76; **World Cup** Weltmeisterschaft (Fußball) **U2:** 24

cupboard [ˈkʌbəd] Schrank **1>Intro:** 11

curly [ˈkɜːli] lockig, gelockt **5>U4:** 70

curtain [ˈkɜːtn] Vorhang, Gardine **1>U6:** 106

cushion [ˈkʊʃn] Kissen **1>U6:** 106

customer [ˈkʌstəmə] Kunde/ Kundin **1>U2:** 41

cut [kʌt] (I cut, I've cut) **1** schneiden **1>U6:** 110; **I cut** ich schnitt **5>U1:** 16; **I've cut** ich habe geschnitten **5>U1:** 16; **cut down trees** Bäume fällen **U5:** 74; **cut off** abschneiden **5>U2:** 31; **2** verringern; Verringerung **U5:** 85

CV (curriculum vitae) [siː ˈviː, kəˈrɪkjələm ˈviːtaɪ] Lebenslauf **4>U5:** 103

cycle [ˈsaɪkl] **1** Rad fahren **U2:** 30; **cycle trail** [ˈsaɪkl treɪl] Radweg **4>U4:** 81; **2** Kreislauf, Zyklus **U5:** 86

cycling [ˈsaɪklɪŋ] Radfahren **4>U2:** 42

cyclist [ˈsaɪklɪst] Radfahrer/ Radfahrerin **4>U2:** 31

→ DICTIONARY

D

dad [dæd] Papa, Vati **1 › U2:** 40

dam [dæm] (Stau-)Damm **U5:** 75

damage ['dæmɪdʒ] beschädigen **5 › U5:** 85

dance [dɑːns] **1** tanzen **4 › U3:** 53; **2** Tanz; Tanzveranstaltung, Ball **4 › U3:** 53

dancer ['dɑːnsə] Tänzer/Tänzerin **4 › U5:** 89

dancing ['dɑːnsɪŋ] Tanzen **2 › U4:** 61; **dancing club** ['dɑːnsɪŋ klʌb] Tanzclub, Tanzgruppe **4 › U3:** 53

danger ['deɪndʒə] Gefahr **5 › U1:** 17; **put the animals in danger** die Tiere in Gefahr bringen **U2:** 31

dangerous ['deɪndʒərəs] gefährlich **2 › U1:** 18

dare [deə] sich trauen, wagen **4 › U3:** 54

dark [dɑːk] dunkel **2 › U3:** 51

date [deɪt] Datum **2 › U4:** 72

daughter ['dɔːtə] Tochter **1 › U3:** 60

day [deɪ] Tag **1 › U2:** 42; **day centre** ['deɪ sentə] Altentagesstätte, Seniorentreff **4 › U5:** 90; **four-day trip** viertägige Reise **4 › U2:** 36

DDT [diː diː 'tiː] *Name eines gefährlichen Pflanzenschutzmittels* **U5:** 81

dead [ded] tot **3 › U2:** 33

dear [dɪə]: **Dear ...,** Liebe/r/s ..., **2 › U1:** 16

death [deθ] Tod, Todesfall **5 › U3:** 54

December [dɪ'sembə] Dezember **1 › U5:** 98

decide [dɪ'saɪd] beschließen, (sich) entscheiden **4 › U5:** 89

decoration [dekə'reɪʃn] Dekoration **5 › U3:** 48

deep [diːp] tief **5 › U4:** 73

deforestation [diːfɒrɪ'steɪʃn] Entwaldung *(Zerstörung großer Waldflächen)* **U5:** 74

degree [dɪ'griː] Grad **2 › U6:** 104

deli ['deli] (AE) (Feinkost-)Imbiss **3 › U4:** 76

deliver [dɪ'lɪvə] austragen, zustellen; liefern **3 › U2:** 28

democratic [demə'krætɪk] demokratisch **5 › U3:** 55

demonstration [demən'streɪʃn] Demonstration **4 › U4:** 74

department store [dɪ'pɑːtmənt stɔː] Kaufhaus **U3:** 41

depend [dɪ'pend]: **It depends.** Das kommt (ganz) darauf an. **5 › U1:** 13

dependent [dɪ'pendənt] abhängig **U2:** 38

deposit [dɪ'pɒzɪt] Anzahlung **U4:** 69

describe [dɪ'skraɪb] beschreiben **5 › U5:** 85

desert ['dezət] Wüste **5 › U3:** 44

designer clothes [dɪ'zaɪnə kləʊðz] Markenkleidung **4 › U1:** 10

destroy [dɪ'strɔɪ] zerstören **5 › U2:** 32

detail ['diːteɪl] Detail, Einzelheit **3 › U1:** 23

detailed ['diːteɪld] detailliert **U2:** 29

diagram ['daɪəgræm] Diagramm; Schaubild **4 › U5:** 101

dialling code ['daɪəlɪŋ kəʊd] Vorwahl **3 › U2:** 36

dialogue ['daɪəlɒg] Dialog **2 › U1:** 21

diamond ['daɪəmənd] Diamant **U2:** 27

diary ['daɪəri] Tagebuch **2 › U1:** 18

dictionary ['dɪkʃənri] Wörterbuch **1 › U2:** 37

did [dɪd] (→ do): **I did** ich tat, ich habe getan **2 › U2:** 32; **Did you ...?** Hast du ...? **2 › U2:** 32

didgeridoo [dɪdʒəri'duː] Didgeridoo *(australisches Blasinstrument)* **5 › U3:** 51

didn't ['dɪdnt]: **No, I didn't (= did not).** Nein (habe ich nicht). **2 › U2:** 32

die [daɪ] sterben **2 › A Legend:** 109

difference ['dɪfrəns] Unterschied **2 › U6:** 97

different ['dɪfrənt] **1** andere/r/s **1 › U1:** 24; **2** verschieden, anders **2 › Intro:** 9; **different from** anders als **3 › U3:** 51; **How is it different from ...?** Wie unterscheidet sie sich von ...? **4 › U3:** 48; **they speak differently** sie sprechen unterschiedlich **4 › Intro:** 7

difficult ['dɪfɪkəlt] schwierig, schwer **1 › U5:** 92

digital ['dɪdʒɪtl] Digital- **4 › U5:** 96

diner ['daɪnə] (AE) Café, kleines Restaurant **3 › U4:** 72

dingo, dingoes ['dɪŋgəʊ] Dingo *(austral. Wildhundrasse)* **5 › U5:** 82

dining room ['daɪnɪŋ ruːm] Esszimmer **U1:** 20

dinner ['dɪnə] Abendessen **4 › U1:** 18; **have dinner** zu Abend essen **4 › U1:** 18

director [də'rektə]: **film director** Filmregisseur **U3:** 49

dirty ['dɜːti] schmutzig **4 › U4:** 72

disabled [dɪs'eɪbld] behindert **5 › U4:** 66

disadvantage [dɪsəd'vɑːntɪdʒ] Nachteil **U2:** 26

disagree with [dɪsə'griː] nicht übereinstimmen mit **U2:** 25

disappear [dɪsə'pɪə] verschwinden **U5:** 75

disappointed [dɪsə'pɔɪntɪd] enttäuscht **U2:** 30

disaster [dɪ'zɑːstə] Katastrophe **5 › U1:** 17

disco ['dɪskəʊ] Disko **U3:** 49

discuss [dɪ'skʌs] besprechen, diskutieren **4 › U4:** 70

discussion [dɪ'skʌʃn] Diskussion **U4:** 73

disease [dɪ'ziːz] Krankheit **U1:** 10

dish [dɪʃ] Gericht *(Essen)* **4 › U1:** 14

dishwasher ['dɪʃwɒʃə] Geschirrspülmaschine **2 › U6:** 94

dive [daɪv] tauchen **5 › U3:** 49

divide into [dɪ'vaɪd] einteilen in **U2:** 29

diving ['daɪvɪŋ] Tauchen **5 › U3:** 49

divorced [dɪ'vɔːst]: **get divorced** sich scheiden lassen **4 › U1:** 15

do [duː] (I did, I've done) tun, machen **1 › U4:** 76; **Do exercise 1, please.** Mach/t bitte Übung 1. **1 › Intro:** 13

dock [dɒk] Hafen, Dock **2 › U3:** 46

doctor ['dɒktə] Arzt/Ärztin **1 › U3:** 53

does [dʌz]: **Does she live ...?** Wohnt sie ...? **1 › U5:** 89; **Yes, she does.** Ja (tut sie). **1 › U5:** 89

doesn't ['dʌznt]: **..., doesn't it?** ..., nicht wahr? **5 › U5:** 84; **he doesn't have** er hat kein/e/en **1 › U3:** 57; **No, she doesn't.** Nein (tut sie nicht). **1 › U5:** 89

dog [dɒg] Hund **1 › U1:** 21

doggy bag ['dɒgi bæg] *Tüte zum Mitnehmen von Essensresten ("für den Hund")* 3 > U4: 76

doll [dɒl] Puppe **1 > U4:** 71

dollar ($) ['dɒlə] Dollar *(US-Währung)* **2 > U6:** 96

dominate ['dɒmɪneɪt] dominieren **U3:** 47

don't [dəʊnt]: **Don't do that, please.** Lass/t das. / Mach/t das nicht. 1 > Intro: 13; **I don't have** ich habe kein/e/en **1 > U3:** 55; **I don't like ...** ich mag ... nicht **1 > U5:** 94; **I don't.** Ich nicht. 4 > U1: 10

done [dʌn] (→ do): **I've done** ich habe getan **3 > U3:** 50

door [dɔː] Tür **1 > Intro:** 11

dot [dɒt] Punkt 5 > U2: 41

double ['dʌbl]: **double chair lift** Doppelsesselbahn 5 > U1: 10; **double room** Doppelzimmer **U4:** 69

doubt [daʊt]: **no doubt** kein Zweifel **U3:** 47

doughnut ['dəʊnʌt] Doughnut *(ringförmiges Hefegebäck)*; Berliner, Krapfen **U1:** 11

down [daʊn] hinunter/herunter, hinab/herab **3 > U2:** 34; **down the back of the sofa** in der hintersten Ecke des Sofas U4: 65; **Sit down, please.** Setzt euch./Setz dich. 1 > Intro: 12

download [daʊn'ləʊd] herunter-laden, downloaden **U3:** 42

downtown Brooklyn [daʊn'taʊn] (AE) die (Stadt-)Mitte von Brooklyn **4 > U1:** 10

drama ['drɑːmə] Schauspiel, Theater **4 > U3:** 48; Drama **4 > U4:** 75; **(TV) drama** Fernsehfilm **5 > U4:** 64

dramatic [drə'mætɪk] dramatisch **5 > U4:** 72

dramatically [drə'mætɪkli] drama-tisch **U5:** 79

drank [dræŋk] (→ drink): **I drank** ich trank, ich habe getrunken **3 > U1:** 14

draw [drɔː] (I drew, I've drawn) zeichnen, malen **2 > U6:** 105

dream [driːm] Traum **3 > U5:** 103

dress [dres] **1** sich kleiden **U2:** 27; **2 dress style** Kleidungsstil **U3:** 43

drink [drɪŋk] **1** (I drank, I've drunk) trinken **1 > U4:** 70; **2** Getränk **1 > U3:** 52; **have a drink** etwas trinken **4 > U1:** 10

drive [draɪv] (I drove, I've driven) fahren *(ein Auto, einen Bus usw.)* **2 > U6:** 102

driver ['draɪvə] Fahrer/Fahrerin **4 > U5:** 89

driving ['draɪvɪŋ] Autofahren **2 > U6:** 98; **driving lesson** Fahrstunde **U4:** 62; **driving test** Fahrprüfung **U4:** 60

drought [draʊt] Dürre **5 > U5:** 86

drove [drəʊv] (→ drive): **I drove** ich fuhr, ich bin gefahren **2 > Grammatik:** 179

drug [drʌg] Droge, Rauschgift **5 > U2:** 30

drum [drʌm] Trommel **3 > U5:** 88; **play the drums** Schlagzeug spielen **3 > U5:** 88

drummer ['drʌmə] Schlagzeuger/Schlagzeugerin; Trommler/Trommlerin **4 > U5:** 59

drunk [drʌŋk] (→ drink): **I've drunk** ich habe getrunken **3 > U3:** 53; **get drunk** sich betrinken **U4:** 60

dry [draɪ] trocken **2 > U6:** 104

dull [dʌl] langweilig, stumpfsinnig 3 > U5: 91

during ['djʊərɪŋ] während **4 > U3:** 48

dustman ['dʌstmən] Müllmann **2 > U6:** 98

Dutch [dʌtʃ] Niederländisch **U2:** 25

DVD [diːviː'diː] DVD **1 > U4:** 70; **DVD player** DVD-Spieler **2 > U2:** 29

E

each [iːtʃ] jede/jeder/jedes; je **3 > U1:** 22; **each other** einander, sich **3 > U5:** 106

ear [ɪə] Ohr **U1:** 22

early ['ɜːli] früh, frühzeitig **1 > U6:** 107

earn [ɜːn] verdienen **3 > U2:** 28

earth [ɜːθ]: **Why on earth ...?** Warum in aller Welt ...? **5 > U5:** 89

east [iːst] (nach) Osten; Ost-; östlich **3 > U5:** 89

easy ['iːzi] leicht, einfach **2 > U4:** 66; **(Go) Easy on the mayo.** Wenig Majo(naise). **3 > U4:** 76

easy-going [iːzi 'gəʊɪŋ] locker, gelassen **4 > U3:** 50

eat [iːt] (I ate, I've eaten) essen **1 > U3:** 53; **eat fire** Feuer schlucken/speien **1 > U6:** 105

eaten ['iːtn] (→ eat): **I've eaten** ich habe gegessen **3 > U3:** 53

eco-freak ['iːkəʊ friːk] Öko-Freak **4 > U4:** 73

ecological [iːkə'lɒdʒɪkl] ökologisch **5 > U2:** 35

economic [iːkə'nɒmɪk] wirtschaft-lich, Wirtschafts- **5 > U1:** 8

educate ['edʒukeɪt]: **be educated** zur Schule gehen **U3:** 54

education [edʒu'keɪʃn] (Schul-) Bildung **U2:** 26

effect [ɪ'fekt] Effekt, Auswirkung **U5:** 76

e.g. [iː 'dʒiː] z.B. (= zum Beispiel) **3 > U2:** 36

egg [eg] Ei **3 > U4:** 77

eight [eɪt] acht **1 > Intro:** 15

eighteen [eɪ'tiːn] achtzehn **1 > U2:** 48

eighteenth [eɪ'tiːnθ] achtzehnte/r/s **2 > U4:** 72

eighth [eɪtθ] achte/r/s **2 > U4:** 72

eighty ['eɪti] achtzig **1 > U2:** 48

either ['aɪðə]: **either ... or** entweder ... oder **5 > U1:** 8; **not ... either** auch nicht **U4:** 62

election [ɪ'lekʃn] Wahl **3 > U3:** 48

electric [ɪ'lektrɪk] elektrisch **U2:** 25

electricity [ɪlek'trɪsəti] Strom, Elektrizität **3 > U5:** 94

electronic gadget [ɪlek'trɒnɪk 'gædʒɪt] Elektrogerät, -apparat **2 > U2:** 29

electronics [ɪlek'trɒnɪks] Elektronik **3 > U2:** 29

elegant ['elɪgənt] elegant **5 > U5:** 82

elementary school [elɪ'mentri skuːl] Grundschule (in den USA) **4 > U3:** 48

elephant ['elɪfənt] Elefant **U2:** 24

eleven [ɪ'levn] elf **1 > Intro:** 15

eleventh [ɪ'levnθ] elfte/r/s **2 > U4:** 72

else [els]: **anything else** irgend-etwas anderes, sonst noch irgendetwas **U2:** 30

'em [əm] = them *U5: 81*

email ['iːmeɪl] **1** E-Mail **2 > U1:** 16; **2** als E-Mail verschicken, mailen **2 > U6:** 94

emigrate ['emɪgreɪt] auswandern **5 > U3:** 46

emotion [ɪ'məʊʃn] Gefühl **U3:** 47

empty ['empti] leer **1 > U3:** 57

151

one hundred and fifty-one

DICTIONARY

end [end] **1**enden; beenden
2›U1: 25; **2**Ende **2›A Legend:**
110; **at the end of March** Ende
März **3›U4:** 68; **in the end**
schließlich **4›U1:** 15

ending [ˈendɪŋ] Ende, Schluss
4›U5: 95; **happy ending**
[hæpi ˈendɪŋ] Happy End **U3:** 47

energy [ˈenədʒi] Energie, Kraft
4›U4: 71

engineer [endʒɪˈnɪə] Techniker/in;
Ingenieur/in **4›U5:** 91

England [ˈɪŋɡlənd] England
1›Intro: 16

English [ˈɪŋɡlɪʃ] englisch
1›U1: 30; **English-speaking**
englischsprachig **Intro:** 7; **in
English** auf Englisch **1›U1:** 32

enjoy [ɪnˈdʒɔɪ] genießen
2›U3: 49; **Enjoy!** (AE) Guten
Appetit! **3›U4:** 76; **he enjoys
himself** er amüsiert sich, er hat
Spaß **4›U3:** 52

enormous [ɪˈnɔːməs] ungeheuer
groß **1›U6:** 108

enough [ɪˈnʌf] genug **4›U5:** 92

enter [ˈentə] eingeben **4›U3:** 62

entertainment [entəˈteɪnmənt]
Unterhaltung **U3:** 47

enthusiasm [ɪnˈθjuːziæzəm]
Begeisterung 5›U3: 54

entrance [ˈentrəns] Eingang
4›U2: 33

environment [ɪnˈvaɪrənmənt]
Umgebung; Umwelt **3›U1:** 18

episode [ˈepɪsəʊd] **1**Folge (einer
Serie); **2**Episode **5›U4:** 64

equipment [ɪˈkwɪpmənt] Aus-
rüstung, Ausstattung **4›U2:** 30

especially [ɪˈspeʃəli] besonders
5›U2: 30

estate [ɪˈsteɪt] Siedlung **3›U1:** 8

etc. (= et cetera) [et ˈsetərə] und
so weiter **4›U5:** 89

Ethiopia [iːθiˈəʊpiə] Äthiopien
U1: 14

ethnic [ˈeθnɪk]: **ethnic clothes**
landestypische Kleidung **U3:** 43

ethnology [eθˈnɒlədʒi]: **Museum
of Ethnology** Völkerkunde-
museum 5›U2: 27

euro [ˈjʊərəʊ] Euro **2›U3:** 56

Europe [ˈjʊərəp] Europa
1›Intro: 16

European [jʊərəˈpiːən] europäisch;
Europäer/in **5›U1:** 14;
European Union [jʊərəpiːən
ˈjuːniən] Europäische Union
U1: 11

evacuate [ɪˈvækjueɪt] evakuieren
U5: 79

even [ˈiːvn] sogar **3›U3:** 48;
even if selbst/sogar wenn
U4: 62

evening [ˈiːvnɪŋ] Abend
1›U4: 80; **evening meal**
Abendessen **4›U3:** 50

event [ɪˈvent] Veranstaltung,
Ereignis **U3:** 46

ever [ˈevə] schon einmal, jemals
3›U3: 52; **for ever** [fər ˈevə]
für immer, auf ewig **4›U4:** 71;
larger than ever größer als je
zuvor **5›U1:** 8

every [ˈevri] jede/r/s **1›U3:** 53;
every ten minutes alle zehn
Minuten **3›U1:** 16

everybody [ˈevribɒdi] jeder, alle
2›U5: 83; **Hi, everybody!**
Hallo, zusammen! **4›U1:** 14

everything [ˈevriθɪŋ] alles **1
›U2:** 42; **"everything except
the kitchen sink"** „alles außer
der Küchenspüle" **3›U1:** 14

everywhere [ˈevriweə] überall
2›U6: 99; **everywhere they
go** überall, wo sie hingehen
U3: 52

exactly [ɪɡˈzæktli] genau
5›U5: 82

exam [ɪɡˈzæm] Prüfung
4›U5: 88

example [ɪɡˈzɑːmpl] Beispiel
2›U3: 51; **for example** zum
Beispiel **2›U3:** 51

except [ɪkˈsept] außer **3›U3:** 54;
except for (**U3:** 42)

exchange [ɪksˈtʃeɪndʒ] aus-
tauschen **U4:** 67; **school
exchange** Schüleraustausch
U5: 76

excited [ɪkˈsaɪtɪd] aufgeregt
2›U5: 81

exciting [ɪkˈsaɪtɪŋ] aufregend,
spannend **2›U2:** 35

excuse [ɪkˈskjuːs] Entschuldigung,
Ausrede, Vorwand **4›U3:** 52;
excuse for not trying …
Ausrede, um nicht … zu versuchen **U5:** 76

Excuse me. [ɪkˈskjuːz mi]
Entschuldigung./Entschuldigen
Sie. **2›U1:** 24

exercise [ˈeksəsaɪz] Übung
1›U1: 26

exist [ɪɡˈzɪst] existieren **U2:** 30

exit [ˈeksɪt] Ausgang **U2:** 28

exotic [ɪɡˈzɒtɪk] exotisch
5›U4: 64

expand [ɪkˈspænd] sich ausdehnen
U5: 74

expedition [ekspəˈdɪʃn]
Expedition **5›U5:** 90

expensive [ɪkˈspensɪv] teuer
1›U4: 75

experience [ɪkˈspɪəriəns]
Erfahrung **4›U5:** 90; **Jake's
experience of filming** Jakes
Erfahrungen mit dem Filmen
5›U4: 69; **work experience**
Berufspraktikum **4›Intro:** 6

expert [ˈekspɜːt] Experte/Expertin
U5: 79

expiry date [ɪkˈspaɪəri deɪt]
Verfallsdatum, „Gültig bis"
5›U4: 76

explain [ɪkˈspleɪn] erklären
3›U4: 81

explanation [ekspləˈneɪʃn]
Erklärung U3: 107

explode [ɪkˈspləʊd] explodieren
5›U4: 73

explore [ɪkˈsplɔː] erforschen
3›U3: 51

explorer [ɪkˈsplɔːrə] Entdeckungs-
reisende/-reisender **5›U1:** 7

explosion [ɪkˈspləʊʒn]: **population
explosion** Bevölkerungs-
explosion **U5:** 75

expression [ɪkˈspreʃn] Ausdruck
U4: 62

extinct [ɪkˈstɪŋkt] ausgestorben
U3: 40

extinction [ɪkˈstɪŋkʃn]
Ausrottung, Aussterben **U5:** 74

extra [ˈekstrə] **1**zusätzlich, extra
4›U3: 58; **2**Zusatzleistung,
Extra **4›U2:** 36; **3**Statist/in,
Komparse/Komparsin
5›U4: 67

extraordinary [ɪkˈstrɔːdnri]
außergewöhnlich **5›U1:** 17

extra terrestrial [ekstrə təˈrestriəl]
außerirdisch **U3:** 47

extreme [ɪkˈstriːm] **1**Extrem
5›U5: 82; **2**extrem;
äußerste/r/s **5›U5:** 82

eye [aɪ] Auge **5›U2:** 34

F

face [feɪs] Gesicht **U3:** 42

facilities [fəˈsɪlətiz]: **sports
facilities** Sportanlagen
4›U4: 68

factory [ˈfæktəri] Fabrik
2›U3: 48

fair [feə] **1** fair, gerecht **2 › U1:** 18; **2** hell **5 › U4:** 70

faithfully ['feɪθfəli]: **Yours faithfully, ...** Mit freundlichen Grüßen ... **3 › U4:** 82

fall [fɔːl] **1** (I fell, I've fallen) fallen; hinfallen, stürzen **4 › U3:** 52; **fall ill** krank werden, erkranken **5 › U5:** 85; **2** (AE) Herbst **4 › U2:** 29

fallen ['fɔːlən] (→ fall): **I've fallen** ich bin gefallen **4 › U3:** 52

false [fɔːls] falsch, unwahr **5 › U1:** 18

family ['fæməli] Familie **1 › U2:** 39; **family and consumer science** Hauswirtschaft **4 › U3:** 50; **family name** Familienname **5 › U4:** 76

famous ['feɪməs] berühmt **1 › U6:** 102

fan [fæn] Fan **1 › U1:** 22

fantastic [fæn'tæstɪk] fantastisch, toll **2 › Intro:** 7

far [fɑː] weit **3 › U1:** 14

farm [fɑːm] **1** Bauernhof, Farm **1 › U4:** 69; **2** Landwirtschaft betreiben **5 › U5:** 86

farmer ['fɑːmə] Bauer/Bäuerin, Landwirt/in **4 › U3:** 59

fast [fɑːst] schnell **3 › U2:** 35

fast-food restaurant [fɑːst fuːd 'restrɒnt] Fastfoodrestaurant, Schnellrestaurant **U2:** 30

father ['fɑːðə] Vater **1 › U3:** 60

fault [fɔːlt]: **the tourists' fault** die Schuld der Touristen **U2:** 31

favourite ['feɪvərɪt] Lieblings- **1 › Intro:** 14

February ['februəri] Februar **1 › U5:** 98

fed [fed] (→ feed): **I fed** ich fütterte, ich habe gefüttert **5 › U3:** 54; **I've fed** ich habe gefüttert **5 › U3:** 54

fed up [fed 'ʌp]: **he was fed up** er hatte die Nase voll **1 › U6:** 108

feed [fiːd] (I fed, I've fed) füttern, zu fressen geben **2 › U2:** 32

feel [fiːl] (I felt, I've felt) (sich) fühlen **3 › U3:** 56; sich anfühlen **3 › U4:** 68; **2** glauben **4 › U3:** 56; **feel sorry for yourself** dich selbst bemitleiden **4 › U1:** 15

feeling ['fiːlɪŋ] Gefühl **4 › U3:** 56

feet [fiːt] (→ foot) Füße **1 › U6:** 110

fell [fel] (→ fall): **I fell** ich fiel, ich bin gefallen **4 › U3:** 52

felt [felt] (→ feel): **I felt** ich fühlte (mich), ich habe (mich) gefühlt **3 › U3:** 131; **I've felt** ich habe (mich) gefühlt **3 › U3:** 131

felt-tip ['felt tɪp] Filzstift **1 › U1:** 32

female ['fiːmeɪl] weiblich **4 › U3:** 56

fence [fens] Zaun **5 › U5:** 82

ferry ['feri] Fähre **2 › U3:** 46

festival ['festɪvl] Festival; Fest **5 › U1:** 10

fetch [fetʃ] (ab)holen **3 › U2:** 36; (1 › U5: 93)

few [fjuː] wenige **5 › U2:** 35; **a few** ein paar, einige **2 › U4:** 63

field [fiːld] Feld, Wiese **1 › U4:** 69; **football field** Fußballplatz **1 › U5:** 90

fifteen [fɪf'tiːn] fünfzehn **1 › U2:** 48

fifteenth [fɪf'tiːnθ] fünfzehnte/r/s **2 › U4:** 72

fifth [fɪfθ] fünfte/r/s **2 › U4:** 72

fifty ['fɪfti] fünfzig **1 › U2:** 48

fight [faɪt] **1** (I fought, I've fought) kämpfen; bekämpfen **5 › U1:** 16; **2** Kampf **5 › U5:** 86

fill [fɪl]: **fill the shelves** Regale auffüllen **5 › U3:** 52

film [fɪlm] **1** Film **1 › U2:** 43; **2** filmen **5 › U1:** 13

find [faɪnd] (I found, I've found) finden **1 › U1:** 21; **find out** [faɪnd 'aʊt] herausfinden; entdecken **2 › U3:** 48

fine [faɪn] gut **2 › A Legend:** 111; **I'm fine.** Mir geht's gut. **3 › U2:** 30

finger ['fɪŋgə] Finger **3 › U3:** 56; **Fingers crossed!** Ich drücke die Daumen! **3 › U3:** 56; **I'll cross my fingers for you.** etwa: Ich drück dir die Daumen. **U4:** 62

finish ['fɪnɪʃ] enden; beenden, zu Ende machen **2 › U1:** 14

fire ['faɪə] **1** Feuer **1 › U6:** 105; **be on fire** brennen **5 › U4:** 73; **eat fire** Feuer schlucken/speien **1 › U6:** 105; **2 fire at** ['faɪr ət] schießen auf **U2:** 26

firefighter ['faɪəfaɪtə] Feuerwehrmann/Feuerwehrfrau **4 › U5:** 89

firework ['faɪəwɜːk] Feuerwerkskörper **2 › U4:** 62

first [fɜːst] **1** erste/r/s **2 › U1:** 14; **first name** ['fɜːst neɪm] Vorname **5 › U4:** 68; **May the first (= May 1st)** der erste Mai (1. Mai) **2 › U4:** 72; **2** zuerst **3 › U1:** 10; **First of all ...** zuerst, zuallererst **5 › U2:** 34

fish [fɪʃ] Fisch, Fische **2 › U2:** 33; **fish and chips** Fisch und Pommes frites **1 › U3:** 52; **fish fingers** Fischstäbchen **2 › U5:** 82

fisherman ['fɪʃəmən] Fischer **2 › A Legend:** 110

fishing ['fɪʃɪŋ] Angeln **2 › U6:** 99

five [faɪv] fünf **1 › Intro:** 15

flag [flæg] Flagge, Fahne **1 › U5:** 92

flashlight ['flæʃlaɪt] (AE) Taschenlampe **4 › U2:** 30

flat [flæt] **1** Wohnung **1 › Intro:** 18; **2** flach **5 › U3:** 44

flavour ['fleɪvə] Geschmack **5 › U1:** 8

flew [fluː] (→ fly): **I flew** ich flog, ich bin geflogen **4 › U2:** 36

flight [flaɪt] Flug **5 › U4:** 76

flood [flʌd] Überschwemmung **U2:** 31

floor [flɔː] Boden, Fußboden **5 › U1:** 9; **ground floor** Erdgeschoss **2 › U3:** 51

flower ['flaʊə] Blume, Blüte **2 › U2:** 35; **flower-bed** Blumenbeet **2 › U2:** 35

flown [fləʊn] (→ fly): **I've flown** ich bin geflogen **4 › U2:** 36

fly [flaɪ] (I flew, I've flown) fliegen **4 › U2:** 36; **flying out** Hinflug **5 › U4:** 76

fog [fɒg] Nebel **4 › U3:** 55

foggy ['fɒgi] neblig **2 › U6:** 104

folk music ['fəʊk mjuːzɪk] Folk (auf englischsprachiger Volksmusik basierender Popmusik) **U1:** 103

follow ['fɒləʊ] folgen **1 › U5:** 92

food [fuːd] **1** Essen, Lebensmittel **1 › U3:** 52; **2** Fressen **5 › U2:** 34

foot, feet [fʊt, fiːt] Fuß, Füße **1 › U6:** 110

football ['fʊtbɔːl] Fußball **1 › U1:** 22; **football player** ['fʊtbɔːl pleɪə] Fußballspieler/Fußballspielerin **4 › U5:** 89

footprint ['fʊtprɪnt] Fußabdruck **U5:** 74

→ DICTIONARY

for [fɔː] für **1 › U1:** 26; **Bye for now!** Tschüs erstmal! **5 › U1:** 21; **for ever** [fər 'evə] für immer, auf ewig **4 › U4:** 71; **for example** zum Beispiel **2 › U3:** 51; **for half an hour** seit einer halben Stunde **4 › U2:** 32; **for or against** dafür oder dagegen **5 › U2:** 32; **for shopping** zum Einkaufen **3 › U1:** 10; **for the last time** zum letzten Mal **3 › U3:** 58; **for the weekend** übers Wochenende **4 › U2:** 42; **for three weeks** drei Wochen lang **4 › U3:** 48; **not for long** nicht lange **5 › U1:** 17; **That's all for now.** Das ist im Augenblick alles. **4 › U5:** 102

foreign ['fɒrən]: **foreign language** Fremdsprache **2 › U6:** 96

forest ['fɒrɪst] Wald, Waldgebiet **5 › U1:** 6

forget [fə'get] (I forgot, I've forgotten) vergessen **1 › U6:** 102

forgot [fə'gɒt] (→ forget): **I forgot** ich vergaß, ich habe vergessen **5 › U1:** 17

forgotten [fə'gɒtn] (→ forget): **I've forgotten** ich habe vergessen **5 › U1:** 17

form [fɔːm] **1** Form **2 › U3:** 55; **2** Art **4 › U4:** 71; **3** (sich) bilden **5 › U1:** 6; **4** gründen **U1:** 14

formal ['fɔːməl] offiziell; formell **4 › U5:** 103

Formula One Grand Prix [fɔːmjələ 'wʌn grɑ̃ 'priː] Grand Prix der Formel Eins **U3:** 47

fortunately ['fɔːtʃənətli] zum Glück **5 › U5:** 87

forty ['fɔːti] vierzig **1 › U2:** 48

forum ['fɔːrəm]: **Internet forum** Internetforum **U4:** 60

forward ['fɔːwəd]: **look forward to ...** sich freuen auf ... **3 › U2:** 28; **I'm looking forward to hearing from you.** Ich freue mich darauf, von Ihnen zu hören. **4 › U5:** 103

fought [fɔːt] (→ fight): **I fought** ich kämpfte, ich habe gekämpft **5 › U1:** 16; **I've fought** ich habe gekämpft **5 › U1:** 16

found [faʊnd] gründen **5 › U5:** 85

found [faʊnd] (→ find): **I found** ich fand, ich habe gefunden **2 › U5:** 87; **I've found** ich habe gefunden **3 › U3:** 50

four [fɔː] vier **1 › Intro:** 15

fourteen [fɔː'tiːn] vierzehn **1 › U2:** 48

fourteenth [fɔː'tiːnθ] vierzehn-te/r/s **2 › U4:** 72

fourth [fɔːθ] vierte/r/s **2 › U4:** 72

France [frɑːns] Frankreich **2 › Intro:** 8

free [friː] **1** frei; kostenlos **1 › U2:** 40; **free time** Freizeit **1 › U4:** 76; **you're free** du hast Zeit **4 › U4:** 77; **2** befreien **U2:** 26

freedom ['friːdəm] Freiheit *U2:* 25

freephone ['friːfəʊn] gebühren-freie Telefonnummer **1 › U6:** 115

freezer ['friːzə] Gefriertruhe, -schrank **3 › U5:** 92

French [frentʃ] Französisch, französisch **2 › U1:** 14; **I'm French** ich bin Franzose/Französin **2 › U6:** 99

fresh [freʃ] frisch **U5:** 78

Friday ['fraɪdeɪ] Freitag **1 › U4:** 80

fridge [frɪdʒ] Kühlschrank **1 › U6:** 114

friend [frend] Freund/in **1 › Intro:** 17

friendly ['frendli] freundlich, nett **1 › U2:** 38; **he becomes friendly with her** er freundet sich mit ihr an **4 › U5:** 95

frightened ['fraɪtnd]: **they were frightened** sie hatten Angst **2 › U5:** 82

frightening ['fraɪtnɪŋ] beängsti-gend **U5:** 76

from [frɒm] von, aus **1 › Intro:** 17; **from all over the world** aus der ganzen Welt **3 › U1:** 8; **from now on** ab jetzt **U3:** 47

front [frʌnt] Vorderseite; Vorder-front **5 › U1:** 13; **at the front of the book** vorne im Buch **5 › U1:** 6; **in front of** vor **1 › U2:** 39

fruit [fruːt] Obst **1 › U3:** 53

full [fʊl] vollständig, voll ausge-stattet **3 › U5:** 92; **full (of)** voll (mit, von) **1 › U6:** 107

fun [fʌn] Spaß **1 › U4:** 70; **fun park** Freizeitpark **U5:** 78; **it's fun** es macht Spaß **1 › U2:** 40; **it's good/great fun** es macht großen/sehr großen Spaß **3 › U4:** 70; **she's fun** es macht Spaß, mit ihr zusammen zu sein **3 › U3:** 48

funky ['fʌŋki] toll, super; „in" **3 › U1:** 12

funny ['fʌni] lustig, witzig **1 › U6:** 110; komisch, merkwürdig **2 › U1:** 16

fur [fɜː] Fell, Pelz **5 › U1:** 16

future ['fjuːtʃə] Zukunft **2 › U6:** 101; **future generation** [dʒenə'reɪʃn] zukünftige Generation **U5:** 79

G

gadget ['gædʒɪt]: **electronic gadget** Elektrogerät, -apparat **2 › U2:** 29; **gadgets** (techni-scher) Krimskrams **4 › U1:** 10

gallery ['gæləri] Galerie **3 › U4:** 72

game [geɪm] Spiel **1 › U4:** 69

gameboy ['geɪmbɔɪ] Gameboy **1 › U4:** 73

games console ['geɪmz 'kɒnsəʊl] Spielkonsole **2 › U2:** 29

gang [gæŋ] Clique, (Jugend-)Bande **U1:** 14

garage ['gærɑːʒ] **1** Garage **2 › U1:** 18; **2** (Reparatur-)Werkstatt **4 › U5:** 89

garbage collectors ['gɑːbɪdʒ kə'lektəz] (AE) Müllabfuhr **2 › U6:** 98

garden ['gɑːdn] Garten **1 › U1:** 21

gas [gæs] Gas **4 › U4:** 71

gate [geɪt] **1** Tor, Pforte **2 › U2:** 30; **2** Flugsteig **4 › U1:** 16

gave [geɪv] (→ give): **I gave** ich gab, ich habe gegeben **4 › U3:** 52

GCSE (General Certificate of Secondary Education) [dʒiː siː es 'iː] Schulabschluss-prüfung **4 › U5:** 88

gender ['dʒendə] Geschlecht **5 › U4:** 68

generation [dʒenə'reɪʃn]: **future generation** zukünftige Generation **U5:** 79

gentleman, gentlemen ['dʒentlmən]: **ladies and gentlemen** meine Damen und Herren **U2:** 36

geography [dʒi'ɒgrəfi] Geographie, Erdkunde **2 › U3:** 46

German ['dʒɜːmən] deutsch **1 › U2:** 38; **I'm German** ich bin Deutsche/r **2 › U6:** 99

Germany ['dʒɜːməni] Deutschland **1 › Intro:** 16

get [get] (I got, I've got)
1 bekommen **1 > U5:** 85;
2 (sich) besorgen, (sich) holen
3 > U1: 12; **3** kommen, gelangen
3 > U1: 16; **4** werden **3 > U2:** 33;
Get a life! Fang an zu leben!
4 > U4: 71; **get back** zurück-
kommen/-finden **1 > U5:** 91; **get**
better sich erholen **5 > U3:** 55;
get changed sich umziehen
4 > U5: 92; **get divorced** sich
scheiden lassen **4 > U1:** 15; **get**
married heiraten **5 > U4:** 73;
get on aufsteigen, einsteigen
2 > A Legend: 110; **get on with**
them mit ihnen auskommen
4 > U1: 11; **get out** herauskom-
men **1 > U5:** 91; **Get real!** Mach
dir nichts vor! **5 > U2:** 30; **get**
to erreichen **2 > A Legend:** 110;
get up aufstehen **1 > U4:** 80;
I hope you get better soon. Ich
hoffe, es geht dir bald besser.
3 > U3: 56; **What can I get you?**
Was darf's sein? **3 > U4:** 76
geyser ['giːzə] Geysir **4 > U2:** 28
ghetto ['getəʊ] Getto 3 > U5: 102
ghost town ['gəʊst taʊn] Geister-
stadt **U3:** 43
giant ['dʒaɪənt] Riese/Riesin
U1: 17
gingerbread ['dʒɪndʒəbred] Leb-
kuchen, Honigkuchen 2 > U4: 63
girl [gɜːl] Mädchen **1 > Intro:** 10
girlfriend ['gɜːlfrend] (feste)
Freundin **1 > U1:** 27
give [gɪv] (I gave, I've given)
geben **3 > U1:** 23; **give a talk**
(to) einen Vortrag halten (vor)
3 > U5: 102; **Give my greetings**
to ... Grüße mir ... **1 > U6:** 114
given ['gɪvn] (→ give): **I've given**
ich habe gegeben **4 > U3:** 52
glad [glæd] froh **3 > U1:** 15
glass [glɑːs] Glas **2 > U3:** 51
glass-bottom boat ['glɑːs bɒtəm
bəʊt] Glasbodenboot 5 > U3: 49
glasses ['glɑːsɪz] Brille **4 > U2:** 30
global warming ['gləʊbl 'wɔːmɪŋ]
globale Erwärmung **U5:** 74
go [gəʊ] (I went, I've gone) gehen,
faɦren **1 > U3:** 41; **go away**
verreisen **1 > U5:** 87; **go down**
abnehmen, sinken **U2:** 25;
go on and on immer weitergehen **5 > U4:** 72; **go out**
ausgehen, weggehen
3 > U4: 68; **go out for a meal**
essen gehen **1 > U5:** 86;
go out in the car eine Spazierfahrt machen **1 > U5:** 86;

go red/... rot/... werden
3 > U5: 95; **go shopping**
einkaufen gehen **4 > U1:** 11;
go to church/mosque/... in
die Kirche/Moschee/... gehen
4 > U4: 76; **go to court** vor
Gericht gehen **5 > U3:** 55;
go to the movies (AE) ins Kino
gehen **3 > U5:** 96; **go to the**
shops einen Einkaufsbummel
machen; einkaufen gehen
1 > U4: 76; **go up** zunehmen,
steigen **U2:** 25; **go window-**
shopping ['wɪndəʊ ʃɒpɪŋ] einen
Schaufensterbummel machen
5 > U1: 8; **go wrong** [gəʊ 'rɒŋ]
schief gehen **4 > U5:** 95;
have to go to hospital ins
Krankenhaus müssen
5 > U3: 55
goal [gəʊl] Ziel **3 > U5:** 107
goddess ['gɒdes] Göttin **5 > U2:** 31
godmother ['gɒdmʌðə] Patin,
Patentante **4 > U4:** 75
golf [gɒlf] Golf **2 > U5:** 81
gone [gɒn]: **he's gone** er ist weg
U4: 64
good [gʊd] gut **1 > U1:** 26;
Good afternoon. Guten Tag.
(nachmittags) **1 > U1:** 28;
good at gut in **1 > U1:** 26;
Good evening. Guten Abend.
1 > U1: 28; **Good luck for ...**
Viel Glück bei ... **3 > U4:** 82;
Good morning. Guten Morgen.
1 > U1: 25; **good value** preis-
günstig **2 > U4:** 68; **have a**
good time sich gut amüsieren
2 > U4: 65; **you've been good**
about it etwa: du bist gut damit
umgegangen **U4:** 65
good-looking [gʊd'lʊkɪŋ] gut
aussehend **5 > U4:** 64
Goodbye. [gʊd'baɪ] Auf Wieder-
sehen. **1 > U1:** 28
got [gɒt] (→ get): **I got** ich
bekam, ich habe bekommen
2 > A Legend: 110; **I've got**
ich habe bekommen **3 > U3:** 50;
I haven't got ich habe nicht
2 > U5: 89
govern ['gʌvn] regieren **U2:** 26
government ['gʌvənmənt]
Regierung **5 > U2:** 34
grade [greɪd] **1** Note, Zensur
4 > U3: 51; **2** (AE) Klasse,
Klassenstufe **4 > U3:** 48
gram [græm] Gramm **2 > U4:** 68
grammar ['græmə] Grammatik
4 > U4: 83

grandfather ['grænfɑːðə]
Großvater **1 > U3:** 60
grandma ['grænmɑː] Oma
1 > U2: 39
grandmother ['grænmʌðə]
Großmutter **1 > U3:** 60
grandparents ['grænpeərənts]
Großeltern **5 > U1:** 12
grass [grɑːs] Gras **1 > U5:** 90
great [greɪt] toll **1 > U3:** 53;
bedeutend **4 > U3:** 50; **Great**
Lakes Große Seen **5 > U1:** 6;
Great Wall of China ['greɪt wɔːl
əv 'tʃaɪnə] Große chinesische
Mauer **5 > U5:** 82
green [griːn] grün **1 > Intro:** 14
greenhouse gas ['griːnhaʊs gæs]
Treibhausgas **U5:** 74
greeting ['griːtɪŋ] Gruß(formel),
Begrüßung 2 > U5: 85; **Give my**
greetings to ... Grüße mir ...
1 > U6: 114
grew [gruː] (→ grow): **I grew** ich
wuchs, ich bin gewachsen
5 > U2: 26
grey [greɪ] grau **5 > U4:** 64
ground floor ['graʊnd flɔː]
Erdgeschoss **2 > U3:** 51
group [gruːp] Gruppe **2 > U1:** 17
grow [grəʊ] (I grew, I've grown)
wachsen **5 > U2:** 26; **grow**
crops Feldfrüchte anbauen
U3: 41; **grow louder** lauter
werden **5 > U5:** 87; **Grow up!**
Sei(d) mal vernünftig! **1 > U5:** 90
grown [grəʊn] (→ grow): **I've**
grown ich bin gewachsen
5 > U2: 26
grumpy ['grʌmpi] mürrisch,
brummig **1 > U5:** 90
guess [ges]: **Guess what!**
Stell dir vor! **4 > U3:** 51; **I guess**
(AE) ich schätze, ich nehme an
3 > U4: 70
guest [gest] Gast **5 > U4:** 73
guide [gaɪd] (Museums-)Führer/in
U2: 28; **film guide** Filmführer,
-programmheft 2 > U4: 73
guidebook ['gaɪdbʊk] Handbuch;
Reiseführer **3 > U1:** 14
guided tour [gaɪdɪd 'tʊə] Führung
U2: 28
guitar [gɪ'tɑː] Gitarre **3 > U5:** 88
Gulf Stream ['gʌlf striːm]
Golfstrom **U5:** 74
guts [gʌts] Mut, Mumm
4 > U3: 54
guy [gaɪ] Typ, Kerl **4 > U3:** 55
Guy Fawkes Night [gaɪ 'fɔːks naɪt]
Guy-Fawkes-Nacht 1 > U5: 98
gym [dʒɪm] Turnhalle **4 > U3:** 50

155

one hundred and fifty-five

→ DICTIONARY

H

habit [ˈhæbɪt]: **eating habit** Essgewohnheit **U3:** 43

had [hæd] (→ have): **I had** ich hatte, ich habe gehabt **1 > U3:** 58; **I've had** ich habe gehabt **3 > U3:** 52; **he had changed** er hatte sich verändert **5 > U1:** 16; **If I had money, ...** Wenn ich Geld hätte, ... **5 > U5:** 89

haggis [ˈhægɪs] Haggis (gefüllter Schafsmagen) **3 > U3:** 53

hair [heə] Haar, Haare **5 > U1:** 16

hairdresser [ˈheədresə] Friseur/ Friseurin **4 > U5:** 89

half [hɑːf]: **half an hour** eine halbe Stunde **3 > U1:** 14; **half board** [hɑːf ˈbɔːd] Halbpension (Hotel) **U4:** 69; **half of them** die Hälfte von ihnen **3 > U1:** 9; **half past one** halb zwei **2 > U3:** 51; **half-brother** Halbbruder **1 > U2:** 39; **half-term holiday** kurze Ferien (nach der Hälfte des Schultrimesters) **4 > U5:** 92

halfway up [hɑːfweɪ ˈʌp] halb oben, auf halber Höhe **U2:** 33

hall [hɔːl] Saal **3 > U3:** 58

Halloween [hæləʊˈiːn] Halloween **1 > U5:** 98

ham [hæm] Schinken **3 > U4:** 76

hamster [ˈhæmstə] Hamster **2 > U2:** 34

hand [hænd] Hand **4 > U3:** 52; **hand luggage** [ˈhænd lʌɡɪdʒ] Handgepäck **4 > U1:** 16; **on the other hand** andererseits **4 > U1:** 8

ha'penny [ˈheɪpni] = halfpenny (ehem. kleinste brit. Münze) **U1:** 17

happen [ˈhæpən] passieren, geschehen **2 > U6:** 95; **it happened to them** es geschah mit ihnen **5 > U3:** 55; **What's happening?** Was ist los?/Was geht hier vor? **2 > U4:** 64

happy [ˈhæpi] glücklich, froh **1 > U1:** 26; **be happy to do something** etwas gern tun **5 > U4:** 77; **Happy birthday (to you)!** Herzlichen Glückwunsch (zum Geburtstag)! **3 > U3:** 56

harbour [ˈhɑːbə] Hafen **5 > U3:** 48

hard [hɑːd] hart; schwierig **2 > U1:** 18

hardware [ˈhɑːdweə] Hardware **1 > U4:** 69

harp [hɑːp] Harfe *U1: 103*

hat [hæt] Hut **3 > U3:** 52

hate [heɪt] hassen, gar nicht mögen **2 > U1:** 17

have [hæv] (I had, I've had) haben **1 > U3:** 54; **have a day out** einen Tagesausflug machen **1 > U5:** 86; **have a drink** etwas trinken **4 > U1:** 10; **Have a good journey.** Gute Reise! **4 > U1:** 16; **have a good time** sich gut amüsieren **2 > U4:** 65; **Have a nice day!** (Einen) Schönen Tag noch! **3 > U4:** 77; **have a picnic** ein Picknick machen **1 > U5:** 84; **have a race** um die Wette laufen **1 > U5:** 92; **have a ride on the Cyclone** mit dem Cyclone fahren **4 > U1:** 10; **have a trip** einen Ausflug machen, eine Reise machen **3 > U1:** 10; **have a wash** sich waschen **1 > U4:** 80; **have breakfast** frühstücken **1 > U4:** 80; **have dinner** zu Abend essen **4 > U1:** 18; **have sandwiches / have a cola** Sandwiches essen / Cola trinken **3 > U1:** 13; **we should have lifestyles ...** wir sollten ein Leben führen ... **4 > U4:** 71

haven't [ˈhævnt] **I haven't got** ich habe nicht **5 > U5:** 89

have to [ˈhæv tə, ˈhæf tə] müssen **2 > U6:** 96

he [hiː] er **1 > U1:** 25; **he's (= he is)** [hiːz] er ist **1 > U1:** 25

head [hed] Kopf **4 > U5:** 96; **head of state** Staatsoberhaupt **5 > U1:** 7

heading [ˈhedɪŋ] Überschrift 5 > U1: 18

headphones [ˈhedfəʊnz] Kopfhörer **2 > U2:** 29

healthy [ˈhelθi] gesund **1 > U3:** 53

hear [hɪə] (I heard, I've heard) hören **2 > U1:** 15

heard [hɜːd] (→ hear): **I heard** ich hörte, ich habe gehört **2 > A Legend:** 109; **I've heard** ich habe gehört **3 > U3:** 52

heart [hɑːt] Herz **5 > U3:** 54; **learn by heart** auswendig lernen 4 > U2: 37

heat [hiːt] Wärme, Hitze **U5:** 84

heavy [ˈhevi] schwer (Gewicht) **U2:** 30

height [haɪt] Höhe; Körpergröße **U3:** 43

held [held] (→ hold): **I held** ich hielt, ich habe gehalten **5 > U3:** 54; **I've held** ich habe (fest)gehalten **5 > U3:** 54

helicopter airport [ˈhelɪkɒptər eəpɔːt] Hubschrauberflugplatz 3 > U3: 49

hello [həˈləʊ] Hallo. (Guten) Tag. **1 > Intro:** 7

helmet [ˈhelmɪt] Helm **1 > U6:** 110

help [help] 1 helfen **1 > U4:** 74; **help out** aushelfen **5 > U3:** 53; **Help yourselves (to cookies)!** Bedient euch! Nehmt euch selbst (Kekse)! **4 > U3:** 53; **2** Hilfe **3 > U4:** 82

helpful [ˈhelpfl] hilfsbereit; hilfreich **5 > U4:** 70

her [hɜː] 1 ihr/ihre **1 > U2:** 39; **2** ihr, sie **2 > U1:** 18

here [hɪə] hier; hierher/hierhin **1 > U1:** 22; **Here you are.** Hier, bitte. **1 > U1:** 32

hers [hɜːz] ihre/ihrer/ihres **5 > U4:** 66; (4 > U3: 52)

herself [hɜːˈself] sich (selbst); selbst **4 > U3:** 52

Hi. [haɪ] Hallo. **1 > U1:** 26

hid [hɪd] (→ hide): **I hid** ich versteckte, ich habe versteckt **5 > U4:** 73

hidden [ˈhɪdn] (→ hide): **I've hidden** ich habe versteckt **5 > U4:** 73

hide [haɪd] (I hid, I've hidden) (sich) verstecken (vor) **5 > U4:** 73

high [haɪ] hoch **2 > U5:** 80; **high school** [ˈhaɪ skuːl] Oberschule (in Nordamerika) **4 > U3:** 48

highway [ˈhaɪweɪ] (AE) Autobahn, Bundesstraße 2 > U6: 94

hike [haɪk] wandern **4 > U2:** 30

hiking [ˈhaɪkɪŋ] Wandern **3 > U2:** 31

hill [hɪl] Hügel, Berg **2 > U3:** 45

him [hɪm] ihm, ihn **2 > Intro:** 8

himself [hɪmˈself] sich (selbst); selbst **3 > U5:** 94

Hindi [ˈhɪndi] Hindi (Amtssprache in Indien) **U3:** 43

Hindu [ˈhɪnduː] Hindu; hinduistisch **U3:** 40

hip-hop [ˈhɪp hɒp] Hiphop **U2:** 27

hippo, hippos [ˈhɪpəʊ] Nilpferd **U2:** 31

his [hɪz] sein/seine **1 > U1:** 27; seine/seiner/seines **5 > U4:** 66; (4 > U3: 52)

history [ˈhɪstri] Geschichte, Vergangenheit **2 > U3:** 45

hit [hɪt] 1 Hit, Schlager **1 > U4:** 81; **2 hit the roof** (I hit, I've hit) an die Decke gehen **U4:** 71

156

one hundred and fifty-six

HIV [eɪtʃ aɪ 'vi:] *Virus, das Aids verursacht* **U1:** 15; **HIV positive** [eɪtʃ aɪ vi 'pɒzətɪv] HIV-positiv **U2:** 33

hobby ['hɒbi] Hobby **1>U3:** 58

hold [həʊld] (I held, I've held) (fest)halten **2>U4:** 65; abhalten **5>U5:** 84; **Hold on.** Einen Moment. **3>U2:** 36

hole [həʊl] Loch **5>U5:** 91

holiday ['hɒlədeɪ] Urlaub, Urlaubs-; Ferien **1>U5:** 87; **go on holiday** in Urlaub gehen/fahren **2>Intro:** 8; **holiday home** Ferienhaus 5>U5: 87

holy ['həʊli] heilig **5>U3:** 45

home [həʊm] Heim, Zuhause **1>U4:** 69; **at home** zu Hause, daheim **1>U2:** 36; **come/go home** nach Hause kommen/ gehen **1>U3:** 59; **home match** ['həʊm mætʃ] Heimspiel **4>U4:** 73; **home page** ['həʊm peɪdʒ] Homepage, Startseite **2>U1:** 25

homeroom ['həʊmruːm] (AE) Klassenzimmer **4>U3:** 48

homesick ['həʊmsɪk]: **I'm homesick** ich habe Heimweh **2>U5:** 84

hometown ['həʊmtaʊn] Heimatstadt **U1:** 15

homework ['həʊmwɜːk] Hausaufgabe(n) **1>U5:** 94

honest ['ɒnɪst] ehrlich **5>U2:** 30; **Oh honestly!** Also wirklich! **5>U2:** 32

hoody ['hʊdi] Kapuzenpullover **U4:** 67

Hooray! [hʊ'reɪ] Hurra! 1>U5: 93

hoovering ['huːvərɪŋ] Staubsaugen **5>U3:** 53

hope [həʊp] **1** hoffen **1>U6:** 109; **2** Hoffnung **5>U3:** 50

hormone ['hɔːməʊn] Hormon **5>U2:** 34

horn [hɔːn] Horn 2>A Legend: 110

horoscope ['hɒrəskəʊp] Horoskop **U3:** 43

horrible ['hɒrəbl] schrecklich **U4:** 65

horse [hɔːs] Pferd **1>U5:** 96

hospital ['hɒspɪtl] Krankenhaus **2>U3:** 53; **have to go to hospital** ins Krankenhaus müssen **5>U5:** 55

hot [hɒt] heiß **2>U4:** 62; **hot chocolate** heiße Schokolade **2>U5:** 82; **hot dog** ['hɒt dɒg] Hot dog **1>U3:** 59

hotel [həʊ'tel] Hotel **1>U6:** 114

hotline ['hɒtlaɪn]: **children's hotline** *telefonische Beratung für Jugendliche* 1>U6: 115

hour ['aʊə] Stunde **2>U1:** 18

hours ['aʊəz] Arbeitszeit(en) **5>U3:** 52; **What hours do you work?** Wie sind deine Arbeitszeiten? **5>U3:** 52

house [haʊs] Haus **1>Intro:** 10; **at Bina's house** bei Bina (zu Hause) **1>U2:** 42

how [haʊ] wie **1>U6:** 110; **how many** wie viele **2>U4:** 62; **how much** wie viel **2>U4:** 62; **How much is it?** Was kostet das? **1>U4:** 75; **how to make an igloo** wie man einen Iglu macht **5>U2:** 40

however [haʊ'evə] jedoch, aber **5>U2:** 31

huge [hjuːdʒ] riesig **U2:** 27

human ['hjuːmən] **1** menschlich, Menschen- **2>U3:** 50; **2** Mensch **U2:** 31

humour ['hjuːmə]: **have a good sense of humour** Sinn für Humor haben **5>U4:** 70

hundred ['hʌndrəd] hundert **1>U2:** 48

hungry ['hʌŋgri]: **I'm hungry.** Ich habe Hunger. **1>U3:** 52

hunt [hʌnt] jagen **5>U2:** 26

hunter ['hʌntə] Jäger/in **5>U3:** 54

Huron ['hjʊərən] Hurone/Huronin **5>U1:** 16

hurricane ['hʌrɪkən] Orkan **4>U4:** 74

hurry ['hʌri] sich beeilen **3>U5:** 94; **Hurry!** Beeilt euch! / Beeil dich! **1>U6:** 109

hurt [hɜːt] **1** (I hurt, I've hurt) wehtun; verletzen **3>U3:** 56; **2** verletzt **2>U2:** 31

husband ['hʌzbənd] Ehemann **5>U2:** 31

I

I [aɪ] ich **1>Intro:** 10; **I'd (= I would) like ...** Ich hätte gern .../Ich möchte ... **1>U4:** 75; **I'll (= I will) go** ich werde gehen **1>U6:** 106; **I'll help you** ich helfe dir **2>U6:** 96; **I'm (= I am)** ich bin **1>Intro:** 17

ice [aɪs] Eis (gefrorenes Wasser) **5>U1:** 6; **ice cream** [aɪs 'kriːm] (Speise-)Eis **1>U3:** 55; **ice fishing** ['aɪs fɪʃɪŋ] Eisfischen **5>U2:** 29; **ice hockey** ['aɪs hɒki] Eishockey **4>U4:** 68; **ice rink** ['aɪs rɪŋk] Eisbahn, Schlittschuhbahn **5>U1:** 10; **ice skating** ['aɪs skeɪtɪŋ] Schlittschuhlaufen **5>U1:** 9

iced tea [aɪst 'tiː] Eistee **1>U3:** 55

idea [aɪ'dɪə] Idee, Gedanke; Vorstellung **1>U3:** 54; **have no idea** keine Ahnung haben **1>U6:** 108

idealistic [aɪdɪə'lɪstɪk] idealistisch **U1:** 15

idol ['aɪdl]: **"Canadian idol"** *eine Art „Kanada sucht den Superstar"-Show* 5>U2: 38

if [ɪf] **1** wenn, falls **3>U1:** 19; **What if ...?** Und was, wenn ...? **5>U5:** 91; **2** ob **3>U2:** 37

igloo ['ɪgluː] Iglu **5>U2:** 26

ill [ɪl] krank **1>U3:** 58

illegal [ɪ'liːgl] illegal **U3:** 42

illness ['ɪlnes] Krankheit **U2:** 33

imagination [ɪmædʒɪ'neɪʃn] Fantasie *U2: 105*

imagine (something) [ɪ'mædʒɪn] sich (etwas) vorstellen **5>U5:** 84

IMAX ['aɪmæks] IMAX (Kino-System mit riesigem Bildformat) **3>U4:** 72

immigrant ['ɪmɪgrənt] Immigrant/in, Einwanderer/Einwanderin **4>U1:** 8

immigration (to) [ɪmɪ'greɪʃn] Einwanderung (nach) **5>U3:** 46

important [ɪm'pɔːtnt] wichtig **2>U4:** 72

impossible [ɪm'pɒsəbl] unmöglich **3>U4:** 73

improve [ɪm'pruːv] (sich) verbessern **4>U4:** 68

in [ɪn] in, auf **1>Intro:** 10; **be in love** verliebt sein **5>U4:** 72; **in action** aktiv **4>U2:** 28; **in English/German** auf Englisch/ Deutsch **1>U1:** 32; **in front of** vor **1>U2:** 39; **in the country** auf dem Land **1>U5:** 86; **in the end** schließlich **4>U1:** 15; **in the morning/afternoon/ evening** morgens/nachmittags/ abends **1>U2:** 40; **in the northeast** im Nordosten **4>U4:** 71; **It was in 2005.** Es war (im Jahre) 2005. **2>U2:** 40

→ DICTIONARY

include [ɪnˈkluːd] einschließen, enthalten **4 › U2:** 36

incredible [ɪnˈkredəbl] unglaublich, unwahrscheinlich **U3:** 55

incredibly [ɪnˈkredəbli]: **incredibly (hot)** unglaublich (heiß), unwahrscheinlich (heiß) **5 › U5:** 87

Independence Day [ɪndɪˈpendəns deɪ] Unabhängigkeitstag **4 › U2:** 30

independent [ɪndɪˈpendənt] unabhängig **5 › U1:** 7

India [ˈɪndiə] Indien **3 › U5:** 96

Indian [ˈɪndiən] **1** indisch; Inder/in **2 › U2:** 33; **2** Indianer/ Indianerin; indianisch **5 › U1:** 7

indoors [ɪnˈdɔːz] drinnen, im Haus **U5:** 78

industrial [ɪnˈdʌstriəl]: **industrial city** Industriestadt **4 › U4:** 68; **Industrial Revolution** [ɪnˈdʌstriəl revəˈluːʃn] industrielle Revolution **2 › U3:** 48

industry [ˈɪndəstri] Industrie **2 › U3:** 48; **tourist industry** Tourismusindustrie **U1:** 9

influence [ˈɪnfluəns] Einfluss **U3:** 47

info box [ˈɪnfəʊ bɒks] Infobox **U3:** 43

information [ɪnfəˈmeɪʃn] Informationen, Informations- **4 › U2:** 28; **information office** Informationsbüro **3 › U1:** 14; **information technology (IT)** [ɪnfəmeɪʃn tekˈnɒlədʒi] Informationstechnologie **2 › U1:** 14

injure [ˈɪndʒə] verletzen **U2:** 26

injustice [ɪnˈdʒʌstɪs] Ungerechtigkeit **U1:** 15

inline skating [ˈɪnlaɪn skeɪtɪŋ] Inlineskating **2 › U6:** 102

inside [ɪnˈsaɪd] innerhalb (von); (nach) drinnen **3 › U5:** 95

inspiration [ɪnspəˈreɪʃn] Inspiration **5 › U3:** 54

instead [ɪnˈsted] stattdessen **4 › U3:** 55; **instead of reporting ...** statt ... zu berichten **U4:** 60

instrument [ˈɪnstrəmənt] (Musik-) Instrument **1 › U6:** 105

insurance [ɪnˈʃʊərəns] Versicherung **4 › U5:** 90

intelligent [ɪnˈtelɪdʒənt] intelligent **5 › U4:** 67

interest [ˈɪntrəst] Interesse; Hobby **2 › U2:** 28

interested (in) [ˈɪntrəstɪd] interessiert (an) **1 › U4:** 75

interesting [ˈɪntrəstɪŋ] interessant **1 › U5:** 86

intermediate [ɪntəˈmiːdiət]: **intermediate slopes** Pisten für fortgeschrittene Anfänger/ innen **5 › U1:** 10

international [ɪntəˈnæʃnəl] international **1 › U3:** 65

Internet [ˈɪntənet] Internet **2 › U1:** 25; **on the Internet** im Internet **2 › U1:** 25

interpret [ɪnˈtɜːprɪt] dolmetschen **4 › U3:** 57

interpreter [ɪnˈtɜːprɪtə] Dolmetscher/Dolmetscherin **4 › U5:** 99

interpreting [ɪnˈtɜːprɪtɪŋ] Dolmetschen **4 › U1:** 17

interrupt [ɪntəˈrʌpt] unterbrechen **4 › U5:** 94

interstate [ˈɪntəsteɪt] (AE) Autobahn (zwischen Bundesstaaten) **2 › U6:** 94

interview [ˈɪntəvjuː] **1** Interview **3 › U3:** 50; **job interview** Vorstellungsgespräch **4 › U5:** 102; **2** befragen, interviewen **2 › U3:** 46

into [ˈɪntə] in (... hinein/herein) **2 › U5:** 82

intonation [ɪntəˈneɪʃn] Tongebung, Sprachmelodie **3 › U1:** 16

introduce [ɪntrəˈdjuːs]: **I introduce myself (to them)** ich stelle mich (ihnen) vor **4 › U5:** 88

introduction [ɪntrəˈdʌkʃn] Einführung **U3:** 40

Inuit [ˈɪnuɪt] Inuit (Eskimo/s) **5 › U1:** 6

inventor [ɪnˈventə] Erfinder/in **4 › U3:** 61

invitation [ɪnvɪˈteɪʃn] Einladung **2 › U4:** 64

invite [ɪnˈvaɪt] einladen **5 › U3:** 46

Ireland [ˈaɪələnd] Irland **3 › U3:** 51

Irish [ˈaɪrɪʃ] irisch; Irisch; Ire/Irin **5 › U1:** 8

Iroquois [ˈɪrəkwɔɪ]: **Iroquois Indian** Irokese/Irokesin **5 › U1:** 17

is [ɪz] ist **1 › Intro:** 14; **the meat is sold** das Fleisch wird verkauft **5 › U2:** 34

island [ˈaɪlənd] Insel **3 › U3:** 51

isn't [ˈɪznt] (= is not) ist nicht **1 › U2:** 40; **It's scary, isn't it?** [ˈɪznt ɪt] Es ist unheimlich, nicht wahr? **3 › U2:** 32

it [ɪt] **1** es (er/sie; nicht bei Personen) **1 › Intro:** 14; **2** ihm, es (ihm, ihr/ihn, sie; nicht bei Personen) **1 › U4:** 71; **it's (= it is)** es ist (er/sie ist, nicht bei Personen) **1 › U1:** 25

Italian [ɪˈtæliən] italienisch; Italienisch; Italiener/Italienerin **4 › U1:** 10

Italy [ˈɪtəli] Italien **4 › U1:** 8

its [ɪts] sein/seine, ihr/ihre **1 › U3:** 62

itself [ɪtˈself] sich (selbst); selbst **4 › U4:** 68

J

jacket [ˈdʒækɪt] Jacke **4 › U2:** 31

Jamaican [dʒəˈmeɪkən] jamaikanisch; Jamaikaner/in **5 › U3:** 57

January [ˈdʒænjuəri] Januar **1 › U5:** 98

Japanese [dʒæpəˈniːz] japanisch; Japanisch; Japaner/Japanerin **3 › U2:** 28

jazz [dʒæz] Jazz **3 › U5:** 102

jealous [ˈdʒeləs]: **feel jealous** neidisch sein; eifersüchtig sein **4 › U1:** 11

jeans [dʒiːnz] Jeans **1 › U6:** 107

job [dʒɒb] Aufgabe **1 › U3:** 58; Arbeit(sstelle), Beruf **3 › U1:** 9; **job interview** Vorstellungsgespräch **4 › U5:** 102

join [dʒɔɪn] beitreten, Mitglied werden **3 › U4:** 71; **she joined them** sie gesellte sich zu ihnen **4 › U1:** 14

joke [dʒəʊk] Witz, Scherz **2 › U1:** 25

joking [ˈdʒəʊkɪŋ]: **You must be joking.** Du machst wohl Witze. **3 › U4:** 71

journey [ˈdʒɜːni] (lange) Reise, Fahrt **2 › U5:** 78

judge [dʒʌdʒ] ein Urteil fällen (über), (be)urteilen **U4:** 108

juggle [ˈdʒʌgl] jonglieren **1 › U6:** 105

juggler [ˈdʒʌglə] Jongleur/ Jongleurin **3 › U1:** 15

juice [dʒuːs] Saft **1 › U3:** 53

July [dʒuˈlaɪ] Juli **1 › U5:** 98

jump [dʒʌmp]: **he jumped out of his skin** er erschrak fast zu Tode **4 › U2:** 34

June [dʒuːn] Juni **1 › U5:** 98

just [dʒʌst] **1**gerade, soeben **3>U2:** 31; **2**nur **4>U1:** 11; **Just a minute.** Einen Augenblick. **1>U2:** 43; **Just a moment.** Einen Moment. **4>U1:** 17; **Just phone me.** Ruf(t) mich einfach an. **1>U6:** 110

K

kangaroo [kæŋgə'ruː] Känguru **5>U3:** 44

kayak ['kaɪæk] Kajak **5>U2:** 26

kayaking ['kaɪækɪŋ]: **sea kayaking** Seekajak fahren *U1: 103*

keep [kiːp] (I kept, I've kept) halten; behalten **3>U5:** 94; **keep in touch with** in Kontakt bleiben mit **U4:** 64

ketchup ['ketʃəp] Ketschup **1>U3:** 54

key [kiː] Schlüssel **2>U6:** 97; Schlüssel- **3>U3:** 66

keyboard ['kiːbɔːd] Keyboard **3>U5:** 99

keyword ['kiːwɜːd] Stichwort, Schlüsselwort *U4: 109*

kid [kɪd] Kind, Jugendliche/r **2>U1:** 18; **kids stuff** ['kɪdz 'stʌf] Kinderkram **U2:** 30; **my kid brother** (AE) mein kleiner Bruder **3>U4:** 70

kidding ['kɪdɪŋ]: **You must be kidding.** (AE) Du machst wohl Witze. **4>U3:** 56

kill [kɪl] töten, umbringen **2>U4:** 62

kilo, kilogram ['kiːləʊ, 'kɪləgræm] Kilo(gramm) **U5:** 76

kilometre (km) ['kɪləmiːtə] Kilometer **3>U3:** 49; **kilometres per hour (km/h)** Stundenkilometer **5>U3:** 44

kilt [kɪlt] Schottenrock 3>U3: 53

kind [kaɪnd] nett, freundlich **U4:** 73; **kind of** ['kaɪnd əv] Art (von) **U4:** 60

king [kɪŋ] König **2>U4:** 62

kiss [kɪs] **1**(sich) küssen **5>U4:** 73; **2**Kuss **3>U3:** 54

kitchen ['kɪtʃɪn] Küche **1>U2:** 37

kite [kaɪt] Drachen **1>U4:** 71

kiwi ['kiːwiː] Kiwi **1>U6:** 110

knee [niː] Knie **4>U5:** 96

knew [njuː] (→ know): **I knew** ich wusste, ich habe gewusst **3>U2:** 35

knife, knives [naɪf, naɪvz] Messer **4>U1:** 16

know [nəʊ] (I knew, I've known) wissen, kennen **1>U5:** 92; **know magic** sich mit Zauberei auskennen **5>U2:** 31

know-it-all ['nəʊ ɪt ɔːl] Besserwisser/in 1>U5: 90

koala [kəʊ'ɑːlə] Koala(bär) **5>U3:** 44

kookaburra ['kʊkəbʌrə] „Lachender Hans" (*Eisvogelart*) **5>U3:** 44

kwaito ['kweɪtəʊ] Kwaito (*südafrikanische Musikstilrichtung*) U2: 27

Kyoto Protocol [kiəʊtəʊ 'prəʊtəkɒl] Kyoto-Protokoll U5: 85

L

labour ['leɪbə]: **child labour** Kinderarbeit U3: 42

lacrosse [lə'krɒs] Lacrosse (*Hockey-ähnliche Sportart*) 5>U1: 11

lady ['leɪdi]: **first lady of country** die „erste Dame" der Countrymusik **3>U5:** 91

laid [leɪd] (→ lay): **I laid** ich legte, ich habe gelegt **5>U3:** 44; **I've laid** ich habe gelegt **5>U3:** 44

lake [leɪk] (Binnen-)See **2>U6:** 94

land [lænd] **1**Land **5>U5:** 82; **2**landen **2>U6:** 97

landing strip ['lændɪŋ strɪp] (einfache) Landebahn 5>U5: 85

landline ['lændlaɪn] Festnetzverbindung **5>U4:** 76

landowner ['lændəʊnə] Grundbesitzer/in **U1:** 20

language ['læŋgwɪdʒ] Sprache **2>U6:** 96

Lanzarote [lænzə'rɒti] Lanzarote 2>Intro: 11

laptop ['læptɒp]: **laptop computer** Laptop **U2:** 35

large [lɑːdʒ] groß **3>U5:** 92

last [lɑːst] letzte/r/s **2>U1:** 19; **last name** Nachname 5>U4: 76; **last night** gestern Abend **3>U1:** 24

late [leɪt] spät **1>U2:** 40; **late parking** [leɪt 'pɑːkɪŋ] das Überziehen der Parkzeit **1>U6:** 109

later ['leɪtə] später **3>U1:** 10

latest ['leɪtɪst] neueste/r/s **3>U5:** 107

Latin ['lætɪn] Latein U1: 14

laugh [lɑːf] lachen **2>U3:** 50

lawyer ['lɔːjə] Rechtsanwalt/-anwältin **U2:** 27

lay [leɪ]: **lay eggs** (I laid, I've laid) Eier legen **5>U3:** 44; **lay the table** den Tisch decken **5>U3:** 53

lay [leɪ] (→ lie): **I lay** ich lag, ich habe gelegen **2>U5:** 82

layout ['leɪaʊt] Layout (*Text- und Bildgestaltung*) **3>U3:** 50

lazy ['leɪzi] faul, träge **4>U5:** 93

lead [liːd] (I led, I've led) führen **5>U5:** 90; **lead singer** [liːd 'sɪŋə] Leadsänger/in **3>U5:** 88

leader ['liːdə] Leiter/in **3>U2:** 33

leaf, leaves [liːf, liːvz] Blatt, Blätter **2>U4:** 62

learn [lɜːn] lernen **2>U1:** 14; **learn about** etwas erfahren über **1>U6:** 102; **learn by heart** auswendig lernen **4>U2:** 37

learning buddy ['lɜːnɪŋ bʌdi] Lernpate/Lernpatin **4>U3:** 51

least [liːst] wenigste/r/s; am wenigsten **3>U5:** 92; **at least** zumindest; wenigstens; mindestens **4>U4:** 71

leave [liːv] (I left, I've left) **1**(stehen/liegen) lassen **1>U4:** 71; **leave a message** eine Nachricht hinterlassen **3>U2:** 35; **leave behind** zurücklassen **U1:** 10; **2**verlassen **2>U3:** 50; **leave the house** das Haus verlassen **1>U4:** 80; **3**weggehen von **5>U5:** 91

leaves [liːvz] (→ leaf) Blätter **2>U4:** 62

led [led] (→ lead): **I led** ich führte, ich habe geführt **5>U5:** 90; **I've led** ich habe geführt **5>U5:** 90

left [left]: **on the left** auf der linken Seite, links **3>U2:** 35; **to the left** links **1>U5:** 92; **turn left** nach links abbiegen **2>U3:** 52

left [left] (→ leave): **I left** ich ließ, ich habe gelassen **2>U3:** 49

leg [leg] Bein **3>U3:** 56

legend ['ledʒənd] Legende, Sage **2>A Legend:** 108

lemon soda [lemən 'səʊdə] (AE) Zitronensprudel **3>U4:** 76

lemonade [lemə'neɪd] Limonade **1>U3:** 55

leopard ['lepəd] Leopard **U2:** 24

less [less] weniger **3>U5:** 92

DICTIONARY

lesson [ˈlesn] (Unterrichts-)
Stunde **1›U1:** 32; **lessons**
Unterricht **5›U1:** 10
let [let] (I let, I've let) lassen
3›U2: 33; **Let's ...** [lets]
Lass(t) uns ... **1›U2:** 41
letter [ˈletə] Brief **1›U6:** 106
lettuce [ˈletɪs] (Kopf-)Salat
1›U3: 53
leukaemia [luːˈkiːmɪə] Leukämie
(Blutkrebs) **U5:** 79
level [ˈlevl]: **radioactive level**
Wert/Menge an Radioaktivität
U5: 78; **sea level** Meeresspiegel
U5: 75
library [ˈlaɪbrəri] Bibliothek,
Bücherei **1›U6:** 104
lie [laɪ] (I lay, I've lain) liegen
2›U5: 81
life [laɪf] Leben **2›U3:** 48
lifestyle [ˈlaɪfstaɪl] Lifestyle,
Lebensstil **4›U1:** 11; **we should
have lifestyles ...** wir sollten
ein Leben führen ... **4›U4:** 71
lift [lɪft] Fahrstuhl, Aufzug
2›U3: 51; **Lift off!** Start!
1›Intro: 15
light [laɪt] **1**Licht, Lampe
2›U5: 82; **2**hell **2›U6:** 97
like [laɪk] **1**mögen **1›U5:** 85;
I like reading. Ich lese gern.
2›U2: 28; **I like her best**
sie gefällt mir am besten
4›U5: 93; **2**wie **2›U3:** 51;
it looks to me like ... für mich
sieht es aus, als ob ... **U4:** 64;
like this so, auf diese Weise
4›U5: 88; **What's he like?**
Wie ist er? **2›U2:** 36
line [laɪn] Linie **3›U1:** 16; Zeile
3›U1: 15
link [lɪŋk] Link; Verbindung
2›U1: 25
lion [ˈlaɪən] Löwe **U2:** 24
list [lɪst] Liste **2›U4:** 64
listen [ˈlɪsn] zuhören **2›U3:** 50;
listen to hören, sich anhören
1›U4: 70
litre [ˈliːtə] Liter **5›U5:** 87; **one
litre of water** ein Liter Wasser
5›U5: 87
little [ˈlɪtl] **1**klein **4›U1:** 8; **Little
Italy** [lɪtl ˈɪtəli] „Klein-Italien"
4›U1: 8; **2**wenig **3›U5:** 92;
a little ein bisschen, ein wenig
2›U4: 63
live **1**[lɪv] leben, wohnen
1›U5: 89; **2**[laɪv] live
5›U1: 10;

lively [ˈlaɪvli] lebhaft **4›U4:** 68
living room [ˈlɪvɪŋ ruːm]
Wohnzimmer **1›U2:** 37
local [ˈləʊkl] örtlich, am/vom Ort
1›U6: 102
location [ləʊˈkeɪʃn] Schauplatz,
Lage **5›U4:** 64
logo [ˈləʊgəʊ] (Marken-)Logo
4›U1: 10
Londoner [ˈlʌndənə] Londoner/in
3›U1: 8; **I'm a Londoner.**
Ich bin Londoner/in. **3›U1:** 8
lonely [ˈləʊnli] einsam **3›U4:** 68
long [lɒŋ] lang; lange **1›U5:** 86;
take long lange dauern
4›U2: 32
look [lʊk] **1**gucken, schauen
1›U2: 41; **2**nachschauen
1›U3: 54; **3**aussehen
3›U1: 14; **it looks to me like ...**
für mich sieht es aus, als ob ...
U4: 64; **look after** sich küm-
mern um; betreuen **1›U6:** 107;
look around sich umschauen,
umherschauen **3›U2:** 30;
look at (sich) anschauen
1›U1: 26; **look for** suchen
3›U3: 51; **look forward to ...**
sich freuen auf ... **3›U2:** 28;
**I'm looking forward to hearing
from you.** Ich freue mich darauf,
von Ihnen zu hören. **4›U5:** 103;
look up aufblicken **4›U5:** 95
looks [lʊks]: **good looks** gutes
Aussehen **U3:** 42
lorry [ˈlɒri] Lastwagen
4›U5: 99; **lorry driver**
Lastwagenfahrer/in **4›U5:** 99
lose [luːz] (I lost, I've lost) ver-
lieren **4›U4:** 68
lost [lɒst] verloren **1›U5:** 90;
We're lost. Wir haben uns ver-
laufen. **2›U3:** 52
lost [lɒst] (→ lose): **I lost** ich
verlor, ich habe verloren
4›U4: 68; **I've lost** ich habe
verloren **4›U4:** 68
lot [lɒt]: **a lot (of)** viele; viel; eine
Menge **2›U2:** 34
lots (of) [lɒts] viele; viel; eine
Menge **1›U3:** 54
lottery ticket [ˈlɒtəri tɪkɪt]
Lotterieschein, Lottoschein
U4: 109
loud [laʊd] laut **3›U5:** 90
lounge [laʊndʒ] Gesellschafts-/
Aufenthaltsraum **4›U5:** 93

love [lʌv] lieben, sehr mögen
2›U2: 29; **be in love** verliebt
sein **5›U4:** 72; **love triangle**
Dreiecksverhältnis **5›U4:** 72;
Love, ... Liebe Grüße ...
5›U1: 21; (1›U5: 93)
low [ləʊ] niedrig **5›U1:** 7
luck [lʌk]: **Good luck for ...** Viel
Glück bei ... **3›U4:** 82; **Wish
me luck!** Wünsch mir Glück!
U4: 62
luckily [ˈlʌkɪli] glücklicherweise
3›U1: 14
lucky [ˈlʌki] glücklich, Glücks-
1›U2: 42; **You're lucky to live
here.** Du hast (das) Glück, hier
zu wohnen. **3›U1:** 11; **You're
lucky!** Du hast Glück! **1›U2:** 40
luggage [ˈlʌgɪdʒ] Gepäck
4›U1: 16
lunch [lʌntʃ] Mittag(essen)
2›U1: 15; **lunch box** Butter-
brotdose **1›U3:** 56
lunchtime [ˈlʌntʃtaɪm]: **at
lunchtime** zur Mittagszeit
3›U1: 10
lung [lʌŋ] Lunge **U5:** 74
luxury yacht [ˈlʌkʃəri jɒt]
Luxusjacht **U1:** 14
lyrics [ˈlɪrɪks] (Lied-)Text
4›U3: 55

M

macabre [məˈkɑːbrə] makaber
U5: 79
machine [məˈʃiːn] Maschine,
Gerät **2›U3:** 50
mad [mæd]: **mad (about)** verrückt
(nach) **2›U2:** 29; **mad (at)**
wütend (auf) **4›U3:** 54
madam [ˈmædəm]: **Dear Sir/
Madam, ...** Sehr geehrte Damen
und Herren, ... **3›U4:** 82
made [meɪd] (→ make): **I made**
ich machte, ich habe gemacht
2›U3: 49; **I've made** ich habe
gemacht **3›U3:** 50; **clothes
made of seal fur** Kleidung aus
Seehundfell **5›U2:** 34
magazine [mægəˈziːn] Zeitschrift
1›U4: 69
magic [ˈmædʒɪk] Zauberei
5›U2: 31; **magic
show** Zaubershow **2›U4:** 61
mail [meɪl] Post **5›U3:** 45;
(2›U6: 98)
maize [meɪz] Mais **1›U5:** 90

majority [mə'dʒɒrəti] Mehrheit **Intro:** 7

make [meɪk] (I made, I've made) machen **1 › U2:** 37; **it makes me think of you** es lässt mich an dich denken **3 › U4:** 74; **make a camp** ein Lager aufschlagen **5 › U5:** 90; **make a list** eine Liste schreiben **2 › U4:** 64; **make friends** Freunde finden; sich anfreunden **3 › U3:** 58; **make it into a film** einen Film daraus machen **U4:** 64; **make sure** sichergehen **U4:** 64; **make up** [meɪk ˈʌp] erfinden **3 › U3:** 52; **What makes a good soap opera?** Was macht eine gute Seifenoper aus? **5 › U4:** 72

maker ['meɪkə] Hersteller/in, Produzent/in **U3:** 46

Maldives ['mɔːldiːvz]: **the Maldives** die Malediven **U5:** 74

male [meɪl] männlich **5 › U4:** 68

mall [mɔːl] (AE) Einkaufszentrum **2 › U6:** 94; **shopping mall** (**3 › U4:** 73)

man, men [mæn, men] Mann, Männer **1 › U6:** 113; **my old man** (infml) mein „Alter" (Ehemann oder Vater) **U5:** 81

manager ['mænɪdʒə] Geschäftsführer/in; Manager/in **4 › U5:** 103

many ['meni] viele **2 › U3:** 48

map [mæp] Landkarte, Stadtplan **2 › U3:** 52

maple syrup [meɪpl ˈsɪrəp] Ahornsirup **5 › U1:** 12

March [mɑːtʃ] März **1 › U5:** 98

market ['mɑːkɪt] Markt **1 › U6:** 102; **market hall** Markthalle **1 › U6:** 107

marketing ['mɑːkɪtɪŋ] Marketing **5 › U3:** 51

marriage ['mærɪdʒ] Hochzeit; Ehe **U3:** 43

married ['mærid] verheiratet **5 › U4:** 70; **get married** heiraten **5 › U4:** 73

marry ['mæri] heiraten **U1:** 21

mascot ['mæskət] Maskottchen **1 › U4:** 74

mask [mɑːsk] Maske **2 › U4:** 63

match [mætʃ] **1** Spiel, Wettkampf **1 › U5:** 86; **2 Match the texts with the photos.** Ordne den Texten die Fotos zu. **5 › U5:** 83

math [mæθ] (AE) Mathe(matik) **4 › U3:** 50

maths [mæθs] Mathe(matik) **1 › U1:** 26

matter ['mætə]: **It doesn't matter.** Das macht doch nichts. **2 › U5:** 84; **matter to you** dir wichtig sein, dich betreffen **U3:** 46

may [meɪ]: **May I ...?** Dürfte ich ...? **4 › U1:** 16

May [meɪ] Mai **1 › U5:** 98

mayo ['meɪəʊ] Majo(naise) **3 › U4:** 76

maze [meɪz] Irrgarten **1 › U5:** 90

me [miː] mich, mir **1 › U3:** 58; **It's me.** Ich bin's. **3 › U2:** 30; **Me too!** Ich auch! **3 › U2:** 33; **Me?** Ich? **4 › U1:** 11; **Not me!** Ich nicht! **4 › U1:** 10

meal [miːl] Mahlzeit, (zubereitetes) Essen **1 › U3:** 53

mean [miːn] **1** (I meant, I've meant) bedeuten, meinen **2 › U1:** 16; **2** geizig **3 › U3:** 53

meaning ['miːnɪŋ] Bedeutung **4 › U3:** 60

meant [ment]: **I meant** ich meinte, ich habe gemeint **4 › U5:** 95; **I've meant** ich habe gemeint **4 › U5:** 95

meat [miːt] Fleisch **5 › U2:** 32

mechanic [məˈkænɪk] Mechaniker/Mechanikerin **4 › U5:** 89

medal [gəʊld ˈmedl]: **gold medal** Goldmedaille **U3:** 47

media ['miːdiə]: **(the) media** (die) Medien **5 › U3:** 44

medicine ['medsn] Medikament/e **5 › U2:** 34

meet [miːt] (I met, I've met) (sich) treffen (mit) **1 › U4:** 70; **Meet Christine.** Darf ich vorstellen – Christine. **5 › U1:** 9; **Nice to meet you.** Schön, dich/Sie kennen zu lernen. **5 › U1:** 13

meeting ['miːtɪŋ] Treffen **4 › U3:** 53

megaphone ['megəfəʊn] Megaphon **4 › U4:** 74

melt [melt] schmelzen **5 › U2:** 26

member ['membə] Mitglied **3 › U3:** 48

men [men] (→ man) Männer **1 › U6:** 113

menu ['menjuː] Speisekarte **U3:** 49

mess [mes] Durcheinander **1 › U6:** 106

message ['mesɪdʒ] Nachricht **1 › U6:** 114

messy ['mesi] chaotisch, durcheinander **U4:** 65

met [met] (→ meet): **I met** ich traf, ich habe getroffen **2 › U6:** 98; **I've met** ich habe getroffen **3 › U3:** 52

metal ['metl] Metall **5 › U2:** 30

meter ['miːtə] (AE) Meter **4 › U2:** 28

metre ['miːtə] Meter **2 › A Legend:** 109; **a 3.8 metre crocodile** ein drei Meter achtzig langes Krokodil **5 › U3:** 54

Mexican ['meksɪkən] mexikanisch; Mexikaner/in **4 › U1:** 10

miaow [miˈaʊ] miau **1 › U5:** 90

mice [maɪs] (→ mouse) Mäuse **2 › U2:** 35

microwave ['maɪkrəweɪv] Mikrowelle **3 › U5:** 92

midday [mɪdˈdeɪ] Mittag **4 › U2:** 33

middle ['mɪdl] Mitte **1 › U5:** 91; **middle class** [mɪdl ˈklɑːs] Mittelschicht **U3:** 46; **middle school** ['mɪdl skuːl] „Mittelschule" (für 11- bis 14-jährige in den USA) **4 › U3:** 48; **the Middle East** [mɪdl ˈiːst] der Nahe Osten **U5:** 75

mile [maɪl] Meile **3 › U4:** 81

milk [mɪlk] Milch **1 › U3:** 55

milkman ['mɪlkmən] Milchmann **2 › U6:** 98

milkshake ['mɪlkʃeɪk] Shake **1 › U3:** 55

million ['mɪljən] Million **1 › U4:** 74

millionaire [mɪljəˈneə] Millionär/in **U3:** 42

mind [maɪnd]: **come to mind** in den Sinn kommen, einfallen **U3:** 40; **he didn't mind** es machte ihm nichts aus **U4:** 64; **never mind** macht nichts **1 › U2:** 42

mine [maɪn] meine/meiner/meines **5 › U4:** 66; (**4 › U3:** 52)

mineral water ['mɪnərəl wɔːtə] Mineralwasser **1 › U3:** 55

mini- ['mɪni] Mini- **4 › U3:** 56

minibus ['mɪnibʌs] Kleinbus **4 › U4:** 71

minigolf ['mɪnigɒlf] Minigolf **2 › Intro:** 11

mining town ['maɪnɪŋ taʊn] Bergbaustadt **5 › U5:** 82

minority [maɪˈnɒrəti] Minderheit **Intro:** 7

minus ['maɪnəs] minus **2 › U6:** 104

161

one hundred and sixty-one

→ DICTIONARY

minute ['mɪnɪt] Minute **1 ▸ U2:** 43
miss [mɪs] **1** verpassen; vermissen **2 ▸ U1:** 15; **miss the point** nicht verstehen, worum es geht **U4:** 65; **2** fehlen **U2:** 35
missing ['mɪsɪŋ] fehlend **4 ▸ U4:** 72
mission control [mɪʃn kən'trəʊl] Raumflugkontrollstation **3 ▸ U4:** 72
mist [mɪst] (leichter) Nebel **3 ▸ U2:** 34
mistake [mɪ'steɪk] Fehler **3 ▸ U4:** 75
mix [mɪks] **mix everything** alles miteinander vermischen **1 ▸ U6:** 110
mixer ['mɪksə] Mixer **1 ▸ U6:** 110
moan [məʊn] klagen, jammern **2 ▸ U5:** 89
mobile (phone) ['məʊbaɪl, məʊbaɪl 'fəʊn] Handy, Mobiltelefon **3 ▸ U2:** 34
model ['mɒdl] Modell; Nachbildung **2 ▸ U4:** 62; **model train** [mɒdl 'treɪn] Modelleisenbahn **1 ▸ U4:** 76
modern ['mɒdn] modern **2 ▸ U3:** 48
mom [mɒm] (AE) Mama, Mutti **3 ▸ U5:** 94
moment ['məʊmənt] Moment **3 ▸ U3:** 54; **at that moment** in dem Moment **3 ▸ U3:** 54; **at the moment** zurzeit, gerade **3 ▸ U3:** 130
Monday ['mʌndeɪ] Montag **1 ▸ U4:** 80
money ['mʌni] Geld **1 ▸ U4:** 71
monitor ['mɒnɪtə] Monitor, Bildschirm **3 ▸ U5:** 100
monkey ['mʌŋki] Affe **U2:** 31
monsoon wind [mɒn'suːn wɪnd] Monsunwind **U3:** 41
monster ['mɒnstə] Monster **3 ▸ U3:** 51
month [mʌnθ] Monat **1 ▸ U5:** 98
monument ['mɒnjumənt] Denkmal **3 ▸ U2:** 35
moo [muː] muh **1 ▸ U5:** 90
moon [muːn] Mond **3 ▸ U4:** 72; **moon rock** ['muːn rɒk] Mondgestein **3 ▸ U4:** 72
moor [mʊə] (Hoch-)Moor **2 ▸ U3:** 45
more [mɔː] mehr, weitere **2 ▸ U6:** 104; **more and more** immer mehr **U2:** 26; **more interesting** interessanter **2 ▸ U3:** 50; **one more** noch ein/e **3 ▸ U2:** 38

morning ['mɔːnɪŋ] Morgen **1 ▸ U6:** 107
mosque [mɒsk] Moschee **4 ▸ U4:** 76
mosquito, mosquitoes [mə'skiːtəʊ] Mücke; *Gerät, das Ultraschall-Störgeräusche produziert* **U4:** 67
most [məʊst] der/die/das meiste, die meisten **2 ▸ U3:** 48; am meisten **4 ▸ U3:** 57; **most popular** beliebteste/r/s **2 ▸ U3:** 51
mostly ['məʊstli] hauptsächlich, meistens **3 ▸ U2:** 29
mother ['mʌðə] Mutter **1 ▸ U1:** 24; **mother language** Muttersprache **U3:** 43
motor industry ['məʊtə 'ɪndəstri] Autoindustrie **U3:** 46
motorbike ['məʊtəbaɪk] Motorrad **4 ▸ U4:** 81
motorway ['məʊtəweɪ] Autobahn **U4:** 62
mountain ['maʊntən] Berg **2 ▸ Intro:** 9; **mountain bike** ['maʊntən baɪk] Mountainbike **1 ▸ U2:** 48; **mountain biking** ['maʊntən baɪkɪŋ] Mountainbikefahren **3 ▸ U2:** 31
mouse, mice [maʊs, maɪs] Maus, Mäuse **2 ▸ U2:** 35
move [muːv] (sich) bewegen **5 ▸ U5:** 90; **move from ... to** (um)ziehen von ... nach **U4:** 64
movie ['muːvi] (AE) Film **3 ▸ U5:** 96
Mozambique [məʊzæm'biːk] Mosambik **U2:** 30
MP3 player [em piː 'θriː pleɪə] MP3-Player **3 ▸ U5:** 90
Mr ['mɪstə] Herr *(Anrede)* **1 ▸ U1:** 28
Mrs ['mɪsɪz] Frau *(Anrede für verheiratete Frauen)* **1 ▸ U1:** 24
Ms [mɪz, məz] Frau *(Anrede allgemein)* **3 ▸ U2:** 36
much [mʌtʃ] viel **1 ▸ U5:** 91; **How much is it?** Was kostet das? **1 ▸ U4:** 75
mug [mʌg] überfallen und ausrauben **U4:** 60
multicultural [mʌlti'kʌltʃərəl] multikulturell **5 ▸ U1:** 8
multinational [mʌlti'næʃnəl] multinational, aus vielen Nationen **U1:** 9
mum [mʌm] Mama, Mutti **1 ▸ U1:** 28
Munich ['mjuːnɪk] München **2 ▸ U6:** 93

museum [mjuˈziːəm] Museum **1 ▸ U5:** 99
music ['mjuːzɪk] Musik **1 ▸ U4:** 70
musical ['mjuːzɪkl] **1** musikalisch **5 ▸ U4:** 68; **2** Musical **4 ▸ U3:** 48
musician [mjuˈzɪʃn] Musiker/in **U1:** 16
Muslim ['mʊzlɪm, 'mʌzlɪm] Moslem/in; moslemisch **U3:** 40
must [mʌst] müssen **2 ▸ U1:** 17
mustn't ['mʌsnt]: **you mustn't** du darfst/Sie dürfen nicht **2 ▸ U2:** 34
my [maɪ] mein/meine **1 ▸ Intro:** 14
myself [maɪ'self] mir/mich (selbst); selbst **4 ▸ U3:** 52

N

naive [naɪ'iːv] naiv **U1:** 15
name [neɪm] Name **1 ▸ U2:** 40
narrow ['nærəʊ] schmal, eng **5 ▸ U5:** 88
narwhal ['nɑːwəl] Narwal **5 ▸ U2:** 28
national ['næʃnəl] national, National- **5 ▸ U1:** 17; **national anthem** [næʃnəl 'ænθəm] Nationalhymne **5 ▸ U5:** 93; **national holiday** gesetzlicher Feiertag **4 ▸ U2:** 30; **national park** Nationalpark **4 ▸ U2:** 28
nationality [næʃə'næləti] Nationalität; Staatsbürgerschaft **5 ▸ U4:** 67
Native American ['neɪtɪv ə'merɪkən] amerik. Ureinwohner/in, Indianer/in **5 ▸ U1:** 8
native people ['neɪtɪv 'piːpl] Ureinwohner/innen **5 ▸ U1:** 14
natural catastrophe [nætʃrel kə'tæstrəfi] Naturkatastrophe **U2:** 31
nature ['neɪtʃə] Natur **5 ▸ U2:** 34
near [nɪə] in der Nähe von, nahe **1 ▸ U5:** 89
nearest ['nɪərɪst]: **Where's the nearest ...?** Wo ist der/die/das nächste ...? **2 ▸ U3:** 52
nearly ['nɪəli] fast **5 ▸ U5:** 86
necessary ['nesəsəri] notwendig, nötig **5 ▸ U2:** 34
need [niːd] brauchen **1 ▸ U6:** 110
needn't ['niːdnt] nicht brauchen, nicht müssen **3 ▸ U2:** 33
neighbour ['neɪbə] Nachbar/in **1 ▸ U2:** 39
nervous ['nɜːvəs] nervös, ängstlich **4 ▸ U3:** 55

Netherlands ['neðələndz]: **the Netherlands** die Niederlande **U1:** 15

network ['netwɜːk] Netz, Netzwerk 1 › **U6:** 115

never ['nevə] nie, niemals 1 › **U5:** 86; **Better late than never.** Lieber spät als gar nicht. 1 › **U5:** 93; **never mind** macht nichts 1 › **U2:** 42

new [njuː] neu 1 › **Intro:** 18; **if you're new to it** wenn es dir neu ist 3 › **U4:** 74; **New Delhi** [njuː 'deli] Neu-Delhi **U3:** 40; **New Year** [njuː 'jɪə] Neujahr 4 › **U1:** 9; **New Zealand** [njuː 'ziːlənd] Neuseeland 5 › **U4:** 80; **they were new to me** sie waren mir neu 3 › **U1:** 15

news [njuːz] Nachricht(en); Neuigkeit(en) 4 › **U3:** 51

newspaper ['njuːzpeɪpə] Zeitung 2 › **U4:** 63

next [nekst] **1** nächste/r/s 1 › **U4:** 74; **2** als Nächstes 1 › **U6:** 110; **next door** nebenan 5 › **U4:** 64; **next to** ['neks tə] neben 1 › **U2:** 37

Niagara Falls [naɪˈæɡərə ˈfɔːlz] Niagarafälle 5 › **U1:** 6

nice [naɪs] nett 1 › **U1:** 24; **Nice of you to say so.** Nett, dass du das sagst. 3 › **U5:** 94; **Nice to meet you.** Schön, dich/Sie kennen zu lernen. 5 › **U1:** 13

nickname ['nɪkneɪm] Spitzname **U1:** 14

night [naɪt] Nacht, (später) Abend 2 › **U4:** 62; **at night** nachts, in der Nacht 5 › **U1:** 13

nil [nɪl] **1:0 (one nil) to ...** eins zu null für ... 4 › **U4:** 74

nine [naɪn] neun 1 › **Intro:** 15

nineteen [naɪnˈtiːn] neunzehn 1 › **U2:** 48

nineteenseventies [naɪntiːn'sevəntiz]: **the 1970s** die Siebzigerjahre 5 › **U2:** 35

nineteenth [naɪnˈtiːnθ] neunzehnte/r/s 2 › **U4:** 72

ninety ['naɪnti] neunzig 1 › **U2:** 48

ninth [naɪnθ] neunte/r/s 2 › **U4:** 72

no [nəʊ] **1** nein 1 › **U1:** 22; **2** kein/e 1 › **U4:** 71

nobody ['nəʊbədi] niemand 3 › **U3:** 53

noise [nɔɪz] Lärm, Geräusch 2 › **A Legend:** 109

noisy ['nɔɪzi] laut, lärmend 2 › **U3:** 51

normal ['nɔːml] normal 5 › **U2:** 28

north [nɔːθ] (nach) Norden; Nord-; nördlich 2 › **U3:** 45; **North Sea** [nɔːθ 'siː] Nordsee 3 › **U3:** 48

northeast [nɔːθˈiːst]: **in the northeast** im Nordosten 4 › **U4:** 71

Northern Ireland [nɔːðən 'aɪələnd] Nordirland 2 › **U1:** 12

Northern Lights [nɔːðən 'laɪts] Nordlicht 3 › **U3:** 48

northwest [nɔːθ'west] Nordwesten, Nordwest- **U3:** 40

Norway ['nɔːweɪ] Norwegen **U5:** 78

not [nɒt] nicht 1 › **U1:** 22; **not ... any** kein/keine 3 › **U4:** 73; **not ... yet** noch nicht 3 › **U2:** 30; **not at all** überhaupt nicht 4 › **U2:** 34

note [nəʊt] Notiz, (kurzer) Brief 1 › **U6:** 115; **take notes** sich Notizen machen 4 › **U1:** 11; **take notes on the weather** sich Notizen über das Wetter machen 4 › **U2:** 29

nothing ['nʌθɪŋ] nichts 3 › **U2:** 34

notice ['nəʊtɪs] bemerken 4 › **U1:** 14

noticeboard ['nəʊtɪsbɔːd] Anschlagbrett, Schwarzes Brett 4 › **U3:** 53

noun [naʊn] Nomen, Hauptwort 5 › **U5:** 97

November [nəʊ'vembə] November 1 › **U5:** 98

now [naʊ] jetzt 1 › **U1:** 26; **Bye for now!** Tschüs erstmal! 5 › **U1:** 21; **right now** gerade jetzt **U4:** 64; **That's all for now.** Das ist im Augenblick alles. 4 › **U5:** 102

nowhere ['nəʊweə] nirgendwo(hin) 3 › **U5:** 90

nuclear ['njuːkliə]: **nuclear power station** Kernkraftwerk 4 › **U4:** 71

number ['nʌmbə] Zahl, Nummer 1 › **Intro:** 15

Nuremberg ['njʊərəmbɜːg] Nürnberg 3 › **U3:** 59

nurse [nɜːs] Krankenpfleger/Krankenschwester 4 › **U5:** 89

O

occasion [ə'keɪʒn] Gelegenheit, Anlass 3 › **U3:** 56

ocean ['əʊʃn] Ozean **U5:** 74

o'clock [ə'klɒk]: **at two o'clock** um zwei Uhr 1 › **U3:** 64

October [ɒk'təʊbə] Oktober 1 › **U5:** 98

of [ɒv, əv] von 1 › **U4:** 76; **a bottle/carton/... of ...** eine Flasche/eine Packung/... 1 › **U3:** 55; **a photo of my dog** ein Foto meines Hundes 2 › **U3:** 48; **the U.S. state of Rhode Island** der U.S.-Bundesstaat Rhode Island 3 › **U4:** 69

of course [əf 'kɔːs] natürlich, selbstverständlich 2 › **U4:** 62

offer ['ɒfə]: **special offer** Sonderangebot 2 › **U2:** 68

office ['ɒfɪs] Büro 4 › **Intro:** 6; **information office** Informationsbüro 3 › **U1:** 14; **ticket office** Fahrkartenschalter, Verkaufsstelle 3 › **U1:** 16

officer ['ɒfɪsə] (Polizei-)Beamter/Beamtin 2 › **U3:** 52

official language [ə'fɪʃl 'læŋgwɪdʒ] Amtssprache 5 › **U1:** 7

often ['ɒfn] oft 1 › **U4:** 70

oil [ɔɪl] ...l 3 › **U3:** 48

oink [ɔɪŋk] grunz 1 › **U5:** 90

OK [əʊ'keɪ] O.K., in Ordnung 1 › **U1:** 26; **Are you OK?** Ist alles in Ordnung bei dir? 3 › **U2:** 36

old [əʊld] alt 1 › **U2:** 38; **my old man** (infml) mein „Alter" (Ehemann oder Vater) **U5:** 81; **old people's home** [əʊld 'piːplz həʊm] Altenheim 5 › **U3:** 52; **sixteen-year-old** [sɪks'tiːn jɪər əʊld] Sechzehnjährige/r **U4:** 70

Olympic [ə'lɪmpɪk]: **the Olympic Games** die Olympischen Spiele 5 › **U3:** 45

on [ɒn] auf; an 1 › **U1:** 23; **be on fire** brennen 5 › **U4:** 73; **go on and on** immer weitergehen 5 › **U4:** 72; **on holiday** im Urlaub 1 › **U6:** 115; **on November 8th** am 8. November 2 › **U4:** 72; **on Saturday** am Samstag 1 › **U4:** 81; **on Sundays** sonntags, am Sonntag 1 › **U4:** 70; **on the Internet** im Internet 2 › **U1:** 25; **on the right/left** auf der rechten/linken Seite, rechts/links 3 › **U2:** 35; **on the telephone** am Telefon 3 › **U2:** 36;

163

one hundred and sixty-three

DICTIONARY

on time pünktlich **4 > U3:** 54;
on TV im Fernsehen **2 > U1:** 18
once [wʌns] einmal **3 > U3:** 48;
at once sofort **4 > U2:** 31; **for once** [fə 'wʌns] ausnahmsweise (ein)mal **U4:** 60
one [wʌn] ein, eine/r/s, eins
1 > Intro: 15; **a small one, two small ones** ein/e kleine/r/s, zwei kleine **3 > U4:** 76; **one morning/night/...** eines Morgens/Nachts/... **3 > U5:** 90;
the small one/s der/die/das kleine, die kleineren **2 > U4:** 68
online [ɒn'laɪn] online **5 > U4:** 67
only ['əʊnli] **1** nur, bloß **1 > U2:** 43;
2 erst **5 > U3:** 46; **3 the only company** die einzige Firma **U1:** 11
onto ['ɒntʊ, 'ɒntə] auf (... hinauf/ herauf) **3 > U5:** 103
oops [ʊps] hoppla **2 > U5:** 86
open ['əʊpən] **1** öffnen, aufmachen **1 > U1:** 26; eröffnen **4 > U4:** 68; sich öffnen **5 > U5:** 83;
2 geöffnet **1 > U2:** 40
open-top ['əʊpən'tɒp] ohne Verdeck, offen **5 > U3:** 48
opening times ['əʊpənɪŋ taɪmz] Öffnungszeiten **3 > U1:** 17
opera ['ɒprə] Oper **5 > U4:** 72;
opera house ['ɒprə haʊs] Opernhaus **5 > U3:** 48
opinion [ə'pɪnjən] Meinung **5 > U1:** 21; **give an opinion** eine Meinung abgeben **5 > U1:** 21;
in my opinion meiner Meinung nach **5 > U4:** 64
opposite ['ɒpəzɪt] Gegenteil **2 > U2:** 35
optimistic [ɒptɪ'mɪstɪk] optimistisch **U4:** 65
option ['ɒpʃn] (Wahl-)Möglichkeit **4 > U5:** 90
or [ɔː] oder **1 > Intro:** 19
orange ['ɒrɪndʒ] Apfelsine, Orange **1 > U3:** 53
order ['ɔːdə] **1** bestellen **2 > U4:** 64; **2** Reihenfolge **2 > U1:** 23; **in order to help** um zu helfen **U1:** 14
organisation [ɔːgənaɪ'zeɪʃn] Organisation **1 > U4:** 74
organise ['ɔːgənaɪz] organisieren, veranstalten **2 > U1:** 17; **she organises herself** sie hat ihr Leben im Griff **4 > U3:** 54
organiser ['ɔːgənaɪzə] Organisator/in, Veranstalter/in **4 > U3:** 59

origin ['ɒrɪdʒɪn] Herkunft **U3:** 49
original [ə'rɪdʒənl] originell **5 > U4:** 66
Oscar ['ɒskə] Oscar (amerikanischer Filmpreis) **U2:** 105
ostrich ['ɒstrɪʃ] Strauß (Vogel) **U2:** 27
other ['ʌðə] andere, weitere **1 > U2:** 37; **the other way round** anders herum **U3:** 47
ought to ['ɔːt tə]: **you ought to** du solltest (eigentlich) **U4:** 64
our ['aʊə] unser/unsere **1 > U1:** 20
ours ['aʊəz] unsere/unserer/ unseres **5 > U4:** 66; (**4 > U3:** 52)
ourselves [aʊə'selvz] uns (selbst); selbst **4 > U3:** 53
out [aʊt]: **go out** ausgehen, weggehen **3 > U4:** 68; **go out for a meal** essen gehen **1 > U5:** 86; **go out in the car** eine Spazierfahrt machen **1 > U5:** 86; **have a day out** einen Tagesausflug machen **1 > U5:** 86
out of ['aʊt əv] aus (... hinaus/ heraus) **3 > U1:** 14; **out of work** [aʊt əv 'wɜːk] arbeitslos **3 > U2:** 28; **sixth out of 200** Sechste/r von 200 **U1:** 14
out-of-town [aʊt əv 'taʊn]: **an out-of-town shopping centre** ein außerhalb der Stadt gelegenes Einkaufszentrum **4 > U4:** 68
outback ['aʊtbæk]: **the outback** das Outback (das Landesinnere Australiens) **5 > U3:** 44
outdoor ... ['aʊtdɔː] ... im Freien **5 > U1:** 10
outer fence [aʊtə 'fens] Außenzaun **U2:** 31
outside [aʊt'saɪd] außerhalb (von) **3 > U3:** 54; (nach) draußen **2 > U3:** 51
outsider [aʊt'saɪdə] Außenseiter/ in **U4:** 61
over ['əʊvə] über, mehr als **2 > U1:** 14; **from all over the world** aus der ganzen Welt **3 > U1:** 8; **over there** [əʊvə 'ðeə] dort/ da drüben **1 > U5:** 93
overtake [əʊvə'teɪk] (I overtook, I've overtaken) überholen **U5:** 84
overtaken [əʊvə'teɪkən] (→ overtake): **I've overtaken** ich habe überholt **U5:** 84
overtook [əʊvə'tʊk] (→ overtake): **I overtook** ich überholte **U5:** 84

own [əʊn] **1** besitzen **5 > U3:** 51;
2 your own dialogue dein eigener Dialog **3 > U3:** 55
owner ['əʊnə] Besitzer/in **2 > U2:** 32
oxygen ['ɒksɪdʒən] Sauerstoff **U5:** 74

P

pack [pæk] packen **3 > U1:** 14; einpacken **4 > U2:** 31
packet ['pækɪt] Schachtel; Paket, Päckchen **2 > U1:** 18
pad [pæd] Schützer **1 > U6:** 110
paddle ['pædl] Paddel **U1:** 103
page [peɪdʒ] Seite **1 > U1:** 26
paid [peɪd] (→ pay): **I paid** ich zahlte, ich habe gezahlt **4 > U1:** 12; **I've paid** ich habe gezahlt **4 > U1:** 12
paint [peɪnt] malen **1 > U4:** 76
pair [peə] Paar **4 > U4:** 72; **a pair of shoes** ein Paar Schuhe **4 > U4:** 72
Pakistan [pækɪ'stɑːn] Pakistan **1 > U2:** 39
pancake ['pænkeɪk] (kleiner) Pfannkuchen **3 > U4:** 73
paradise ['pærədaɪs] Paradies **U5:** 81
paragraph ['pærəgrɑːf] Abschnitt **3 > U2:** 29
pardon ['pɑːdn]: **Pardon?** Wie bitte? **3 > U2:** 36
parents ['peərənts] Eltern **1 > U2:** 39
park [pɑːk] **1** parken **4 > U2:** 35;
2 Park **1 > U5:** 87
parking lot ['pɑːkɪŋ lɒt] (AE) Parkplatz **U5:** 81
parliament ['pɑːləmənt] Parlament **2 > U4:** 62
part [pɑːt] **1** Teil **4 > U4:** 68;
2 Rolle **5 > U4:** 68; **take part in** teilnehmen an **U1:** 14
partly ['pɑːtli] teilweise **5 > U1:** 8
partner ['pɑːtnə] Partner/in **1 > U1:** 23; Partner- **2 > U1:** 15
party ['pɑːti] Party **1 > U2:** 49; Feier **1 > U6:** 112
pass [pɑːs]: **pass a test** eine Prüfung bestehen **U4:** 62; **pass through** gehen/fahren/fließen durch **U5:** 75
passport ['pɑːspɔːt] (Reise-)Pass **4 > U1:** 16
past [pɑːst] Vergangenheit **2 > U3:** 48

164

one hundred and sixty-four

path [pɑːθ] Weg, Pfad **3>U2:** 33

patient [ˈpeɪʃnt] Patient/in **5>U5:** 85

pause [pɔːz] Pause **3>U5:** 96

pave [peɪv] pflastern *(mit Pflastersteinen) U5: 81*

pay [peɪ] (I paid, I've paid) bezahlen, zahlen **2>U6:** 96

P. E. (Physical Education) [ˈpiːˌiː ˌfɪzɪkl edʒuˈkeɪʃn] Turnen, Turnunterricht **4>U3:** 50

peace [piːs] Friede(n) **U1:** 10

peaceful [ˈpiːsfl] friedlich **4>U4:** 74

pee [piː] pinkeln **U4:** 64

pen [pen] Füller **1>U1:** 32

pence [pens] Pence **2>U5:** 88

pencil [ˈpensl] Bleistift **1>U1:** 32; **pencil case** [ˈpensl keɪs] Federmäppchen **1>U1:** 32

penguin [ˈpeŋgwɪn] Pinguin **U2:** 28

penknife, penknives [ˈpennaɪf, -naɪvz] Taschenmesser **4>U1:** 16

people [ˈpiːpl] **1** Leute, Menschen **1>U4:** 70; **2** Volk **5>U3:** 50

pepper [ˈpepə] Paprika(schote) **1>U3:** 53

pepperoni [pepəˈrəʊni] (scharfe) Salami **U4:** 64

per [pɜː] pro **4>U2:** 36; **per cent (%)** [pəˈsent] Prozent **5>U1:** 7

perfect [ˈpɜːfɪkt] vollkommen, perfekt **5>U4:** 73

perfectly [ˈpɜːfɪktli] vollkommen, absolut **U4:** 64

perform [pəˈfɔːm] spielen, aufführen **U2:** 105

perhaps [pəˈhæps] vielleicht **1>U1:** 24

permit [ˈpɜːmɪt] (schriftliche) Genehmigung, Erlaubnis **4>U2:** 30

person [ˈpɜːsn] Person, Mensch **3>U3:** 61

pessimistic [pesɪˈmɪstɪk] pessimistisch **5>U2:** 27

pet [pet] Haustier, zahmes Tier **2>U2:** 34; **pet shop** Tierhandlung **1>U6:** 104

phenomenal [fəˈnɒmɪnəl] phänomenal **5>U3:** 48

phone [fəʊn] **1** anrufen, telefonieren **1>U5:** 93; **2** Telefon **4>U2:** 34; **answer the phone** ans Telefon gehen **3>U2:** 37; **phone book** Telefonbuch **1>U2:** 44; **phone number** [ˈfəʊn nʌmbə] Telefonnummer **3>U2:** 36

phonetic script [fəˈnetɪk ˈskrɪpt] Lautschrift **4>U1:** 19

photo [ˈfəʊtəʊ] Foto **1>Intro:** 11; **take photos** Fotos machen **1>U4:** 76

photography [fəˈtɒgrəfi] Fotografie **5>U4:** 70

phrase [freɪz] (Rede-)Wendung, Ausdruck **2>U1:** 21

piano [piˈænəʊ] Klavier **3>U5:** 88

pick [pɪk] wählen, aussuchen **3>U2:** 32; ernten **U1:** 20; **pick the pepperoni off** die Salami (von der Pizza) runternehmen **U4:** 64; **pick up** [pɪk ˈʌp] abholen **4>U4:** 76

picnic [ˈpɪknɪk] Picknick **1>U5:** 84; **have a picnic** ein Picknick machen **1>U5:** 84

picture [ˈpɪktʃə] Bild **1>Intro:** 10

pie [paɪ]: **apple pie** gedeckter Apfelkuchen **3>U4:** 76

piece [piːs] Stück **3>U4:** 76

pig [pɪg] Schwein **1>U5:** 90

pilot [ˈpaɪlət] Pilot/in **5>U5:** 85

pingo [ˈpɪŋgəʊ] *eine Art Hügel mit Eiskern in Dauerfrostgebieten* **5>U2:** 37

pink [pɪŋk] rosa **1>Intro:** 14

pioneer [paɪəˈnɪə] Pionier/ Pionierin **4>U2:** 30

pirate [ˈpaɪrət] Pirat/in **2>A Legend:** 109

pity [ˈpɪti]: **It's a pity.** Es ist schade. **4>U2:** 34

pizza [ˈpiːtsə] Pizza **2>U5:** 86

pizzeria [piːtsəˈriːə] Pizzeria **4>U1:** 22

place [pleɪs] Ort, Stelle **1>U4:** 78

plan [plæn] **1** planen **1>U6:** 112; **2** Plan, Vorhaben **1>U6:** 109

plane [pleɪn] Flugzeug **2>Intro:** 9

plant [plɑːnt] **1** pflanzen **4>U4:** 70; **2** Pflanze **5>U2:** 26; **steel plant** Stahlfabrik **U3:** 46

plasma TV [ˈplæzmə tiːviː] Plasma-Fernseher **2>U6:** 94

plate [pleɪt] Teller **2>U4:** 63

platypus [ˈplætɪpəs] Schnabeltier **5>U3:** 44

play [pleɪ] **1** spielen **1>U4:** 70; **play sport** Sport treiben **1>U4:** 70; **play the violin** Geige spielen **3>U5:** 88; **2** (Theater-)Stück, Schauspiel **5>U4:** 67

player [ˈpleɪə] Spieler/Spielerin **4>U5:** 89

playground [ˈpleɪgraʊnd] Spielplatz **U5:** 78

please [pliːz] bitte **1>U1:** 26

pleased [pliːzd]: **be pleased about** sich freuen über **SUM:** 94

p.m. [piː ˈem] nachmittags, abends **3>U1:** 17

pocket money [ˈpɒkɪt mʌni] Taschengeld **1>U5:** 85

poem [ˈpəʊɪm] Gedicht **2>U5:** 89

point [pɔɪnt] Punkt **1>U3:** 53; **miss the point** nicht verstehen, worum es geht **U4:** 65; **That's not the point.** Darum geht es nicht. **5>U2:** 32

Poland [ˈpəʊlənd] Polen **U1:** 11

polar bear [ˈpəʊlə beə] Eisbär **5>U5:** 26

police [pəˈliːs] Polizei **2>U3:** 51; **police station** Polizeiwache, Polizeirevier **2>U3:** 52; **the police were there** die Polizei war da **4>U4:** 74

Polish [ˈpəʊlɪʃ] Pole/Polin; polnisch; Polnisch **U1:** 11

politician [pɒləˈtɪʃn] Politiker/in **5>U3:** 55

poll [pəʊl] Umfrage **U1:** 15

pollution [pəˈluːʃn] (Umwelt-) Verschmutzung **4>U4:** 69

pony-trekking [ˈpəʊni trekɪŋ] Ponyreiten *(übers Land)* **3>U2:** 31

poor [pʊə] arm **2>A Legend:** 108; schlecht **3>U1:** 8

pop [pɒp] Pop(musik) **1>U2:** 45

popcorn [ˈpɒpkɔːn] Popcorn **3>U5:** 96

popular [ˈpɒpjələ] beliebt **1>U3:** 53

population [pɒpjuˈleɪʃn] Bevölkerung, Bevölkerungszahl **3>U2:** 29

port [pɔːt] Hafen(stadt) **3>U2:** 29

portion [ˈpɔːʃn] Portion **1>U3:** 53

portray [pɔːˈtreɪ] darstellen, porträtieren **U4:** 60

positive [ˈpɒzətɪv] positiv **U2:** 30

possible [ˈpɒsəbl] möglich **5>U5:** 86

post [pəʊst] schicken *(per Post oder E-Mail)* **U1:** 14

post office [ˈpəʊst ɒfɪs] Postamt **2>U3:** 52

postcard [ˈpəʊstkɑːd] Postkarte **1>U5:** 93

postcode [ˈpəʊstkəʊd] Postleitzahl **2>U5:** 85

165

one hundred and sixty-five

DICTIONARY

poster ['pəʊstə] Poster **1 › U3:** 61;
tourist poster Touristenposter
U1: 13

postman ['pəʊstmən] Briefträger,
Postbote **3 › U3:** 54

pot [pɒt]: **coffee/tea pot** Kaffee-/
Teekanne **4 › U5:** 94

potato, potatoes [pə'teɪtəʊ]
Kartoffel **1 › U3:** 53

pot-luck meal [pɒtlʌk 'miːl] *Essen,
zu dem alle Gäste etwas mitbringen* **2 › U6:** 97

pound [paʊnd] Pfund *(britische
Währung)* **1 › U2:** 43

poverty ['pɒvəti] Armut **U1:** 14

power ['paʊə] Strom **4 › U4:** 69;
power station ['paʊə steɪʃn]
Kraftwerk **4 › U4:** 69

practice ['præktɪs] Training;
Übung **3 › U4:** 71

practise ['præktɪs] üben, trainie-
ren **3 › U1:** 17

prefer [prɪ'fɜː] vorziehen
5 › U3: 47; **prefer watching
TV** lieber fernsehen **3 › U4:** 69

pregnant ['pregnənt] schwanger
U4: 60

prejudiced ['predʒədɪst]: **be
prejudiced against** Vorurteile
haben gegen, voreingenommen
sein gegen **U4:** 60

prepare [prɪ'peə] vorbereiten
3 › U5: 102

preposition [prepə'zɪʃn] Präpo-
sition **2 › U1:** 23

present ['preznt] **1** Geschenk
2 › U4: 66; **2** Gegenwart
2 › U3: 48

president ['prezɪdənt] Präsident/
in **U1:** 15

pretty ['prɪti] hübsch **U5:** 78;
pretty well ziemlich gut **U4:** 60

price [praɪs] (Kauf-)Preis
1 › U4: 75

primary school ['praɪməri skuːl]
Grundschule **4 › U5:** 88

prime minister [praɪm 'mɪnɪstə]
Premierminister/in, Minister-
präsident/in **5 › U3:** 54;
(**3 › U1:** 9)

prince [prɪns] Prinz **U3:** 40

print [prɪnt] drucken **2 › U6:** 95

prison ['prɪzn] Gefängnis
5 › U3: 47; **be in prison** im
Gefängnis sein **5 › U3:** 47

prisoner ['prɪznə] Gefangene/r
5 › U4: 64

private school [praɪvət 'skuːl]
Privatschule **U4:** 73

probably ['prɒbəbli] wahrschein-
lich **3 › U3:** 56

problem ['prɒbləm] Problem
1 › U4: 70

produce [prə'djuːs] erzeugen,
produzieren **4 › U4:** 71

product ['prɒdʌkt]: **cleaning
product** Reinigungsmittel
5 › U4: 72

programme ['prəʊgræm]
1 (Fernseh-)Sendung **1 › U2:** 42;
2 Programm **3 › U2:** 33

progress ['prəʊgres] Fortschritt(e)
U5: 85

project ['prɒdʒekt] Projekt
1 › U2: 37

projector [prə'dʒektə] Projektor
3 › U5: 102; **on a projector** an
einem Projektor **3 › U5:** 102

prompt [prɒmpt] (Rollen-)Stich-
wort **5 › U3:** 53

pronunciation [prənʌnsi'eɪʃn]
Aussprache **3 › U2:** 36

protect [prə'tekt] (be)schützen
U3: 40

protective clothing [prətektɪv
'kləʊðɪŋ] Schutzkleidung **U5:** 78

protest [prə'test] protestieren
5 › U2: 34

protest ['prəʊtest] Protest
5 › U2: 35; **protest march**
['prəʊtest mɑːtʃ] Protestmarsch
4 › U3: 55

Protestant ['prɒtɪstənt]
Protestant/in; protestantisch
U1: 10

proud [praʊd] stolz **3 › U3:** 48

prove [pruːv] beweisen
4 › U4: 74

province ['prɒvɪns] Provinz
4 › U2: 28

PS [piː 'es] PS **2 › U6:** 98

psychological [saɪkə'lɒdʒɪkl]
psychisch **5 › U3:** 55

psychology [saɪ'kɒlədʒi]
Psychologie **4 › U1:** 15

pub [pʌb] Kneipe, Lokal **2 › U1:** 19

public ['pʌblɪk] öffentlich
4 › U2: 31; **public holiday**
gesetzlicher Feiertag **1 › U5:** 86

publicity [pʌb'lɪsəti] Werbung;
Publicity **4 › U4:** 74

pull [pʊl] ziehen **4 › U2:** 34;
pull down [pʊl 'daʊn] abreißen
4 › U4: 70

pullover ['pʊləʊvə] Pullover
U5: 84

pump [pʌmp] pumpen **U3:** 46

pupil ['pjuːpl] Schüler/in
1 › U5: 96

push [pʊʃ] **1** schieben **1 › U6:** 110;
2 stoßen **5 › U2:** 31

put [pʊt] (I put, I've put) stellen,
legen, (an einen Platz) tun
1 › U3: 58; **put (a fire) out**
(ein Feuer) löschen **5 › U5:** 87;
put in hineintun, -stecken
1 › U4: 71; **put out** hinausstellen
5 › U3: 53; **put up** (auf)bauen
U5: 81; **put up a tent** ein Zelt
aufstellen **4 › U2:** 34; **Put your
hands up, please.** Meldet euch.
1 › Intro: 12

put (→ put): **I put** ich stellte, ich
habe gestellt **3 › U3:** 54; **I've
put** ich habe gestellt **4 › U2:** 34

puzzle ['pʌzl] Rätsel **3 › U5:** 98

Q

quarter ['kwɔːtə] Viertel
3 › U1: 14; **quarter to/past**
Viertel vor/nach **2 › U5:** 82

queen [kwiːn] Königin **5 › U1:** 7

question ['kwestʃən] Frage
2 › U1: 16

queue [kjuː] (Warte-)Schlange
3 › U1: 14

quick [kwɪk] schnell **3 › U3:** 54

quiet ['kwaɪət] ruhig, leise, still
2 › U5: 78

quite [kwaɪt] ziemlich **3 › U1:** 13

quiz [kwɪz] Quiz **1 › U2:** 44

R

race [reɪs] **1** rasen **5 › U5:** 87;
he races against them er
läuft mit ihnen um die Wette
1 › U5: 92; **2** Rennen; (Wett-)
Lauf **5 › U2:** 29; **have a race**
um die Wette laufen **1 › U5:** 92

racehorse ['reɪs hɔːs] Rennpferd
U1: 19

radio ['reɪdiəʊ] Radio, Rundfunk
1 › U2: 48; **radio station**
['reɪdiəʊ steɪʃn] Radiosender
3 › U5: 89

radioactive [reɪdiəʊ'æktɪv] radio-
aktiv **4 › U4:** 71; **radioactive
level** [reɪdiəʊ'æktɪv levl] Wert/
Menge an Radioaktivität **U5:** 78

radioactivity [reɪdiəʊæk'tɪvəti]
Radioaktivität **U5:** 78

railway ['reɪlweɪ] Eisenbahn
U2: 24

rain [reɪn] **1** regnen **2 › U5:** 81;
2 Regen **5 › U5:** 82

rainbow ['reɪnbəʊ] Regenbogen 5>U5: 82; **rainbow nation** ['reɪnbəʊ neɪʃn] Regenbogennation *(Name für Südafrika aufgrund seiner ethnischen Vielfalt)* **U2:** 25

rainforest ['reɪnfɒrɪst] Regenwald **U5:** 74

rainy ['reɪni] regnerisch **2>U5:** 84

raise [reɪz] *(Spendengelder)* sammeln; *(Kinder)* großziehen **U1:** 14

ran [ræn] (→ run): **I ran** ich rannte, ich bin gerannt **1>U6:** 109

ranch [rɑːntʃ] Ranch **3>U3:** 52

rand [rænd] Rand *(südafrikanische Währung)* **U2:** 28

rang [ræŋ] (→ ring): **it rang** es klingelte, es läutete **SUM:** 92

ranger ['reɪndʒə] Aufseher/in *(in Nationalparks)* **4>U2:** 28; **ranger station** ['reɪndʒə steɪʃn] Wache der Parkaufsicht **4>U2:** 30

rank [ræŋk] einstufen, (ein)ordnen **U4:** 61

rap [ræp] Rap **3>U5:** 89

rat [ræt] Ratte **2>U2:** 35

rate [reɪt]: **rate (of HIV/AIDS)** (HIV/Aids-)Quote **U2:** 26

rather ['rɑːðə]: **they would rather have ...** sie hätten lieber ... **U5:** 76

reach [riːtʃ] erreichen **5>U5:** 90

reactor [ri'æktə] Reaktor **U5:** 79

read [riːd] (I read, I've read) lesen, vorlesen **1>U4:** 70

read [red] (→ read): **I read** ich las, ich habe gelesen **4>U1:** 12; **I've read** ich habe gelesen **4>U1:** 12

reader ['riːdə] Leser/in **5>U1:** 11

reading ['riːdɪŋ] Lesen **2>U2:** 28

ready ['redi] fertig **1>U5:** 92

real ['riːəl] echt, richtig **3>U1:** 12; eigentlich **5>U4:** 67

realistic [riːə'lɪstɪk] realistisch **4>U5:** 95

reality [ri'æləti] Wirklichkeit *U3:* 107

really ['rɪəli] sehr, echt **2>U2:** 35; wirklich **3>U2:** 33

reason ['riːzn] Grund **5>U2:** 30

receive [rɪ'siːv] erhalten **U2:** 35

reception [rɪ'sepʃn] Rezeption, Empfang *(Hotel)* **U1:** 20

receptionist [rɪ'sepʃənɪst] Empfangsmitarbeiter/in *(Hotel)* **U1:** 20

rechargeable [riː'tʃɑːdʒɪbl]: **rechargeable battery** Akku *(Batterie, die wieder aufgeladen werden kann)* **U2:** 35

recommend [rekə'mend] empfehlen **U4:** 69

record [rɪ'kɔːd] aufnehmen, aufzeichnen **2>U4:** 73

record ['rekɔːd] Schallplatte **3>U5:** 107

recycled [riː'saɪkld] recycelt, wiederverwertet **3>U1:** 13

red [red] rot **1>Intro:** 10

reduce [rɪ'djuːs] reduzieren, verringern **U5:** 75

referee [refə'riː] Referenz(geber/in) **5>U4:** 76

reference ['refərəns] Referenz, Zeugnis **4>U5:** 95

reggae ['regeɪ] Reggae(musik) **3>U1:** 13

region ['riːdʒən] Gegend, Region **5>U1:** 6

registration [redʒɪ'streɪʃn] Anwesenheitskontrolle *(in der Schule)* 2>U1: 25

regular ['regjələ] normal **3>U5:** 96; **regular customer** Stammkunde/Stammkundin **4>U5:** 94

relationship [rɪ'leɪʃnʃɪp] Beziehung, Verhältnis **5>U4:** 73

relative ['relətɪv] Verwandte/r **4>U1:** 12

relax [rɪ'læks] (sich) entspannen **3>U1:** 12

relaxed [rɪ'lækst] locker, entspannt **4>U4:** 74

release [rɪ'liːs] abgeben, freisetzen **U5:** 74

religion [rɪ'lɪdʒən] Religion **U3:** 40

remember [rɪ'membə] sich erinnern; daran denken **2>U4:** 62

remind [rɪ'maɪnd]: **remind you of ...** dich an ... erinnern **U4:** 63

remote control [rɪməʊt kən'trəʊl] Fernbedienung **U4:** 65

rent [rent] **1** mieten, leihen **2>U6:** 96; **2** Miete, Pacht (-gebühr) **U1:** 20

repair [rɪ'peə] reparieren **1>U6:** 105

repeat [rɪ'piːt] wiederholen **4>U2:** 36

replace [rɪ'pleɪs]: **replace ... with ...** ersetzen durch U3: 53

replacement [rɪ'pleɪsment] Ersatz(gerät) **U2:** 35

report [rɪ'pɔːt] **1** berichten **U3:** 53; **2** Bericht **2>U1:** 18

reporter [rɪ'pɔːtə] Reporter/in **3>U3:** 61

republic [rɪ'pʌblɪk] Republik **U1:** 9

rescue ['reskjuː] retten **5>U5:** 91

reserve [rɪ'zɜːv] Reservat, Schutzgebiet **U3:** 40

restaurant ['restrɒnt] Restaurant **2>U2:** 33

result [rɪ'zʌlt] Ergebnis **U3:** 46

return [rɪ'tɜːn] **1** zurückkehren; zurückkommen **5>U5:** 91; **2** zurückschicken **U2:** 35; **3** Hin- und Rückflug/-fahrt **5>U4:** 76; **return date** Datum des Rückflugs/der Rückfahrt **5>U4:** 76

revision [rɪ'vɪʒn] Wiederholung **5>U2:** 28

rhinoceros, rhinoceroses [raɪ'nɒsərəs, raɪ'nɒsərəsɪz] Nashorn **U2:** 24

rhyme (with) [raɪm] (sich) reimen (auf) **3>U1:** 19

rich [rɪtʃ] reich **2>A Legend:** 108; **rich in ...** reich an ... **5>U5:** 82

ride [raɪd]: **1 ride a bike** (I rode, I've ridden) Rad fahren **1>U3:** 58; **2 have a ride on the Cyclone** mit dem Cyclone fahren **4>U1:** 10

right [raɪt]: **1 on the right** auf der rechten Seite, rechts **3>U2:** 35; **to the right** rechts **1>U5:** 92; **turn right** nach rechts abbiegen **2>U3:** 52; **2** richtig, korrekt **2>U1:** 25; **oh, right ...** ah ja, ach so **U4:** 62; **You're right.** Du hast Recht./Stimmt. **1>U1:** 27; **3 right now** gerade jetzt **U4:** 64

ring [rɪŋ] (it rang, it has rung) klingeln, läuten **SUM:** 92

rise [raɪz] (it rose, it has risen) wachsen, (an)steigen **U5:** 75

risen ['rɪzn] (→ rise): **it has risen** es ist gewachsen, es ist (an)gestiegen **U5:** 75

risk [rɪsk] Risiko **3>U2:** 33; **take risks** Risiken eingehen **3>U2:** 33

rival ['raɪvl] Rivale/Rivalin **5>U4:** 66

river ['rɪvə] Fluss **2>U5:** 80

road [rəʊd] Straße **1>Intro:** 18

DICTIONARY

rock [rɒk] **1** Fels **5 › U3:** 45;
rock painting Felszeichnung
5 › U5: 82; **2** Rock(musik)
3 › U1: 13; **rock and roll** Rock
and Roll **3 › U5:** 102

rocky ['rɒki] felsig **4 › U4:** 68

rodeo ['rəʊdiəʊ] Rodeo **3 › U4:** 69

role [rəʊl] Rolle **4 › U2:** 42;
role-play ['rəʊl pleɪ] Rollenspiel
3 › U1: 17

roll [rəʊl] Brötchen **1 › U3:** 54

roller coaster ['rəʊlə kəʊstə]
Achterbahn **4 › U1:** 10

Roman ['rəʊmən] römisch
1 › U6: 102

romantic [rəʊ'mæntɪk] romantisch
U3: 42

roof [ruːf] Dach **5 › U5:** 87; **hit
the roof** an die Decke gehen
U4: 71

room [ruːm] Zimmer, Raum
1 › U1: 32; Platz, Raum
4 › U1: 12

rope [rəʊp] Seil 2 › A Legend: 110

rose [rəʊz] (→ rise): **it rose** es
wuchs, es stieg (an) U5: 75

round [raʊnd] um ... herum
2 › U3: 46; **look round the
shops** sich die Geschäfte
ansehen **4 › U1:** 10

row [rəʊ] Reihe **3 › U5:** 96

row [raʊ] Streit U4: 60

royal ['rɔɪəl]: **Royal Flying Doctor
Service** Königlicher Fliegender
Ärzteservice *(in Australien)*
5 › U5: 85

rubber ['rʌbə] Radiergummi
1 › U1: 32

rubbish ['rʌbɪʃ] **1** Abfall, Müll
2 › U4: 62; **2** Blödsinn, Quatsch;
Mist **5 › U1:** 20

rucksack ['rʌksæk] Rucksack
3 › U1: 14

rugby ['rʌgbi] Rugby **3 › U1:** 27

ruined ['ruːɪnd]: **ruined house**
verfallenes Haus U1: 10

rule [ruːl]: **break the rules** gegen
die Regeln verstoßen U2: 31

ruler ['ruːlə] Lineal **1 › U1:** 32

run [rʌn] (I ran, I've run) rennen,
laufen **1 › U4:** 78; **it can run at
70 km/h** es kann 70 Stundenkilometer schnell laufen
5 › U3: 44; **running water**
fließendes Wasser U2: 24

rupee [ruː'piː] Rupie *(indische
Währung)* U3: 41

Russia ['rʌʃə] Russland U3: 40

RV (= recreational vehicle)
['ɑː 'viː, rekri'eɪʃənl 'viːəkl]
Wohnmobil **3 › U5:** 92

S

sad [sæd] traurig **4 › U1:** 13

safe [seɪf] sicher, in Sicherheit
3 › U1: 8

safety ['seɪfti]: **safety equipment**
Sicherheitsausrüstung U5: 78

said [sed] (→ say): **I said** ich sagte,
ich habe gesagt **1 › U3:** 58; **I've
said** ich habe gesagt **3 › U4:** 73

sail [seɪl] (Schiff, Boot) fahren
5 › U1: 16

sailing ['seɪlɪŋ] Segeln **3 › U2:** 31

salad ['sæləd] Salat **3 › U4:** 73

salary ['sæləri] Gehalt U3: 47

sale [seɪl]: **the Christmas sales**
der Weihnachtsausverkauf
5 › U3: 49

salty ['sɔːlti] salzig **5 › U5:** 90

same [seɪm]: **the same** der-/die-/
dasselbe **1 › U4:** 75; **at the
same time** zur gleichen Zeit,
gleichzeitig **3 › U5:** 95

samosa [sə'məʊsə] Samosa
*(würzig gefüllte, knusprige
Teigtasche)* **3 › U1:** 14

sand [sænd] Sand U5: 75; **sand
storm** Sandsturm U5: 77

sandwich ['sænwɪdʒ] Sandwich
(belegtes Brot) **1 › U3:** 56;
sandwich bar ['sænwɪdʒ baː]
„Sandwichladen", Stehcafé
3 › U1: 12

sandy ['sændi] sandig, Sand- U1: 9

sang [sæŋ] (→ sing): **I sang** ich
sang, ich habe gesungen
3 › U5: 102

sat [sæt] (→ sit): **I sat** ich saß, ich
habe gesessen **3 › U1:** 14

satellite ['sætəlaɪt] Satellit,
Satelliten- **5 › U3:** 55

Saturday ['sætədeɪ] Samstag
1 › U4: 80

sauce [sɔːs] Soße **1 › U3:** 59

sauna ['sɔːnə] Sauna **2 › U6:** 94

sausage ['sɒsɪdʒ] Würstchen,
Wurst **2 › U4:** 62

save [seɪv] **1** retten **5 › U5:** 85;
2 save money Geld sparen
U5: 75

saw [sɔː] (→ see): **I saw** ich sah,
ich habe gesehen **1 › U5:** 91

say [seɪ] (I said, I've said) sagen
1 › U3: 53

scared [skeəd]: **I'm scared** ich
habe Angst **3 › U4:** 74

scary ['skeəri] unheimlich
3 › U2: 31

scene [siːn] Szene **5 › U1:** 13;
(1 › U5: 90)

scheme [skiːm] Projekt,
Programm U4: 69

school [skuːl] Schule **1 › Intro:** 12;
school exchange Schüleraustausch U5: 76

science ['saɪəns] (Natur-)Wissen-
schaft **2 › U1:** 17

scientist ['saɪəntɪst] Wissen-
schaftler/in **5 › U5:** 86

scissors ['sɪzəz] Schere **4 › U1:** 16

score [skɔː] Spielstand, Punktzahl
4 › U4: 74

Scotland ['skɒtlənd] Schottland
2 › U1: 12

Scottish ['skɒtɪʃ] schottisch;
Schotte/Schottin **3 › U3:** 48

screen [skriːn] Bildschirm U2: 35;
screen door zusätzliche Außen-
tür zum Schutz vor Insekten
U5: 81

script [skrɪpt]: **phonetic script**
Lautschrift 4 › U1: 19

sea [siː] Meer, die See **1 › U5:** 87;
sea water Meerwasser, See-
wasser **5 › U5:** 90

sea kayaking ['siː kaɪækɪŋ]
Seekajak fahren *U1: 103*

seal [siːl] Seehund **5 › U2:** 26

search engine ['sɜːtʃ endʒɪn]
Suchmaschine **4 › U3:** 62

seaside ['siːsaɪd]: **at the seaside**
am Meer **1 › U5:** 86

season ['siːzn] **1** Jahreszeit
1 › U5: 99; **2** Saison **4 › U4:** 74

seat [siːt] Sitz, Platz **3 › U5:** 96

second ['sekənd] zweite/r/s
2 › U4: 72

second-hand [sekənd 'hænd]
gebraucht **1 › U4:** 69

secondary school ['sekəndri skuːl]
weiterführende Schule
5 › U4: 66

secret ['siːkrət] heimlich U4: 70

security [sɪ'kjʊərəti] Sicherheit
U2: 27

see [siː] (I saw, I've seen) sehen
1 › Intro: 10; **..., you see.**
..., verstehen Sie? **3 › U5:** 94;
I see. Verstehe. **4 › U2:** 32;
See you ... Wir sehen uns ...
1 › U4: 69; **See you later.** Bis
später. **1 › U1:** 28; **Then we'll
see.** Dann sehen wir weiter.
4 › U5: 96

seem [siːm] scheinen, erscheinen
3 › U1: 14

seen [siːn] (→ see): **I've seen** ich
habe gesehen **3 › U3:** 52

selfish ['selfɪʃ] egoistisch U1: 14

sell [sel] (I sold, I've sold) verkau-
fen **1 › U4:** 69

send [send] (I sent, I've sent) senden, schicken **1 ▸ U4:** 74

sense [sens]: **have a good sense of humour** Sinn für Humor haben **5 ▸ U4:** 70

sensible ['sensəbl] vernünftig **U4:** 64

sent [sent] (→ send): **I sent** ich schickte, ich habe geschickt **2 ▸ U3:** 47; **I've sent** ich habe geschickt **3 ▸ U3:** 53

sentence ['sentəns] Satz **2 ▸ U1:** 20

separate ['sepəreɪt] trennen **U1:** 20

September [sep'tembə] September **1 ▸ U5:** 98

serious ['sɪərɪəs] ernst, ernsthaft **5 ▸ U3:** 50

serve [sɜːv] **1** servieren; **2** bedienen **4 ▸ U5:** 93

service ['sɜːvɪs]: **Royal Flying Doctor Service** Königlicher Fliegender Ärzteservice *(in Australien)* **5 ▸ U5:** 85

set [set] Satz *U3: 107*

settlement ['setlmənt] Siedlung **5 ▸ U5:** 87

seven ['sevn] sieben **1 ▸ Intro:** 15

seventeen [sevn'tiːn] siebzehn **1 ▸ U2:** 48

seventeenth [sevn'tiːnθ] siebzehnte/r/s **2 ▸ U4:** 72

seventh ['sevnθ] siebte/r/s **2 ▸ U4:** 72

seventy ['sevnti] siebzig **1 ▸ U2:** 48

several ['sevrəl] mehrere, verschiedene **U4:** 61

sex [seks] Sex **U2:** 26

shake [ʃeɪk] (I shook, I've shaken) schütteln **U4:** 64

shaken ['ʃeɪkən] (→ shake): **I've shaken** ich habe geschüttelt **U4:** 64; **he had shaken** er hatte geschüttelt **U4:** 64

shall [ʃəl, ʃæl]: **Shall we ...?** Sollen/Wollen wir ...? **4 ▸ U4:** 76

shaman ['ʃeɪmən] Schamane, Schamanin **5 ▸ U2:** 31

share [ʃeə] teilen **5 ▸ U3:** 54

sharp [ʃɑːp] scharf, spitz **5 ▸ U3:** 54

she [ʃiː] sie **1 ▸ U1:** 25; **she's (= she is)** [ʃiːz] sie ist **1 ▸ U1:** 25

sheep [ʃiːp] Schaf, Schafe **1 ▸ U5:** 90

shelf, shelves [ʃelf, ʃelvz] Regal, Regale **5 ▸ U3:** 52

Sheriff ['ʃerɪf] Sheriff **1 ▸ U2:** 49

shine [ʃaɪn] (it shone, it has shone) scheinen, glänzen, leuchten **5 ▸ U2:** 29; **the sun is shining** die Sonne scheint **1 ▸ U2:** 42

ship [ʃɪp] Schiff **2 ▸ A Legend:** 111

shirt [ʃɜːt] Hemd; Fußballtrikot **1 ▸ U6:** 107

shiver ['ʃɪvə] zittern **4 ▸ U2:** 34

shoe [ʃuː] Schuh **3 ▸ U5:** 107

shone [ʃɒn] (→ shine): **it shone** es leuchtete, es hat geleuchtet **5 ▸ U2:** 29; **it has shone** es hat geleuchtet **5 ▸ U2:** 29

shook [ʃʊk] (→ shake): **I shook** ich schüttelte **U4:** 64

shop [ʃɒp] Laden, Geschäft **1 ▸ Intro:** 18; **go to the shops** einen Einkaufsbummel machen; einkaufen gehen **1 ▸ U4:** 76; **shop assistant** ['ʃɒp əsɪstənt] Verkäufer/Verkäuferin **4 ▸ U5:** 89

shopping ['ʃɒpɪŋ] Einkaufen **3 ▸ U1:** 10; **go shopping** einen Einkaufsbummel machen; einkaufen gehen **4 ▸ U1:** 11; **shopping centre** Einkaufszentrum **1 ▸ U6:** 109; **shopping mall** (AE) Einkaufszentrum **3 ▸ U4:** 73

short [ʃɔːt] kurz **2 ▸ Intro:** 7

shortage ['ʃɔːtɪdʒ] Mangel **U5:** 74

shortbread ['ʃɔːtbred] *eine Art Butterkeks* **2 ▸ U4:** 68

should [ʃʊd, ʃəd]: **I should** ich soll/sollte **3 ▸ U2:** 32

shouldn't [ʃʊdnt]: **I shouldn't** ich soll/sollte nicht **3 ▸ U2:** 33

shout [ʃaʊt] schreien, laut rufen **3 ▸ U2:** 34

show [ʃəʊ] **1** (I showed, I've shown) zeigen **2 ▸ U6:** 94; **show off** [ʃəʊ 'ɒf] angeben **4 ▸ U1:** 10; **2** (Fernseh-, Radio-) Sendung **1 ▸ U5:** 94

shower ['ʃaʊə] Dusche **3 ▸ U5:** 92

shown [ʃəʊn] (→ show): **I've shown** ich habe gezeigt **5 ▸ U5:** 84

Shut up! [ʃʌt 'ʌp] Halt den Mund! **4 ▸ U1:** 12

shy [ʃaɪ] schüchtern **4 ▸ U3:** 53

sick [sɪk]: **That makes me sick.** Das macht mich ganz krank. Das widert mich an. **5 ▸ U2:** 34

side [saɪd] Seite **2 ▸ U6:** 98

sight [saɪt] Sehenswürdigkeit **3 ▸ U1:** 8

sign [saɪn] **1** Schild **1 ▸ U5:** 91; **2** Anzeichen **5 ▸ U3:** 44; **3** unterschreiben **4 ▸ U1:** 17

silent ['saɪlənt] still, ruhig **U5:** 78

silly ['sɪli] dumm, albern **3 ▸ U4:** 68

simple ['sɪmpl] einfach **4 ▸ U2:** 30

simplified ['sɪmplɪfaɪd] vereinfacht *U3: 107*

simulation [sɪmjʊ'leɪʃn] Simulation **3 ▸ U4:** 72

since [sɪns] seit **4 ▸ U2:** 33

sing [sɪŋ] (I sang, I've sung) singen **1 ▸ U6:** 105

singer ['sɪŋə] Sänger/in **3 ▸ U1:** 15

single ['sɪŋgl] **1** einzig; einzeln **5 ▸ U4:** 64; **2** ledig **5 ▸ U4:** 70; **3** einfache/r Fahrt/Flug **5 ▸ U4:** 76; **4** Single (Musikstück; Platte) **3 ▸ U5:** 107

sink [sɪŋk]: **kitchen sink** Küchenspüle **3 ▸ U1:** 14

sir [sɜː]: **Dear Sir/Madam, ...** Sehr geehrte Damen und Herren, ... **3 ▸ U4:** 82

sister ['sɪstə] Schwester **1 ▸ U2:** 39; **brothers or sisters** Geschwister **4 ▸ U1:** 8

sit [sɪt] (I sat, I've sat) sich setzen; sitzen **1 ▸ U1:** 25; **Sit down, please.** Setzt euch./Setz dich. **1 ▸ Intro:** 12

sitar [sɪ'tɑː] Sitar *(indische Laute)* **3 ▸ U5:** 107

situation [sɪtʃu'eɪʃn] Situation **2 ▸ A Legend:** 109

six [sɪks] sechs **1 ▸ Intro:** 15

sixteen [sɪk'stiːn] sechzehn **1 ▸ U2:** 48

sixteenth [sɪk'stiːnθ] sechzehnte/r/s **2 ▸ U4:** 72

sixth [sɪksθ] sechste/r/s **2 ▸ U4:** 72

sixty ['sɪksti] sechzig **1 ▸ U2:** 48

size [saɪz] Größe **U2:** 29

skateboard ['skeɪtbɔːd] Skateboard **2 ▸ Intro:** 11

skateboarding ['skeɪtbɔːdɪŋ] Skateboardfahren **3 ▸ U1:** 12

skates [skeɪts] Inlineskates, Rollschuhe **2 ▸ Intro:** 8

skating ['skeɪtɪŋ] Roll-, Schlittschuhlaufen **2 ▸ U1:** 18

ski resort [skiː rɪ'zɔːt] Skiort **5 ▸ U4:** 69

skiing ['skiːɪŋ] Skifahren **5 ▸ U1:** 9

skills [skɪlz] Fähigkeiten, Erfahrung **5 ▸ U4:** 68; Kenntnisse, Fertigkeiten **5 ▸ U3:** 51

169

one hundred and sixty-nine

DICTIONARY

skin [skɪn] Haut **5 › U2:** 26
sky [skaɪ] Himmel **U5:** 78
skyscraper ['skaɪskreɪpə]
Wolkenkratzer, Hochhaus
4 › U1: 8
slam [slæm]: **slam the door** die
Tür zuknallen **4 › U1:** 13
sled [sled] Schlitten **5 › U2:** 29
sleep [sliːp] (I slept, I've slept)
schlafen **2 › U5:** 82
sleeping ['sliːpɪŋ] Schlafen
2 › U5: 82; **sleeping-bag**
['sliːpɪŋbæg] Schlafsack
4 › U2: 30
slept [slept] (→ sleep): **I slept** ich
schlief, ich habe geschlafen
2 › U5: 87; **I've slept** ich habe
geschlafen **4 › U2:** 34
slogan ['sləʊgən] Slogan, Werbe-
spruch **1 › U6:** 112
slope [sləʊp] Piste **5 › U1:** 10
slow [sləʊ] langsam **5 › U2:** 40
small [smɔːl] klein **1 › U2:** 37
smart [smɑːt] (AE) clever, klug
4 › U3: 54
smell [smel] **1** riechen, duften
5 › U3: 49; **2** Geruch **U1:** 20
smile [smaɪl] lächeln **1 › U6:** 109
smoke [sməʊk] **1** rauchen
2 › U1: 18; **2** Rauch **5 › U5:** 87;
"Smoking kills." ['sməʊkɪŋ]
„Rauchen tötet." **2 › U1:** 18
smoker ['sməʊkə] Raucher/in
U3: 43
smoothie ['smuːði] *Getränk aus
Obst mit Jogurt* 1 › U6: 110
smuggler ['smʌglə] Schmuggler/
in **2 › U3:** 45
snack [snæk] Snack **1 › U3:** 53
snake [sneɪk] Schlange
4 › U2: 28
sneaker ['sniːkə] (AE) Turnschuh
4 › U1: 10
snorkel ['snɔːkl] schnorcheln
5 › U3: 49
snorkelling ['snɔːkəlɪŋ]
Schnorcheln **5 › U3:** 49
snow [snəʊ] **1** schneien
2 › U6: 104; **2** Schnee
5 › U2: 26
snowboarding ['snəʊbɔːdɪŋ] Snow-
boarden, Snowboardfahren
5 › U1: 10
snowy ['snəʊi] verschneit
2 › U6: 99
so [səʊ] so **1 › U5:** 90; also, daher
3 › U1: 14; **so far** ['səʊ fɑː]
bisher **U4:** 65; **so that** damit
3 › U5: 88; **So what?** Na und?
U5: 76

soap [səʊp] **1** Seife **5 › U4:** 77;
2 soap (opera) Seifenoper
5 › U4: 72; (**2 › U1:** 19)
social ['səʊʃl] sozial, gesellschaft-
lich **5 › U2:** 31; **social studies**
[səʊʃl 'stʌdɪz] Sozialwissenschaft-
en **4 › U3:** 50
sock [sɒk] Socke **2 › U4:** 63
soda ['səʊdə]: **lemon soda** (AE)
Zitronensprudel **3 › U4:** 76
sofa ['səʊfə] Sofa **U4:** 65
soft [sɒft] weich(herzig), ver-
weichlicht **3 › U2:** 32
software ['sɒftweə] Software
1 › U4: 69
soggy ['sɒgi] matschig, durch-
geweicht **U4:** 65
sold [səʊld] (→ sell): **I sold** ich
verkaufte, ich habe verkauft
2 › U5: 87
solo singer ['səʊləʊ sɪŋə] Solo-
Sänger/in *U1: 103*
some [sʌm] **1** einige, ein paar
1 › Intro: 11; **2** etwas **3 › U1:** 8
somebody ['sʌmbədi] jemand
2 › U5: 82
somehow ['sʌmhaʊ] irgendwie
U4: 64
someone ['sʌmwʌn] jemand
U4: 64
something ['sʌmθɪŋ] etwas
2 › U1: 16; **something special/...**
etwas Besonderes/... **4 › U1:** 14
sometimes ['sʌmtaɪmz] manchmal **1 › U5:** 86
somewhere ['sʌmweə]
irgendwo(hin) **3 › U5:** 88
son [sʌn] Sohn **1 › U3:** 60
song [sɒŋ] Lied **2 › U1:** 25
soon [suːn] bald **2 › U2:** 35
sorry ['sɒri]: **feel sorry for
yourself** dich selbst bemitleiden
4 › U1: 15; **I'm sorry.** Es tut mir
leid. **1 › U1:** 27; **I'm sorry for
them** sie tun mir leid
4 › U2: 43; **I'm sorry you ...**
Tut mir leid, dass du ...
3 › U4: 74
sort of ['sɔːt ɒv] Art (von) **U2:** 27
sound [saʊnd] **1** klingen, sich
anhören **3 › U1:** 14; **It sounds
fun.** Es hört sich gut an. / Es
klingt gut. **3 › U1:** 14; **2** Laut
3 › U2: 36; **3** Sound **4 › U3:** 56
soup [suːp] Suppe **2 › U4:** 62
south [saʊθ] (nach) Süden;
Süd-; südlich **3 › U3:** 48; **South
Africa** [saʊθ 'æfrɪkə] Südafrika
Intro: 7; **South African**
[saʊθ 'æfrɪkən] südafrikanisch;
Südafrikaner/in **Intro:** 7

southeast [saʊθ'iːst]: **the
southeast** der Südosten
5 › U3: 45
southwest [saʊθ'west] Südwesten
4 › U5: 88
souvenir [suːvə'nɪə] Souvenir,
Andenken **1 › U6:** 102
Soviet Union [səʊviət 'juːnɪən]
Sowjetunion **U5:** 78
space [speɪs] **1** Platz, Raum
2 › U6: 96; **2** Weltraum
3 › U4: 69; **Space Center**
Weltraumzentrum **3 › U4:** 69;
space shuttle ['speɪs 'ʃʌtl]
Spaceshuttle **3 › U4:** 72
spaghetti [spə'geti] Spaghetti
1 › U3: 59
Spain [speɪn] Spanien **2 › Intro:** 11
Spanish ['spænɪʃ] spanisch; Spanisch; Spanier/Spanierin(nen)
3 › U4: 70
speak [spiːk] (I spoke, I've spoken)
sprechen **2 › U1:** 18; **French-
speaking** französischsprachig
5 › U1: 6
speaker ['spiːkə] Sprecher/in
Intro: 7
special ['speʃl] besondere/r/s
1 › U4: 74; **special offer**
Sonderangebot **2 › U4:** 68;
That's special! Das ist etwas
Besonderes! **3 › U1:** 13; **What's
special about ...?** Was ist das
Besondere an ...? **5 › U2:** 27
spectacular [spek'tækjələ] sensa-
tionell, spektakulär **4 › U1:** 8
spell [spel] buchstabieren
1 › U1: 32
spelling ['spelɪŋ] Rechtschreibung
4 › U1: 19
spend [spend] (I spent, I've spent)
1 verbringen **3 › U2:** 28;
2 ausgeben **5 › U2:** 32; **spend
money on** Geld ausgeben für
U1: 14
spent [spent] (→ spend): **I spent**
ich verbrachte, ich habe verbracht **3 › U2:** 28; **I've spent**
ich habe verbracht **3 › U4:** 71
spin [spɪn] drehen 2 › U4: 69
spire ['spaɪə] Turm; Kirchturm-
spitze **U1:** 9
split up [splɪt 'ʌp] (they split up,
they've split up) sich trennen
U1: 103
spoke [spəʊk] (→ speak): **I spoke**
ich sprach, ich habe gesprochen
3 › U4: 71
spoken ['spəʊkən] (→ speak): **I've
spoken** ich habe gesprochen
3 › U4: 134

sport [spɔːt] Sport(art) **1 ▸ U4:** 70

sports centre ['spɔːts sentə] Sport-
zentrum **1 ▸ U6:** 104

sports facilities ['spɔːts fə'sɪlətiz]
Sportanlagen **4 ▸ U4:** 68

spot [spɒt] Fleck *U5: 81*

spray [spreɪ] (be)sprühen, (be)
spritzen **5 ▸ U5:** 87

spread [spred] (it spread, it has
spread) sich ausbreiten *U3:* 48

spring [sprɪŋ] Frühling **1 ▸ U5:** 86

square [skweə] **1** Platz *(in einer
Stadt)* *U5:* 78; **square (sq)**
2 Quadrat, Quadrat- **5 ▸ U5:** 84

stadium ['steɪdiəm] Stadion
4 ▸ U4: 68

stage [steɪdʒ] Bühne **3 ▸ U5:** 103

stall [stɔːl] (Verkaufs-)Stand
1 ▸ U4: 69

stallholder ['stɔːlhəʊldə]
Standbesitzer/in **1 ▸ U4:** 69

stamp [stæmp] Briefmarke
2 ▸ U5: 85

stand [stænd] (I stood, I've stood)
stehen **1 ▸ U6:** 105; **stand up**
[stænd 'ʌp] aufstehen, aufrecht
stehen **1 ▸ U4:** 78

star [stɑː] Star **1 ▸ U4:** 74

start [stɑːt] **1** beginnen, starten
1 ▸ U5: 53; **2** Start **1 ▸ U5:** 92;
they started eating sie fingen
an zu essen **2 ▸ U3:** 50

starve [stɑːv] verhungern *U1:* 10

state [steɪt] Staat; Bundesstaat
3 ▸ U4: 69; **state capital**
Hauptstadt des Bundesstaates
3 ▸ U5: 89

station ['steɪʃn] Bahnhof
2 ▸ U3: 48; Haltestelle
3 ▸ U1: 14; **(cattle/sheep)**
station *große australische
Farm* 5 ▸ U5: 84; **radio station**
Radiosender **3 ▸ U5:** 89;
TV station Fernsehsender
5 ▸ U1: 8

Statue of Liberty ['stætʃuː əv
'lɪbəti] Freiheitsstatue 4 ▸ U1: 8

stay [steɪ] **1** bleiben **1 ▸ U5:** 87;
stay (with) übernachten (bei),
wohnen (bei) **2 ▸ Intro:** 8;
2 Aufenthalt *U2:* 35

steak [steɪk] Steak *U2:* 27

steal [stiːl] (I stole, I've stolen)
stehlen **5 ▸ U3:** 46

steam roll ['stiːm rəʊl] glatt
walzen *U5: 81*

steel [stiːl] Stahl *U3:* 46;
steel-making ['stiːl meɪkɪŋ]
Stahlproduktion(s-) *U3:* 46;
steel plant Stahlfabrik *U3:* 46

steep [stiːp] steil **3 ▸ U2:** 34

stepfather ['stepfɑːðə] Stiefvater
1 ▸ U3: 60

stepmother ['stepmʌðə]
Stiefmutter **1 ▸ U3:** 60

stick [stɪk] Stock *U3: 107*

sticker ['stɪkə] Sticker, Aufkleber
2 ▸ U2: 29

still [stɪl] **1** bewegungslos, still
1 ▸ U6: 105; **2** noch **2 ▸ U2:** 35;
3 trotzdem **5 ▸ U2:** 29

stingray ['stɪŋreɪ] Stachelrochen
5 ▸ U3: 54

stole [stəʊl] (→ steal): **I stole**
ich stahl, ich habe gestohlen
5 ▸ U3: 46

stolen ['stəʊlən] (→ steal): **I've**
stolen ich habe gestohlen
5 ▸ U3: 46

stop [stɒp] **1** aufhören **3 ▸ U2:** 38;
Stop it! Hör(t) auf! **1 ▸ U5:** 90;
they stopped eating ... sie
hörten auf, ... zu essen *U5:* 78;
2 anhalten, stoppen **4 ▸ U1:** 11

store [stɔː] (AE) Laden, Geschäft
4 ▸ U2: 30

storm [stɔːm] Unwetter, Gewitter
5 ▸ U2: 31

story ['stɔːri] Geschichte,
Erzählung **2 ▸ A Legend:** 108

storyline ['stɔːrɪlaɪn] Handlungs-
strang, Handlung **5 ▸ U4:** 64

storyteller ['stɔːritelə] Erzähler/in
1 ▸ U5: 90

stove [stəʊv] Herd **3 ▸ U5:** 92

straight [streɪt]: **go straight on**
geradeaus (weiter)gehen
2 ▸ U3: 52; **straight out of the**
box direkt aus der Verpackung
U4: 65

strange [streɪndʒ] merkwürdig,
seltsam **3 ▸ U4:** 68

strawberry ['strɔːbəri] Erdbeere
3 ▸ U5: 96

street [striːt] Straße **2 ▸ Intro:** 9

stress [stres] **1** betonen
4 ▸ U5: 99; **2** Stress *U4:* 60

strict [strɪkt] streng *U4:* 73

string [strɪŋ] Schnur, Bindfaden
2 ▸ U4: 63

strive [straɪv]: **strive for** streben
nach *U2: 25*

strong [strɒŋ] stark **5 ▸ U4:** 72

student ['stjuːdnt] Schüler/in;
Student/in **2 ▸ U1:** 14

studio ['stjuːdiəʊ] Studio
3 ▸ U5: 96

study ['stʌdi] studieren
5 ▸ U3: 55

stuff [stʌf]: **... and stuff.** ... und
so. **4 ▸ U3:** 51; **kids stuff**
['kɪdz 'stʌf] Kinderkram *U2:* 30

stupid ['stjuːpɪd] blöd, dämlich
1 ▸ U1: 23

style [staɪl] Stil **1 ▸ U6:** 108

subject ['sʌbdʒɪkt] (Schul-)Fach
2 ▸ U1: 20

suburb ['sʌbɜːb] Vorort
2 ▸ U6: 94

subway ['sʌbweɪ] (AE) U-Bahn
4 ▸ U1: 8

successful [sək'sesfl] erfolgreich
3 ▸ U5: 91; **she was successful**
sie hatte Erfolg **3 ▸ U5:** 91

suddenly ['sʌdnli] plötzlich, auf
einmal **2 ▸ U2:** 30

suffer ['sʌfə] leiden **5 ▸ U2:** 31

sugar ['ʃʊgə] Zucker **3 ▸ U4:** 76

suggest [sə'dʒest] vorschlagen
U4: 109

summary ['sʌməri] Zusammen-
fassung 1 ▸ U1: 34

summer ['sʌmə] Sommer
1 ▸ U5: 86

sun [sʌn] Sonne **1 ▸ U2:** 42

sunbathe ['sʌnbeɪð] sonnenbaden,
in der Sonne liegen **5 ▸ U2:** 29

Sunday ['sʌndeɪ] Sonntag
1 ▸ U4: 69

sung [sʌŋ] (→ sing) es wird
gesungen *U5: 81*

sunglasses ['sʌnglɑːsɪz] Sonnen-
brille **4 ▸ U2:** 30

sunny ['sʌni] sonnig **2 ▸ U6:** 104

super ['suːpə] super, toll
1 ▸ U3: 58

supermarket ['suːpəmɑːkɪt]
Supermarkt **1 ▸ U5:** 87

support [sə'pɔːt] Fan sein von;
unterstützen **5 ▸ U1:** 11

suppose [sə'pəʊz]: **I suppose** ich
glaube, ich nehme an **SUM:** 93

sure [ʃʊə] (AE) klar; echt
3 ▸ U4: 71; **I'm sure** ich bin
sicher **1 ▸ U5:** 92; **make sure**
sichergehen *U4:* 64

surf [sɜːf] surfen **4 ▸ U5:** 88;
surf the Internet (for ...) im
Internet (nach ...) suchen
3 ▸ U5: 92

surname ['sɜːneɪm] Nachname,
Familienname **5 ▸ U4:** 68

surprise [sə'praɪz] Überraschung;
Überraschungs- **1 ▸ U3:** 58

surprised [sə'praɪzd] überrascht
2 ▸ U6: 98

surprising [sə'praɪzɪŋ] über-
raschend, verwunderlich *U1:* 20

survey ['sɜːveɪ] Umfrage, Unter-
suchung 5 ▸ U4: 75

→ DICTIONARY

swam [swæm] (→ swim): **I swam** ich schwamm, ich bin geschwommen **2›Grammatik:** 179

swap [swɒp] **1** tauschen **2›U5:** 81; **2** Tausch **2›U5:** 81

sweatshirt ['swetʃɜːt] Sweatshirt **1›U3:** 62

sweatshop ['swetʃɒp] Sweatshop *(Ausbeutungsbetrieb)* U3: 42

Sweden ['swiːdn] Schweden **U5:** 78

sweet [swiːt] **1** süß, niedlich **2›U2:** 35; **2** Süßigkeit, Bonbon **1›U4:** 79

sweetie ['swiːti] „Schätzchen", Süße/Süßer **3›U3:** 54

swim [swɪm] (I swam, I've swum) schwimmen **1›U5:** 85

swimmer ['swɪmə] Schwimmer/in **5›U4:** 70

swimming ['swɪmɪŋ] Schwimmen **2›U1:** 17; **swimming costume** ['swɪmɪŋ kɒstjuːm] Badeanzug **5›U3:** 49; **swimming pool** Schwimmbad, Freibad; Schwimmbecken **2›Intro:** 11

swinging hot spot [swɪŋɪŋ 'hɒt spɒt] *(infml)* „heißer Schuppen" *(Club/Disko, wo viel los ist)* U5: 81

switch [swɪtʃ]: **switch off** ausschalten **SUM:** 98

Switzerland ['swɪtsələnd] die Schweiz **U5:** 78

swum [swʌm] (→ swim): **I've swum** ich bin geschwommen **2›Grammatik:** 179

syllable ['sɪləbl] Silbe **4›U5:** 99

symbol ['sɪmbl] Symbol *U1: 103*

Syria ['sɪriə] Syrien **U5:** 74

system ['sɪstəm] System **5›U1:** 10

T

table ['teɪbl] Tisch **1›Intro:** 10; **table tennis** Tischtennis **1›U6:** 105

taco ['tækəʊ] Taco *(knuspriger, gefüllter Teigfladen)* **3›U4:** 73

take [teɪk] (I took, I've taken) **1** nehmen, mitnehmen **2›U3:** 47; **2** bringen, mitbringen **2›U6:** 96; **3** einnehmen **5›U1:** 17; **4** dauern **4›U2:** 32; **Don't take long.** Mach' nicht so lange. **4›U2:** 31; **take a message** etwas ausrichten **3›U2:** 36; **take a test** eine Prüfung machen **U4:** 60;

take notes sich Notizen machen **4›U1:** 11; **take notes on the weather** sich Notizen über das Wetter machen **4›U2:** 29; **take over** übernehmen **5›U3:** 54; **take part in: he took part in** teilnehmen an: er nahm teil an **U1:** 14; **take photos** Fotos machen **1›U4:** 76; **take place** stattfinden, spielen *(Handlung)* **5›U4:** 64; **take risks** Risiken eingehen **3›U2:** 33; **take the dog for a walk** mit dem Hund rausgehen/spazierengehen **2›U1:** 19

take-away ... ['teɪk əweɪ] ... zum Mitnehmen **1›U3:** 53

taken ['teɪkən] (→ take): **I've taken** ich habe genommen **3›U3:** 50

talk (to) [tɔːk] **1** reden (mit), sprechen (mit) **2›U2:** 32; **2** Vortrag **3›U5:** 102; **give a talk** einen Vortrag halten **3›U5:** 102

tall [tɔːl] groß (gewachsen); hoch **5›U4:** 70

tank [tæŋk] Tank **5›U5:** 87

taste [teɪst] schmecken **U2:** 27

taught [tɔːt] (→ teach): **I taught** ich brachte bei, ich habe beigebracht **4›U3:** 52; **I've taught** ich habe beigebracht **4›U3:** 52

tax [tæks] Steuer(n) **U1:** 15

taxi ['tæksi] Taxi **2›U6:** 97

tea [tiː] Tee **2›U5:** 82

teach [tiːtʃ] (I taught, I've taught) beibringen, unterrichten, lehren **4›U3:** 52

teacher ['tiːtʃə] Lehrer/in **1›Intro:** 10

team [tiːm] Team, Mannschaft **1›U1:** 23

tease [tiːz] ärgern, auf den Arm nehmen **4›U1:** 10

technology [tek'nɒlədʒi] technisches Werken; Technik, Technologie **4›U3:** 50; **information technology (IT)** Informationstechnologie **2›U1:** 14

teddy bear ['tedi beə] Teddybär **1›U4:** 73

teenage ['tiːneɪdʒ]: **teenage girl** Mädchen im Teenager-Alter **U4:** 60

teenager ['tiːneɪdʒə] Teenager **3›U1:** 8

teeth [tiːθ] (→ tooth) Zähne **1›U4:** 80

telephone ['telɪfəʊn] Telefon **1›U6:** 115

television ['telɪvɪʒn] Fernsehen, Fernsehgerät **U2:** 35

tell (about) [tel] (I told, I've told) erzählen, berichten (über) **2›U1:** 16

temperature ['temprətʃə] Temperatur **2›U6:** 104

ten [ten] zehn **1›Intro:** 15

tennis ['tenɪs] Tennis **1›U4:** 76; **tennis shoe** Turnschuh **3›U5:** 107

tent [tent] Zelt **2›U5:** 82

tenth [tenθ] zehnte/r/s **2›U4:** 64

terrible ['terəbl] schrecklich, furchtbar **1›U1:** 23

terrific [tə'rɪfɪk] fantastisch, toll **1›U4:** 69

test [test] testen, prüfen **2›U5:** 82; **pass a test** [pɑːs] eine Prüfung bestehen **U4:** 62; **take a test** eine Prüfung machen **U4:** 60

text [tekst] **1** Text **3›U1:** 21; **text message** SMS-Nachricht **1›U6:** 105; **2** eine SMS senden, simsen **5›U5:** 84

than [ðæn, ðən]: **bigger than** größer als **1›U5:** 90

thank [θæŋk] danken **2›U6:** 95; **Thank you.** Danke (schön). **1›U1:** 26

Thanks. [θæŋks] Danke. **1›U3:** 58

Thanksgiving (Day) [θæŋks'gɪvɪŋ] Erntedankfest **1›U5:** 98

that [ðæt] **1** das; der/die/das (da) **1›U4:** 75; **2** der/die/das *(in Relativsätzen)* **3›U4:** 74; **3** dass **3›U1:** 14; **so that** damit **3›U5:** 88; **that's (= that is)** das ist **1›U4:** 75; **That's when ...** Das ist der Moment, wo ... **5›U1:** 14; **That's where ...** Da/Dort ... **5›U5:** 84; **That's why ...** Deshalb ..., Darum ... **4›U1:** 15

the [ðə] der/die/das **1›Intro:** 10; **the cheapest** am billigsten **1›U6:** 107; **the next day** am nächsten Tag **3›U1:** 13

theatre ['θɪətə] Theater **2›U5:** 78

their [ðeə] ihr/ihre **1›U3:** 56

theirs [ðeəz] ihre/ihrer/ihres **5›U4:** 66; (4›U3: 52)

them [ðem] sie, ihnen **1›U4:** 71

theme park ['θiːm pɑːk] Freizeitpark **1›U5:** 86

themselves [ðəm'selvz] sich (selbst); selbst **3›U5:** 88

then [ðen] **1** dann **1 ▸ U3:** 59; **2** damals, da **5 ▸ U1:** 14; **back then** damals **U2:** 26

theory ['θɪəri] Theorie **5 ▸ U4:** 72

there: Hi, there. Hallo. **3 ▸ U2:** 33; [ðeə] da, dort **1 ▸ U2:** 39; **there's/there are** es gibt **1 ▸ U4:** 74; **There you are!** Da bist du ja! **4 ▸ U1:** 13

these [ði:z] diese **2 ▸ U6:** 93

they [ðeɪ] sie **1 ▸ U1:** 24; **they're (= they are)** [ðeə] sie sind **1 ▸ U1:** 24

thick [θɪk] dick **U5:** 79

thief, thieves [θi:f, θi:vz] Dieb/in **U2:** 27

thing [θɪŋ] Ding, Sache **1 ▸ U1:** 20; **that's a good thing** das ist gut **4 ▸ U4:** 74

think [θɪŋk] (I thought, I've thought) denken, glauben; meinen **2 ▸ U1:** 15; **Do you think so?** Findest du? **3 ▸ U3:** 52; **I think it's great.** Ich finde es toll. **3 ▸ U1:** 11; **she doesn't know what to think** sie weiß nicht, was sie davon halten soll **3 ▸ U3:** 58; **she thinks to herself** sie denkt sich **4 ▸ U3:** 52; **think of** denken an **4 ▸ U1:** 13; **What do you think of her?** Was hältst du von ihr? **4 ▸ U3:** 56

third [θɜ:d] dritte/r/s **2 ▸ U4:** 72; **a third** ein Drittel **5 ▸ U5:** 82

thirsty ['θɜ:sti]: **I'm thirsty.** Ich habe Durst. **1 ▸ U3:** 55

thirteen [θɜ:'ti:n] dreizehn **1 ▸ U2:** 48

thirteenth [θɜ:'ti:nθ] dreizehnte/r/s **2 ▸ U4:** 72

thirtieth ['θɜ:tiəθ] dreißigste/r/s **2 ▸ U4:** 72

thirty ['θɜ:ti] dreißig **2 ▸ U4:** 72

this [ðɪs] dies **1 ▸ U3:** 58; **Do it this way.** Mach(t) es so. **1 ▸ U6:** 110; **this morning/ evening/...** heute Morgen/ Abend/... **3 ▸ U3:** 56

those [ðəʊz] diese, jene, die (da) **4 ▸ U2:** 30

thought [θɔ:t] (→ think): **I thought** ich dachte, ich habe gedacht **2 ▸ U5:** 87; **I've thought** ich habe gedacht **3 ▸ U4:** 74

thousand ['θaʊznd] tausend **1 ▸ U5:** 90

threaten ['θretn] (be)drohen **U5:** 74

three [θri:] drei **1 ▸ Intro:** 15

threw [θru:] (→ throw): **I threw** ich warf, ich habe geworfen **4 ▸ U4:** 72

thriller ['θrɪlə] Thriller, Krimi **1 ▸ U2:** 45

through [θru:] durch, hindurch **2 ▸ U4:** 66

throw [θrəʊ] (I threw, I've thrown) werfen **4 ▸ U4:** 72

throwaway ['θrəʊəweɪ] Wegwerf- **4 ▸ U3:** 61

thrown [θrəʊn] (→ throw): **I've thrown** ich habe geworfen **4 ▸ U4:** 72

Thursday ['θɜ:zdeɪ] Donnerstag **1 ▸ U4:** 80

ticket ['tɪkɪt] Eintrittskarte; Fahrkarte **2 ▸ U2:** 29; **ticket office** ['tɪkɪt ɒfɪs] Fahrkartenschalter, Verkaufsstelle **3 ▸ U1:** 16

tidy ['taɪdi] aufräumen **2 ▸ U6:** 96

tiger ['taɪgə] Tiger **U3:** 40

till [tɪl] bis **1 ▸ U2:** 40

time [taɪm] **1** Zeit, Uhrzeit **1 ▸ U3:** 64; **have a good time** sich gut amüsieren **5 ▸ U5:** 88; **on time** pünktlich **4 ▸ U3:** 54; **time of day** Tageszeit **5 ▸ U5:** 83; **What time is it?** Wie spät ist es? **1 ▸ U3:** 64; **2** Mal **3 ▸ U3:** 58; **three times a week** dreimal die Woche **2 ▸ U1:** 14

timetable ['taɪmteɪbl] Stundenplan, Tagesablauf **1 ▸ U6:** 102

tin [tɪn] Dose, Büchse **2 ▸ U4:** 68

tinned [tɪnd]: **tinned vegetables** Dosengemüse **U5:** 78

tiny ['taɪni] winzig **5 ▸ U5:** 87

tip [tɪp] **1** Hinweis, Tipp **1 ▸ U5:** 92; **2** Trinkgeld **4 ▸ U5:** 94

tired ['taɪəd] müde **1 ▸ U4:** 75

tiring ['taɪərɪŋ] ermüdend **5 ▸ U3:** 52

title ['taɪtl] **1** Titel **5 ▸ U3:** 56; **2** Anrede **5 ▸ U4:** 68

to [tu] **1** zu, nach; an **1 ▸ U3:** 57; **from ... to ...** von ... bis ... **2 ▸ U1:** 14; **they were new to me** sie waren mir neu **3 ▸ U1:** 15; **to the right/left** rechts/links **1 ▸ U5:** 92; **2 to go/do/...** zu gehen/machen/... **3 ▸ U3:** 50; **a stupid thing to say** eine dumme Bemerkung **3 ▸ U5:** 94; **Nice of you to say so.** Nett, dass du das sagst. **3 ▸ U5:** 94; **things to eat** Sachen zu essen **3 ▸ U4:** 73; **to see** um zu sehen **4 ▸ U2:** 28

today [tə'deɪ] heute **1 ▸ U2:** 42

toffee ['tɒfi] Karamell **3 ▸ U5:** 96

together [tə'geðə] zusammen **3 ▸ U1:** 9

toilet ['tɔɪlət] Toilette **1 ▸ U2:** 37

told [təʊld] (→ tell): **I told** ich erzählte, ich habe erzählt **2 ▸ U3:** 47; **I've told** ich habe erzählt **4 ▸ U3:** 54

tomato, tomatoes [tə'mɑ:təʊ] Tomate **1 ▸ U3:** 53

tomorrow [tə'mɒrəʊ] morgen **1 ▸ U6:** 106

tonight [tə'naɪt] heute Nacht, heute Abend **2 ▸ U5:** 82

tons of ... ['tʌnz əv] Tonnen ..., tonnenweise ... **U5:** 87

too [tu:] **1** auch **1 ▸ Intro:** 16; **2 too expensive** zu teuer **1 ▸ U4:** 75

took [tʊk] (→ take): **I took** ich nahm, ich habe genommen **2 ▸ U3:** 47

tool [tu:l] Werkzeug **1 ▸ U4:** 69

tooth, teeth [tu:θ, ti:θ] Zahn, Zähne **1 ▸ U4:** 80

top [tɒp] Spitze **3 ▸ U2:** 34; **at the top** auf der Spitze **3 ▸ U2:** 34; **top ten** die Top zehn, die wichtigsten zehn **4 ▸ U5:** 89

topic ['tɒpɪk] Thema **4 ▸ U3:** 57

torch [tɔ:tʃ] Taschenlampe **2 ▸ U5:** 82

torn [tɔ:n]: **it's torn** er ist gerissen/zerrissen **4 ▸ U5:** 92

total ['təʊtl] total, ganz **U5:** 76

touch [tʌtʃ] berühren, anfassen **3 ▸ U4:** 72; **keep in touch with** in Kontakt bleiben mit **4 ▸ U4:** 64

tour [tʊə] **1** Führung, Besichtigung **2 ▸ U3:** 51; **2 tour the USA** eine Tournee durch die USA machen **3 ▸ U5:** 102

tourism ['tʊərɪzəm] Tourismus **1 ▸ U6:** 103

tourist ['tʊərɪst] Tourist/Touristin **3 ▸ U1:** 8; **tourist industry** Tourismusindustrie **U1:** 9; **tourist office** ['tʊərɪst ɒfɪs] Fremdenverkehrsamt; Auskunft **2 ▸ U3:** 52; **tourist poster** Touristenposter **U1:** 13

towards [tə'wɔ:dz] auf ... zu, in Richtung **4 ▸ U2:** 35

tower ['taʊə] Turm **U1:** 9

town [taʊn] Stadt **1 ▸ Intro:** 16; **go to town** in die (Innen-)Stadt fahren **1 ▸ U6:** 106; **town centre** Stadtmitte **2 ▸ U6:** 99

DICTIONARY

township ['taʊnʃɪp] Township *(von Schwarzen und Farbigen bewohnte Siedlung)* U2: 26

toy [tɔɪ] Spielzeug 1>U4: 68

track [træk] Stück, Track *(auf einer CD)* 4>U3: 56

tradition [trə'dɪʃn] Tradition 5>U2: 31

traditional [trə'dɪʃənl] traditionell U2: 30

traffic ['træfɪk] Verkehr 3>U1: 8

tragically ['trædʒɪkli]: **Tragically, he was killed.** Tragischerweise wurde er getötet. 5>U3: 54

trail [treɪl] Wanderweg, Pfad 4>U2: 31; **cycle trail** Radweg 4>U4: 81

train [treɪn] 1 Zug 1>U1: 32; 2 ausbilden 5>U3: 50

trainer ['treɪnə] Sportschuh 3>U1: 13

training ['treɪnɪŋ] Ausbildung U2: 31

tram [træm] Tram, Straßenbahn 2>U3: 48

translate [træns'leɪt] übersetzen U2: 34

transport [træn'spɔːt] befördern, transportieren 5>U5: 85

transport ['trænspɔːt] Verkehrsmittel 3>U1: 19

travel ['trævl] reisen 2>U6: 97

treat [triːt] behandeln 5>U2: 31

tree [triː] Baum 4>U2: 28

trend [trend] Trend U3: 47

triangle ['traɪæŋgl] Dreieck 5>U4: 72; **love triangle** Dreiecksverhältnis 5>U4: 72

trick [trɪk]: **play tricks with them** ihnen Streiche spielen 5>U3: 56

trip [trɪp] Ausflug 2>U1: 17

trouble ['trʌbl]: **get into trouble** in Schwierigkeiten geraten, Probleme bekommen U2: 30; **the trouble is that ...** das Problem ist, dass ... U5: 76

trousers ['traʊzəz] Hose 4>U4: 72

true [truː] wahr 3>U5: 94

try [traɪ] versuchen, (aus)probieren 2>U3: 50; **try phoning** versuchen, zu telefonieren 3>U2: 34

T-shirt ['tiː ʃɜːt] T-Shirt 1>U2: 50

tube [tjuːb]: **the tube** „die Röhre" *(die Londoner U-Bahn)* 3>U1: 14

Tuesday ['tjuːzdeɪ] Dienstag 1>U4: 80

tunnel ['tʌnl] Tunnel 5>U1: 10

Turkey ['tɜːki] Türkei 2>Intro: 11

Turkish ['tɜːkɪʃ] türkisch; Türkisch; Türke/Türkin 5>U4: 70

turn [tɜːn]: **1 turn left/right** nach links/rechts abbiegen 2>U3: 52; **turn on** [tɜːn 'ɒn] einschalten 5>U1: 10; **turn the music down** die Musik leiser stellen 4>U5: 91; **2 it's your turn** du bist dran U1: 13

turnoff ['tɜːnɒf]: **TV turnoff week** Fernsehausschaltwoche 2>U1: 18

TV [tiː'viː] Fernseher, Fernsehapparat 1>U2: 42; **on TV** im Fernsehen 2>U1: 18; **TV station** Fernsehsender 5>U1: 8

twelfth [twelfθ] zwölfte/r/s 2>U4: 72

twelve [twelv] zwölf 1>Intro: 15

twentieth ['twentiəθ] zwanzigste/r/s 2>U4: 72

twenty ['twenti] zwanzig 1>U2: 48

twice [twaɪs] zweimal 3>U3: 48; **She gets twice the money that Amy gets.** Sie bekommt doppelt so viel Geld wie Amy. 3>U5: 98

twin town [twɪn 'taʊn] Partnerstadt 3>U3: 49

two [tuː] zwei 1>Intro: 15

two-way radio [tuː weɪ 'reɪdiəʊ] Funksprechgerät 5>U5: 84

type [taɪp] Art, Sorte 5>U4: 76

typical ['tɪpɪkl] typisch 1>U4: 74

tyre ['taɪə] Reifen 4>U4: 72

U

Ukraine [juː'kreɪn] Ukraine U5: 78

unarmed [ʌn'ɑːmd] unbewaffnet U2: 26

uncle ['ʌŋkl] Onkel 1>U3: 60

under ['ʌndə] unter 2>U2: 30

underground ['ʌndəgraʊnd] 1 unterirdisch 5>U1: 10; 2 U-Bahn 3>U1: 14

underline [ʌndə'laɪn] unterstreichen 3>U3: 66

understand [ʌndə'stænd] (I understood, I've understood) verstehen 1>U6: 107

understood [ʌndə'stʊd] (→ understand): **it is understood** es wird verstanden **Intro:** 7

unemployed [ʌnɪm'plɔɪd] arbeitslos 5>U2: 30

unemployment [ʌnɪm'plɔɪmənt] Arbeitslosigkeit 5>U3: 50

unfair [ʌn'feə] unfair, ungerecht 4>U1: 15

unfortunately [ʌn'fɔːtʃənətli] leider; unglücklicherweise 4>U3: 50

unfriendly [ʌn'frendli] unfreundlich 1>U1: 23

unhappy [ʌn'hæpi] unglücklich 4>U1: 12

uniform ['juːnɪfɔːm] Uniform 2>U1: 16

uninhabitable [ʌnɪn'hæbɪtəbl] unbewohnbar U5: 79

unit ['juːnɪt] Kapitel, Lektion 1>U1: 20

united [juː'naɪtɪd] vereint *U2: 25;* **United Kingdom (UK)** [junaɪtɪd 'kɪŋdəm] Vereinigtes Königreich 2>U1: 12; **United Nations, UN** [junaɪtɪd 'neɪʃnz, juː 'en] Vereinte Nationen U3: 42; (5>U1: 8)

university [juːnɪ'vɜːsəti] Universität 5>U3: 54

unless [ən'les] außer, wenn ... nicht U4: 60

unlucky [ʌn'lʌki] glücklos, unglücklich 2>U6: 101

unofficial [ʌnə'fɪʃl] inoffiziell 5>U5: 82

unpack [ʌn'pæk] auspacken 3>U2: 30

unrealistic [ʌnrɪə'lɪstɪk] unrealistisch U5: 76

up [ʌp] hinauf/herauf, nach oben 2>U3: 51; **up to** bis (zu) 3>U5: 92

update ['ʌpdeɪt] Aktualisierung 1>U3: 63

us [ʌs] uns 1>U5: 89

USA [juː es 'eɪ] USA, die Vereinigten Staaten 1>U5: 98

use [juːz] verwenden, benutzen 2>U2: 35

use [juːs] Gebrauch, Anwendung U3: 49; **it's no use being ...** es hat keinen Sinn, ... zu sein U4: 62

used [juːst]: **get used to** sich gewöhnen an U4: 64; **they used to be British** sie waren (früher) britisch U3: 46

useful ['juːsfl] nützlich 3>U2: 28

useless ['juːsles] nutzlos U2: 30

usually ['juːʒuəli] normalerweise 1>U6: 114

V

vacation [veɪˈkeɪʃn] (AE) Ferien, Urlaub **3 › U4:** 75
vacuum cleaner [ˈvækjuəm kliːnə] Staubsauger **2 › U3:** 50
Valentine's Day [ˈvæləntaɪnz deɪ] Valentinstag **3 › U3:** 53
valley [ˈvæli] Tal **5 › U5:** 82
value [ˈvæljuː]: **good value** preis-günstig **2 › U4:** 68
vandal [ˈvændl] Rowdy, Randalie-rer/in **4 › U4:** 75
varied [ˈveərɪd] abwechslungs-reich **4 › U3:** 56
vegetable [ˈvedʒtəbl] Gemüse **1 › U3:** 53
vegetarian [vedʒəˈteərɪən] Vegeta-rier/in **5 › U2:** 34
veggie (= vegetable) [ˈvedʒi] Gemüse **3 › U4:** 76
verb [vɜːb] Verb **2 › U3:** 51
verse [vɜːs] Strophe **5 › U5:** 93
version [ˈvɜːʃn] Version *U5:* 81
very [ˈveri] sehr **1 › U1:** 23; **the very first day** der allererste Tag **U2:** 31
vet's assistant [ˈvets əsɪstənt] Tierarzthelfer/Tierarzthelferin **4 › U5:** 89
video [ˈvɪdiəʊ] Video **1 › U2:** 40; **video game** Videospiel **1 › U4:** 71; **video recorder** [ˈvɪdiəʊ rɪˈkɔːdə] Videorekorder **1 › U2:** 42
view [vjuː] Aussicht, Sicht **3 › U2:** 34; **views of the country** Aussichten auf das Land **5 › U5:** 82
viewer [ˈvjuːə] Fernsehzuschau-er/in **5 › U4:** 72
village [ˈvɪlɪdʒ] Dorf **1 › U2:** 38
violence [ˈvaɪələns] Gewalt, Gewalttätigkeit **4 › U4:** 74
violent [ˈvaɪələnt] gewalttätig, gewaltsam **4 › U4:** 75
violin [vaɪəˈlɪn] Geige **3 › U5:** 88
violinist [vaɪəˈlɪnɪst] Geigen-spieler/in, Geiger/in **4 › U3:** 59
visit [ˈvɪzɪt] **1** besuchen **1 › U5:** 85; besichtigen **3 › U4:** 70; **2** Besuch **4 › U2:** 31
visitor [ˈvɪzɪtə] Besucher/Besucherin, Gast **3 › U4:** 72; **visitor center** [ˈvɪzɪtə sentə] Besucherzentrum **4 › U2:** 33
voice [vɔɪs] Stimme **2 › U3:** 51
volleyball [ˈvɒlibɔːl] Volleyball **2 › Intro:** 11

voluntary [ˈvɒləntri]: **voluntary work** ehrenamtliche Arbeit **U4:** 60
vote [vəʊt] wählen; abstimmen **5 › U3:** 50

W

wait [weɪt] warten **1 › U5:** 92; **wait for** warten auf **2 › U4:** 66
wake [weɪk] (I woke, I've woken) wecken **2 › U1:** 15; **wake up** aufwachen **U1:** 19
Wales [weɪlz] Wales **2 › Intro:** 9
walk [wɔːk] **1** (spazieren) gehen **1 › U5:** 86; **2** Spaziergang **2 › U1:** 19; **take the dog for a walk** mit dem Hund rausgehen/spazierengehen **2 › U1:** 19
Walkman [ˈwɔːkmən] Walkman **1 › U4:** 69
wall [wɔːl] Mauer **1 › U5:** 91; Wand **5 › U5:** 87
wallpaper [ˈwɔːlpeɪpə] Tapete **1 › U6:** 106
want [wɒnt] wollen **1 › U4:** 73; **he wants me to come** er möchte, dass ich komme **4 › U3:** 54; **want to swap** tauschen wollen **2 › U6:** 95
war [wɔː] Krieg **5 › U1:** 7
warden [ˈwɔːdn] Herbergsmutter/-vater **4 › U5:** 93
warm [wɔːm] warm **2 › U5:** 81
warn [wɔːn] warnen **5 › U5:** 86
was [wɒz] war **1 › U3:** 58; **I was reading** ich las (gerade) **4 › U1:** 14; **I was staying** ich übernachtete (gerade) **5 › U2:** 29; **it was built** es wurde gebaut **4 › U4:** 70; **it was said** (so) wurde gesagt **5 › U1:** 17
wash [wɒʃ] **1** waschen **1 › U4:** 79; **wash the floor** den Boden wischen **5 › U3:** 52; **wash up** abwaschen, spülen **1 › U3:** 58; **2** sich waschen **U1:** 20; **have a wash** sich waschen **1 › U4:** 80
wasn't (= was not) [wɒznt] war nicht **2 › U2:** 31
waste [weɪst] Abfall **4 › U4:** 71
watch [wɒtʃ] zuschauen, sich ansehen **2 › U4:** 65; **watch TV** fernsehen **1 › U4:** 70
water [ˈwɔːtə] Wasser **1 › U4:** 73
waterfall [ˈwɔːtəfɔːl] Wasserfall **4 › U2:** 28

wave [weɪv] Welle *U1: 103*
way [weɪ] Weg **1 › U5:** 92; **by the way** übrigens **4 › U2:** 34; **Do it this way.** Mach(t) es so. **1 › U6:** 110; **on the way** auf dem Weg, unterwegs **1 › U6:** 109
we [wiː] wir **1 › Intro:** 11; **we're (= we are)** [wɪə] wir sind **1 › U1:** 23
weak [wiːk] schwach **5 › U5:** 90
wealthy [ˈwelθi] reich, wohl-habend **U2:** 24
wear [weə] (I wore, I've worn) tragen, anhaben *(Kleidung)* **2 › U1:** 16
weather [ˈweðə] Wetter **1 › U6:** 114
Web (= World Wide Web) [web] Netz (= Internet) **2 › U1:** 24
webcode [ˈwebkəʊd] Webcode **5 › U1:** 7
website [ˈwebsaɪt] Website **2 › U1:** 16
wedding [ˈwedɪŋ] Hochzeit **5 › U4:** 72
Wednesday [ˈwenzdeɪ] Mittwoch **1 › U4:** 80
week [wiːk] Woche **1 › U4:** 72
weekday [ˈwiːkdeɪ] Wochentag **1 › U4:** 80
weekend [wiːkˈend] Wochenende **1 › U4:** 80; **at the weekend** am Wochenende **1 › U5:** 84
weird [wɪəd] seltsam **U4:** 64
welcome [ˈwelkəm] willkommen heißen **U2:** 31; **Welcome!** Will-kommen! **1 › U5:** 93; **Welcome to ...** Willkommen auf/in/zu ... **5 › U2:** 26; **You're welcome.** Nichts zu danken; Bitte schön. **3 › U3:** 56
well [wel] gut **4 › U2:** 30; nun, also **1 › U2:** 40; **Well done!** [wel ˈdʌn] Gut gemacht! **1 › U5:** 93; **well-paid** [welˈpeɪd] gut bezahlt **4 › U5:** 91
Welsh [welʃ] Walisisch; walisisch; Waliser/Waliserin **2 › U1:** 16
went [went] (→ go): **I went** ich ging, ich bin gegangen **2 › Intro:** 8
were [wɜː] warst, wart, waren **1 › U4:** 75; **If I were you, I'd ...** An deiner Stelle/Wenn ich du wäre, würde ich ... **U1:** 67; **they were built** sie wurden gebaut **4 › U4:** 70; **they were watching TV** sie sahen (gerade) fern **4 › U1:** 13; **we were flying** wir flogen (gerade) **5 › U2:** 29

DICTIONARY

weren't (= were not) [wɜːnt] warst/wart/waren nicht **2 › U2:** 31

west [west] (nach) Westen; West-; westlich **3 › U5:** 89

western ['westən] Western 1 › U2: 45

wet [wet] nass, feucht **2 › U2:** 30

wetsuit ['wetsuːt] Surf-/Tauch-(schutz)anzug **4 › U5:** 92

whale [weɪl] Wal **5 › U2:** 31

what [wɒt] **1** was **1 › Intro:** 10; **2** welche/r/s **1 › U2:** 42; **So what?** Na und? **U5:** 76; **What a ...** Was für ein/e ... **1 › U6:** 109; **What about you?** Und du? **4 › U3:** 56; **What about ...?** Wie wäre es mit ...? **1 › U3:** 54; **What if ...?** Und was, wenn ...? **5 › U5:** 91; **What time is it?** Wie spät ist es? **1 › U3:** 64; **What's that?** Was ist das? **1 › Intro:** 11; **What's your hobby?** Welches Hobby hast du? **1 › U4:** 76; **What's your name?** Wie heißt du? **1 › U1:** 22

wheel [wiːl] Rad **2 › U4:** 69; **big wheel** Riesenrad **U5:** 78

when [wen] **1** wann **1 › U3:** 64; **2** wenn **1 › U6:** 107; **3** als **2 › U5:** 82; **That's when ...** Das ist der Moment, wo ... **5 › U1:** 14

where [weə] wo **1 › U2:** 40; **Where are you from?** Wo kommst du her? **1 › U1:** 22

whereas [weər'æz] während, wohingegen **U4:** 63

whether ['weðə] ob **U4:** 64

which [wɪtʃ] **1** welche/r/s **2 › U5:** 76; **2** der/die/das *(in Relativsätzen)* **3 › U1:** 13

while [waɪl] **1** während **4 › U5:** 92; **2** Weile, Zeit **U4:** 64

whisky ['wɪski] Whisky **3 › U3:** 53

white [waɪt] weiß **1 › Intro:** 10; **white coffee** Milchkaffee **5 › U3:** 48

Whites [waɪts]: **the Whites** die Weißen **U2:** 25

who [huː] **1** wer **1 › U3:** 60; **2** der/die/das *(in Relativsätzen)* **3 › U3:** 50; **who's (= who is)** [huːz] wer ist **1 › U5:** 93

whole [həʊl] ganz **5 › U1:** 9

why [waɪ] warum **2 › U1:** 19; **That's why ...** Deshalb ..., Darum ... **4 › U1:** 15; **Why, sure!** (AE) Na klar! **4 › U1:** 14

wide [waɪd] breit **U1:** 9; **widely-spoken** ['waɪdli spəʊkən] weit verbreitet, viel gesprochen **Intro:** 6

wife, wives [waɪf, waɪvz] Ehefrau, Ehefrauen **5 › U2:** 31

wild [waɪld] wild **4 › Intro:** 6

wilderness ['wɪldənəs] Wildnis **4 › U2:** 30

wildlife ['waɪldlaɪf] die Tier- und Pflanzenwelt, die Natur **4 › U2:** 28

will [wɪl]: **I will go** ich werde gehen **1 › U6:** 106

win [wɪn] (I won, I've won) gewinnen, siegen **2 › U6:** 100

wind [wɪnd] Wind **5 › U2:** 26; **wind farm** ['wɪnd fɑːm] Windpark **4 › U4:** 69

window ['wɪndəʊ] Fenster **1 › Intro:** 11; Schaufenster **5 › U1:** 8

windsurfing ['wɪndsɜːfɪŋ] Windsurfen **3 › U2:** 29

windy ['wɪndi] windig **2 › U6:** 104

winner ['wɪnə] Sieger/in **1 › U5:** 93

winning ['wɪnɪŋ] Gewinnen **2 › U1:** 20

winter ['wɪntə] Winter **1 › U5:** 99

wish [wɪʃ] **1 I wish ...** ich wünschte ... **4 › U5:** 88; **Wish me luck!** Wünsch mir Glück! **U4:** 62; **Wish you were here.** Ich wünschte, du wärst hier. **2 › U5:** 85; **2 Best wishes, ...** Viele Grüße ... **3 › U4:** 74

with [wɪð] mit; bei **1 › U1:** 25

without [wɪ'ðaʊt] ohne **2 › U1:** 18; **without producing ...** ohne ... zu produzieren **U5:** 76

woke [wəʊk] (→ wake): **he woke up** er wachte auf **U1:** 19

wolf, wolves [wʊlf, wʊlvz] Wolf, Wölfe **4 › U2:** 28

woman, women ['wʊmən, 'wɪmɪn] Frau, Frauen **2 › U3:** 52

women ['wɪmɪn] (→ woman) Frauen **4 › U1:** 8; **women's prison** Frauengefängnis **5 › U4:** 64

won [wʌn] (→ win): **I won** ich gewann, ich habe gewonnen **4 › U4:** 75; **I've won** ich habe gewonnen **4 › U4:** 75

won't [wəʊnt]: **I won't (= will not) go** ich werde nicht gehen **2 › U1:** 18; **We won't have time.** Wir werden keine Zeit haben. **1 › U6:** 107

wonder ['wʌndə] **1** sich fragen **3 › U3:** 54; **2 no wonder that** kein Wunder, dass **U2:** 25

wonderful ['wʌndəfl] wunderbar, wundervoll **5 › U3:** 54

wood [wʊd] Holz; (kleinerer) Wald **2 › U4:** 62

wooden ['wʊdn] hölzern, aus Holz *U3: 107*

word [wɜːd] Wort **2 › U1:** 24; **words (of a song)** (Lied-)Text **3 › U4:** 74

wore [wɔː] (→ wear): **I wore** ich trug, ich habe getragen **5 › U1:** 16

work [wɜːk] **1** arbeiten **1 › U2:** 40; funktionieren **3 › U2:** 34; **2** Arbeit **2 › U2:** 33; **at work** bei der Arbeit **2 › U2:** 33; **work experience** Berufspraktikum **4 › Intro:** 6

workhouse ['wɜːkhaʊz] Arbeitshaus **U1:** 20

working-class [wɜːkɪŋ'klɑːs] Arbeiter(klasse)- **5 › U4:** 64

world [wɜːld] Welt **2 › U3:** 48; **from all over the world** aus der ganzen Welt **3 › U1:** 8; **in the world** auf der (ganzen) Welt **2 › U3:** 48; **world sport** (der) Weltsport **U3:** 47

worn [wɔːn] (→ wear): **I've worn** ich habe getragen **3 › U3:** 52

worried ['wʌrid] besorgt **5 › U1:** 20; **be worried (about)** sich Sorgen machen (um) **4 › U3:** 54

worry ['wʌri]: **Don't worry.** Mach dir keine Sorgen. **1 › U6:** 109

worse [wɜːs] schlechter, schlimmer **3 › U5:** 90

worst [wɜːst] schlechteste/r/s, schlimmste/r/s; am schlechtesten/schlimmsten **3 › U5:** 90

worth [wɜːθ]: **it's worth doing ...** es lohnt sich, ... zu tun **U5:** 76; **it's worth it** es lohnt sich **4 › U5:** 96

would [wʊd]: **they said that they would ...** sie sagten, sie würden ... **U3:** 42; **Tim would like ...** Tim hätte gern/möchte ... **1 › U4:** 75; **What would you like to do?** Was würdest du gern machen? **2 › U4:** 75

wouldn't ['wʊdnt]: **they wouldn't kill** sie würden nicht töten **5 › U2:** 34; **wouldn't like** nicht mögen, nicht gern haben **3 › U5:** 93

176

one hundred and seventy-six

Wow! [waʊ] Krass!/Wahnsinn!
2 › U6: 94

write [raɪt] (I wrote, I've written)
schreiben **1 › U1:** 26

writer ['raɪtə] Autor/in **U4:** 73

written ['rɪtn] (→ write)**: I've
written** ich habe geschrieben
3 › U3: 50

wrong [rɒŋ] falsch **2 › U1:** 25;
go wrong schief gehen
4 › U5: 95; **What's wrong
with you?** Was ist los mit dir?
4 › U1: 15

wrote [rəʊt] (→ write)**: I wrote** ich
schrieb, ich habe geschrieben
2 › U3: 47

X

X-ray ['eks reɪ] röntgen
4 › U5: 96; **X-ray assistant**
['eks reɪ əsɪstənt] Röntgen-
assistent/in **4 › U5:** 99

Y

yacht [jɒt]**: luxury yacht**
Luxusjacht **U1:** 14

yachting marina ['jɒtɪŋ məri:nə]
Jachthafen **3 › U2:** 29

yard sale ['jɑːd seɪl] (AE)
Trödelverkauf im Garten/Hof
5 › U2: 28

yeah [jeə] ja *(besonders in wörtl.
Rede)* **4 › U2:** 30

year [jɪə] Jahr, Jahrgang
1 › U1: 25; **sixteen-year-old**
[sɪks'ti:n jɪər əʊld] Sechzehn-
jährige/r **U4:** 70

yellow ['jeləʊ] gelb **1 › Intro:** 14

yes [jes] ja **1 › U1:** 22

yesterday ['jestədeɪ] gestern
2 › U2: 30

yet [jet] schon **3 › U3:** 56

yogurt ['jɒgət] Jogurt **1 › U3:** 56

you [juː] **1** du, ihr, Sie **1 › U1:** 23;
you're (= you are) du bist, ihr
seid, Sie sind **1 › U1:** 23; **you
and your ...** du mit deinem/
deiner ... **1 › U4:** 73; **2** dir, euch,
Ihnen; dich, euch, Sie **1 › U2:** 40

young [jʌŋ] jung **1 › U6:** 105

your [jɔː] dein, euer, Ihr
1 › Intro: 11

yours [jɔːz] deine/r/s, eure/r/s,
Ihre/r/s **5 › U4:** 66; (4 › U3: 52);
Yours faithfully, ... Mit freund-
lichen Grüßen ... **3 › U4:** 82

yourself [jɔː'self] dir/dich (selbst);
selbst **3 › U5:** 90

yourselves [jɔː'selvz] euch
(selbst); sich (selbst); selbst
4 › U3: 53

youth [juːθ]**: youth camp** Zelt-
lager für Jugendliche **U4:** 69;
youth club Jugendclub,
-zentrum **2 › U1:** 17

yummy ['jʌmi] lecker **5 › U1:** 12

Z

zap through the channels [zæp]
durch die Programme „zappen"
*(schnell durchschalten, um zu
sehen, was läuft)* **U4:** 65

zebra ['zebrə] Zebra **U2:** 31

zero ['zɪərəʊ] null **2 › U6:** 104

Zimbabwe [zɪm'bɑːbwi]
Simbabwe U2: 30

zip [zɪp] Reißverschluss
2 › U5: 82

zone [zəʊn] Zone **U5:** 79

zoo [zuː] Zoo **1 › U5:** 86

→ NAMES

Girls/Women

Amy ['eɪmi]
Anna ['ænə]
Boniswa [bɒ'niːswʌ]
Charlotte ['ʃɑːlət]
Corinna [kə'rɪnə]
Diana [daɪ'ænə]
Ela ['iːlʌ]
Ella ['elə]
Ellen ['elən]
Ellie ['eli]
Emily ['emɪli]
Emma ['emə]
Gania ['gɑːniə, gə'niːə]
Grace [greɪs]
Hannah ['hænə]
Hasina [hʌ'siːnʌ]
Jenny ['dʒeni]
Jessica ['dʒesɪkə]
Julia ['dʒuːliə]
Kala ['kɑːlʌ]
Kate [keɪt]
Lami ['lɑːmi]
Laura ['lɔːrə]
Loren ['lɔːrən]
Lucinda [luː'sɪndə]
Lucy ['luːsi]
Mafuane [mʌfu'ɑːne]
Makobo [mʌ'kɔːbɒ]
Marion ['mæriən]
Meg [meg]
Neela ['niːlʌ]
Olivia [ə'lɪviə]
Rachel ['reɪtʃəl]
Rebecca [rɪ'bekə]
Ruby ['ruːbi]
Rupa ['ruːpʌ]
Sally ['sæli]
Sarah ['seərə]
Sedna ['sednə]
Selma ['selmə]
Sophie ['səʊfi]
Sue [suː]
Teresa [tə'riːzə, tə'reɪzə]
Thembi ['tembi]
Tina ['tiːnə]
Tuhina [tʊ'hiːnʌ]
Yetunde [je'tʊndeɪ]

Boys/Men

Adam ['ædəm]
Angus ['æŋgəs]
Ben [ben]
Chris [krɪs]
Dan [dæn]
Daniel ['dænjəl]
David, Dave ['deɪvɪd, deɪv]
Dinkar ['dɪŋkʌ]
Eddie ['edi]
Eswar ['esvʌ]
Gavin ['gævɪn]
Goodwin ['gʊdwɪn]
Govind [gɒ'vɪnd]
Jack [dʒæk]
Jakob, Jake ['dʒeɪkəb, dʒeɪk]
James [dʒeɪmz]
Joe [dʒəʊ]
Julian ['dʒuːliən]
Karl [kɑːl]
Kevin ['kevɪn]
Kosan ['kɔːsən, kə'sʌn]
Lalit ['lʌlɪt]
Marcus ['mɑːkəs]
Mark, Marc [mɑːk]
Max [mæks]
Melikhaya [meli'kɑːjʌ]
Mike [maɪk]
Nirvan ['nɪəvən]
Olek ['ɒlək]
Oliver ['ɒlɪvə]
Pat [pæt]
Paul [pɔːl]
Peter ['piːtə]
Phil [fɪl]
Roger ['rɒdʒə]
Stephen ['stiːvən]
Terry ['teri]
Thomas ['tɒməs]
Tim [tɪm]
Tommy, Tom ['tɒmi, tɒm]
Tumelo [tu'meːlɒ]
Uttam ['ʊtʌm]
Vikram ['vɪkrʌm]
William ['wɪljəm]
Zoran ['zɔːrən]

Families

Bai [baɪ]
Bailey ['beɪli]
Briggs [brɪgz]
Cummings ['kʌmɪŋgz]
Curran ['kʌrən]
Ellis ['elɪs]
Gangotri ['gʌŋgɒtri]
Harper ['hɑːpə]
Harrison ['hærɪsən]
Jackson ['dʒæksən]
Johnson ['dʒɒnsən]
Kema ['keːmə]
Nair [neə]
Owen ['əʊɪn]
Philpott ['fɪlpɒt]
Rao [raʊ]
Sands [sændz]
Smith [smɪθ]
Theron [tə'rɒn]
Thomas ['tɒməs]
Timms [tɪmz]
van Tonder [væn 'tɒndə]

People

A. R. Rahman (Allah Rakha Rahman) ['eɪ ɑː rʌ'mɑːn, ʌ'lɑː rʌ'kɑː rʌ'mɑːn]
Adele [ə'del]
Aishwarya Rai ['ʌʃvʌriə 'raɪ]
Amitabh Bachchan [ʌmi'tɑːb 'bʌtʃən]
Amy Grant ['eɪmi 'græːnt]
Andrea Corr ['ændriə 'kɔː]
Angelina Jolie [ændʒə'liːnə dʒəʊ'liː]
Bob Geldof [bɒb 'geldɒf]
Bono ['bɒnəʊ]
Bouga Luv ['bʊgʌ 'lʌv]
Brad Pitt ['bræd 'pɪt]
Counting Crows ['kaʊntɪŋ 'kraʊz]
Dominique Mathebula [dɒmə'niːk mʌtə'buːlʌ]
Ella Huskisson ['elə 'hʌskɪsən]
Elton John [eltən 'dʒɒn]
Frederik Willem de Klerk ['fredərɪk wɪləm də 'kleək]
George Michael ['dʒɔːdʒ 'maɪkəl]
Georgia Nicolson ['dʒɔːdʒə 'nɪkəlzn]
Gina Gallant ['dʒiːnə 'gælənt]
Grigorii Khmel [gri'gɔːri xmel]
Gurinder Chadha [gʊ'rɪndə 'tʃʌdʌ]
Jess Bhamra [dʒes 'bʌmrʌ]
Joni Mitchell ['dʒəʊni 'mɪtʃəl]
Kareena Kapoor [kə'riːnə kə'pɔː]
Katrina Kaif [kə'triːnə 'kaɪf]
Lakshmi Mittal [lʌk'ʃmi mɪ'tʌl]
Louise Rennison [luː'iːz 'renɪsən]
Madonna [mə'dɒnə]
Martin Luther King ['mɑːtɪn luːθə 'kɪŋ]
Meenal Dave [miː'nʌl 'deɪv]
Mohandas Gandhi (Mahatma Gandhi) [mə'hʌndəs 'gɑːndi, mə'hʌtmə 'gɑːndi]
Mosola Manyi [muː'sɒlə 'mʌndʒi]
Mrs Ples ['mɪsɪz 'ples]
Nandila Das [nʌn'diːlə 'dɑːs]
Nelson Mandela [nelsn mæn'delə]
Nick Hornby ['nɪk 'hɔːnbi]
Paul Hewson [pɔːl 'hjuːsən]
Shah Rukh Khan ['ʃɑː rʊk 'kɑːn]
Shakira [ʃə'kiːrə]
Zola ['zəʊlə]

Places

Afghanistan [æfˈɡænɪstɑːn]
Alexandra Township
[ælɪɡˈzɑːndrə ˈtaʊnʃɪp]
Amritsar [æmˈrɪtsə]
Ballymena [bælɪˈmiːnə]
Bangalore [bæŋɡəˈlɔː]
Barrett Way [ˈbærət weɪ]
Belfast [ˈbelfɑːst, belˈfɑːst]
Bihar [biːˈhɑː]
Boulders Beach [ˈbəʊldəz ˈbiːtʃ]
British Columbia [ˈbrɪtɪʃ kəˈlʌmbiə]
Buckingham Palace
[ˈbʌkɪŋəm ˈpæləs]
Cambridge [ˈkeɪmbrɪdʒ]
Cardiff [ˈkɑːdɪf]
Carlow [ˈkɑːləʊ]
Chennai [ˈtʃenaɪ, tʃeˈnaɪ]
Chernobyl [tʃəˈnɒbɪl]
Cork [kɔːk]
County Kerry [ˈkaʊnti ˈkeri]
Culver Studios [ˈkʌlvə ˈstjuːdiəʊz]
Dehradun [deˈrɑːduːn]
Detroit [dɪˈtrɔɪt]
Dingle [ˈdɪŋɡl]
Dublin [ˈdʌblɪn]
Durban [ˈdɜːbən]
Eastbourne [ˈiːstbɔːn]
Eiffel Tower [ˈaɪfl ˈtaʊə]
Elgin School [ˈelɡɪn ˈskuːl]
Enniskillen [enɪsˈkɪlən]
Faxford School [ˈfæksfəd ˈskuːl]
Giant's Causeway
[ˈdʒaɪənts ˈkɔːzweɪ]
Gobi desert [ˈɡəʊbi ˈdezət]
Great Limpopo Transfrontier
Park [ɡreɪt lɪmˈpəʊpəʊ
trənsˈfrʌntɪə pɑːk]
Hackney [ˈhækni]
Hermanus [ˈhɜːmənəs]
Hollywood [ˈhɒliwʊd]
Hotel Nehru [həʊˈtel ˈneəruː]
Howard Street [ˈhaʊəd striːt]
Irish Joker Hotel
[aɪrɪʃ ˈdʒəʊkə həʊˈtel]
Japan [dʒəˈpæn]
Johannesburg,
Joburg [dʒəʊˈhænəzbɜːɡ , ˈdʒəʊbɜːɡ]
Katsina [kʰətˈsiːnə]
Keswick [ˈkezɪk]
Kinsale [kɪnˈseɪl]
Khoka Moya Camp
[kɒkə ˈmɒjə kæmp]
Kolkata [ˈkɒlkʌtʌ]
Kruger National Park
[ˈkruːɡə næʃnəl ˈpɑːk]

Lagos [ˈleɪɡɒs]
Lake District [ˈleɪk dɪstrɪkt]
Langa [ˈlɒŋɡə]
Leeds [liːdz]
Liverpool [ˈlɪvəpuːl]
London [ˈlʌndən]
Madhepura [mʌdeˈpuːrʌ]
Madras [məˈdrɑːs]
Malawi [məˈlɑːwi]
Manhattan [mənˈhætn]
Maropeng [ˈmʌrəpeŋ]
Maxwell Avenue
[ˈmækswəl ˈævənjuː]
Mumbai, Bombay
[mʊmˈbaɪ, bɒmˈbeɪ]
Nairobi [naɪˈrəʊbi]
Nemesis Avenue
[ˈneməsɪs ˈævənjuː]
New York [njuː ˈjɔːk]
Newcastle-Upon-Tyne
[ˈnjuːkɑːsl əpɒn ˈtaɪn]
Nigeria [naɪˈdʒɪərɪə]
O'Neill's [əʊˈniːlz]
Oudtshoorn [əʊtsˈhɔːn]
Paris [ˈpærɪs]
Penguin Palace
Hotel [ˈpeŋɡwɪn ˈpæləs həʊˈtel]
Philadelphia [fɪləˈdelfiə]
Phoenix Park [ˈfiːnɪks ˈpɑːk]
Port Elizabeth [pɔːt iˈlɪzəbəθ]
Pretoria [prɪˈtɔːriə]
Prypiat [ˈprɪpət]
Ringwood Road [ˈrɪŋwʊd ˈrəʊd]
Robben Island [rɒbən ˈaɪlənd]
Sandton [ˈsæntən]
Sarajevo [sʌrəˈjeɪvəʊ]
Sharpeville [ˈʃɑːpvɪl]
Skellig Michael [ˈskelɪɡ ˈmaɪkəl]
Skiddaw Hotel [ˈskidɔː həʊˈtel]
Slavutych [sləˈvuːtɪtʃ]
Southall [ˈsaʊθɔːl]
Soweto [səˈwetəʊ]
Srirampuram [sriːˈræmpəræm]
Taj Mahal [tɑːdʒ məˈhɔːl]
Tokyo [ˈtəʊkiəʊ]
Wembley Stadium
[ˈwembli ˈsteɪdiəm]
Whinash [ˈwɪnæʃ]
Wimbledon [ˈwɪmbldən]
Woking [ˈwəʊkɪŋ]

Other names

Aloo [ˈɑːluː]
B*Witched [bɪˈwɪtʃt]
Bend it like Beckham
[ˈbend ɪt laɪk ˈbekəm]
Bing [bɪŋ]
Bona Vox [ˈbəʊnə ˈvɒks]
Book of Kells [ˈbʊk əv ˈkelz]
Boyzone [ˈbɔɪzəʊn]
Dahi [deɪ]
Golden Globe Award
[ɡəʊldən ˈɡləʊb əˈwɔːd]
Gosht [ɡɒʃt]
Jaguar [ˈdʒæɡjuə]
Kofta [ˈkɒftə]
Komil EP300 [ˈkɒmɪl iː piː θriː ˈhʌndrəd]
Kulfi [ˈkʊlfi]
Land Rover [ˈlænd rəʊvə]
Lassi [ˈlæsi]
Mithai [ˈmɪtaɪ]
Mumbaikar [mʊmˈbaɪkɑː]
Nano [ˈnænəʊ]
Newsweek [ˈnjuːzwiːk]
R.E.M. [ɑːr iː ˈem]
Riverdance [ˈrɪvədɑːns]
Roja [ˈrɔːdʒʌ]
Sabzi [ˈsʌbzi]
SaSa Holidays [ˈsæsə ˈhɒlədeɪz]
Slumdog Millionaire [ˈslʌmdɒɡ miljəˈneə]
Starstream [ˈstɑːstriːm]
Stuart Little [ˈstjuːət ˈlɪtl]
Tata [ˈtɒtə]
TG4 [ˈtiː dʒiː ˈfɔː]
the Corrs [kɔːz]
Titanic [taɪˈtænɪk]
Tsotsi [ˈtsɒtsi]
U2 [juː ˈtuː]
Victor Verster Prison
[vɪktə ˈvɜːstə prɪzn]
Wikipedia [wɪkiˈpiːdiə]
XNO2 [eks en əʊ ˈtuː]
YFM Radio [waɪ ef ˈem ˈreɪdiəʊ]

IRREGULAR VERBS

Infinitive form (Grundform)	Simple past form (Einfache Vergangenheit)	Present perfect form (Vollendete Gegenwart)	
be	I was, you were, she was	I've been	sein
have	I had	I've had	haben
do	I did	I've done [dʌn]	tun, machen
babysit	I babysat	I've babysat	babysitten
become	I became	I've become	werden
begin	I began	I've begun	beginnen, anfangen
blow up	I blew up	I've blown up	sprengen, aufblasen
break	I broke	I've broken	(zer)brechen
bring	I brought	I've brought	(mit)bringen
build	I built	I've built	bauen
burn	I burnt	I've burnt	(ver)brennen
buy	I bought	I've bought	kaufen
catch	I caught	I've caught	fangen
choose	I chose	I've chosen	(aus)suchen, (aus)wählen
come	I came	I've come	kommen
cost	I cost	I've cost	kosten
cut	I cut	I've cut	schneiden
draw	I drew	I've drawn	zeichnen, malen
drink	I drank	I've drunk	trinken
drive	I drove	I've driven ['drɪvn]	fahren
eat	I ate [et]	I've eaten	essen
fall	I fell	I've fallen	fallen
feed	I fed	I've fed	füttern
feel	I felt	I've felt	(sich) fühlen
fight	I fought	I've fought	kämpfen, bekämpfen
find	I found	I've found	finden
fly	I flew	I've flown	fliegen
forget	I forgot	I've forgotten	vergessen
get	I got	I've got	bekommen; holen
give	I gave	I've given	geben
go	I went	I've gone [gɒn]	gehen, fahren
grow	I grew	I've grown	wachsen; werden
hear	I heard [hɜːd]	I've heard [hɜːd]	hören
hit	I hit	I've hit	treffen
hold	I held	I've held	(fest)halten
hurt	I hurt	I've hurt	wehtun; verletzen
keep	I kept	I've kept	(be)halten
know	I knew	I've known	wissen; kennen
lay	I laid	I've laid	legen; decken
lead	I led	I've led	führen
leave	I left	I've left	lassen; verlassen
let	I let	I've let	lassen
lie	I lay	I've lain	liegen
lose	I lost	I've lost	verlieren
make	I made	I've made	machen
mean	I meant [ment]	I've meant [ment]	bedeuten, meinen

Infinitive form (Grundform)	Simple past form (Einfache Vergangenheit)	Present perfect form (Vollendete Gegenwart)	
meet	I met	I've met	(sich) treffen
pay	I paid	I've paid	zahlen, bezahlen
put	I put	I've put	stellen, legen, tun
read	I read [red]	I've read [red]	lesen, vorlesen
ride a bike	I rode a bike	I've ridden a bike	Rad fahren
rise	it rose	it has risen	ansteigen, zunehmen
run	I ran	I've run	rennen, laufen
say	I said [sed]	I've said [sed]	sagen
see	I saw	I've seen	sehen
sell	I sold	I've sold	verkaufen
send	I sent	I've sent	senden, schicken
shake	I shook	I've shaken	schütteln
shine	it shone	it has shone	scheinen, leuchten
show	I showed	I've shown	zeigen
sing	I sang	I've sung	singen
sit	I sat	I've sat	sitzen; sich setzen
sleep	I slept	I've slept	schlafen
speak	I spoke	I've spoken	sprechen
spend	I spent	I've spent	verbringen
spread	it spread	it has spread	(sich) ausbreiten
stand	I stood	I've stood	stehen
steal	I stole	I've stolen	stehlen
swim	I swam	I've swum	schwimmen
take	I took	I've taken	(mit)nehmen; bringen
teach	I taught	I've taught	beibringen, unterrichten
tell	I told	I've told	erzählen; berichten
think	I thought	I've thought	denken, glauben; meinen
throw	I threw	I've thrown	werfen
understand	I understood	I've understood	verstehen
wake	I woke	I've woken	wecken; aufwachen
wear	I wore	I've worn	tragen, anhaben
win	I won	I've won	gewinnen, siegen
write	I wrote	I've written	schreiben

→ CLASSROOM PHRASES

You and your teacher

Sorry I'm late.	Entschuldigung, dass ich zu spät komme.
Sorry, I've forgotten my book.	Entschuldigung, ich habe mein Buch vergessen.
I haven't done my homework.	Ich habe meine Hausaufgaben nicht gemacht.
Can I go to the toilet, please?	Darf ich bitte zur Toilette gehen?
Can I open/close the window, please?	Darf ich bitte das Fenster öffnen/schließen?
I didn't understand what you said.	Ich habe nicht verstanden, was Sie gesagt haben.

You need help

Could you help me, please?	Könnten Sie mir bitte helfen?
Can you write it on the board, please?	Können Sie es bitte an die Tafel schreiben?
Could you explain it to me, please?	Könnten Sie es mir bitte erkären?
Could you spell "…", please?	Könnten Sie bitte „…" buchstabieren?
Sorry, I can't find it. What page?	Entschuldigung, ich kann es nicht finden. Auf welcher Seite?
Which line/paragraph, please?	Welche Zeile/Welcher Absatz, bitte?
Could you say that again, please?	Könnten Sie das bitte wiederholen?
Sorry, could you repeat that, please?	Entschuldigung, könnten Sie das bitte wiederholen?
Could you speak louder, please?	Könnten Sie bitte lauter sprechen?
Could you speak more slowly, please?	Könnten Sie bitte langsamer sprechen?
Can we listen to it again, please?	Können wir es noch einmal hören?
What's "…" in English/in German?	Was heißt „…" auf Englisch/auf Deutsch?
Is "…" the right word for …?	Ist „…" das richtige Wort für …?
Can I say it in German?	Kann ich es auf Deutsch sagen?

Homework and exercises

Can we work together, please?	Können wir bitte zusammen arbeiten?
Can we make notes?	Können wir uns Notizen machen?
Can I read the next sentence?	Kann ich den nächsten Satz lesen?
Can we act the dialogue?	Können wir den Dialog spielen?
Can I borrow your ruler/pencil/..., please?	Kann ich mir bitte dein Lineal/deinen Bleistift/... ausleihen?
I can't do number 3.	Ich kann Nummer 3 nicht lösen.
I don't understand this exercise.	Ich verstehe diese Übung nicht.
I don't know./I'm not sure.	Ich weiß es nicht./Ich bin nicht sicher.
Pardon?	Wie bitte?
Is this right?	Ist das richtig?
Sorry, I haven't finished.	Entschuldigung, ich bin noch nicht fertig.
What's the homework?	Was haben wir (als Hausaufgabe) auf?
It's my turn.	Ich bin an der Reihe.
Can I take ...'s part, please?	Kann ich bitte ...'s Teil/Rolle übernehmen?
Where's there more information about this?	Wo finde ich mehr Informationen dazu?

Talks

I'm going to talk about ...	Ich werde über ... sprechen.
On the one hand ..., but on the other hand ...	Einerseits ..., aber andererseits ...
All in all I think ...	- Insgesamt denke ich ...
I think it's wrong/right to ...	Ich glaube, es ist falsch/richtig ...
Thank you for listening.	Vielen Dank für eure/Ihre Aufmerksamkeit.

→ GRAMMATIK

Wichtige Wörter zur Grammatik (Grammar)

Grammatical terms	Grammatische Begriffe	Beispiele
article	Artikel	the, a/an
adjective	Adjektiv	easy, small, big, quiet, good
adverb	Adverb	simply, carefully, easily
comparative	Komparativ	older, more difficult
superlative	Superlativ	oldest, most difficult
noun	Nomen (Substantiv)	car, town, school, sister, dog
singular	Singular (Einzahl)	a car, a school, a sister, a dog
plural	Plural (Mehrzahl)	some cars, a lot of schools
object	Objekt	The cat drank the milk.
passive	Passiv	am/is/are sold; was/were born
personal pronouns	Personalpronomen	I, you, he, she, it, we, they
preposition	Präposition	after, before, at, next to
reflexive pronouns	Reflexivpronomen	myself, yourself, herself, himself, itself, ourselves, yourselves, themselves
relative pronouns	Relativpronomen	who, which, that
sentence	Satz	I have a big car.
question	Frage	Do you have a car?
answer	Antwort	Yes, I have. I bought it in Spain.
word order	Wortstellung	
signal word	Signalwort	
subject	Subjekt	The cat drank the milk.
tense	Zeitform	
simple present	Präsens (einfache Gegenwart)	He goes home every day.
present progressive	Verlaufsform der Gegenwart	He's going home now.
simple past	Präteritum (einfache Vergangenheit)	He went home yesterday.
past progressive	Verlaufsform der Vergangenheit	He was watching TV.
present perfect	Perfekt (vollendete Gegenwart)	He has (just) gone home.
present perfect progressive	Verlaufsform des present perfect	She has been writing.
past perfect	Plusquamperfekt	had worked, had been

GRAMMATIK

Grammatical terms	Grammatische Begriffe	Beispiele
will-future	Futur	He'll go home after school.
going to-future	Futur mit going to	We're going to go home.
verb	Verb	have, eat, goes, went
infinitive	Infinitiv (Grundform)	have, eat, go
regular verb	regelmäßiges Verb	repair → repaired
irregular verb	unregelmäßiges Verb	make → made
modal verb	modales Hilfsverb	must, have to, should
present participle	Partizip Präsens	driving test, running water
past participle	Partizip Perfekt	played, cleaned, taken, eaten
gerund	Gerundium	Swimming is fun. I like dancing.
direct speech	direkte Rede	Tom says, "I'm late."
reported speech	indirekte Rede	Tom says he's late.
the passive	das Passiv	Emails are sent.
conditional sentences	Bedingungssätze	If I miss the bus, I'll be late for school.
relative clauses	Relativsätze	That's the teacher who we all like.

BILDQUELLEN

Inhalt **Akg-images**, Berlin (S. 26: Peter Magubane, Ian Berry, G.R.N / africanpictures); **Alamy**, Abington, UK (S. 24 o.li. + S. 29 M.: AfriPics.com; S. 27 *Funani*: Gerard Velthuizen, *Mafuane*: Greatstock Photographic Library; S. 30: Jack Picone; S. 34 u.li.: Gallo Images; S. 36 o.: Danita Delimont, u.: Peter Titmuss; S. 41 o.li.: Sylvia Cordaiy Photo Library Ltd; S. 44 u.: Mark Henley / Imagestate Media Partners Limited - Impact Photos; S. 46 li.: GoGo Images Corporation; S. 49 A: Gastromedia, u.: Photos 12; S. 60: Network Photographers; S. 62: Angela Hampton Picture Library; S. 65: Pictorial Press Ltd; S. 67 C: Sean Clarkson; S. 69: Patrick Eden; S. 92: Mike Kemp / RubberBall; S. 95: Bob Pardue – Lifestyle; S. 105 o.re.: Digital Vision; S. 110: Image Source Pink; S. 111 u.li.: David Lyons; S. 116 M.re.: Graham Burns / Photofusion Picture Library); **Associated Press**, Frankfurt/M (S. 77 r.: Xinhua, Li Xin; S. 79: Efrem Lukatsky); **Cartoonstock**, Bath, UK (S. 67: Grizelda; S. 85: Rob Baines); **Chemistryland.com**, USA (S. 84: Ken Costello); **Cinetext Bild- und Textarchiv**, Frankfurt/M (S. 47: rem; S. 64); **Corbis**, Düsseldorf (S. 8 Bild 5: Gideon Mendel; S. 14: Lucy Nicholson/Reuters; S. 16: Emmanuel Kwitema/Reuters; S. 17 u. B: Bob Krist; S. 27 *Gavin*: Image Source; S. 33 o. + 105 o.li.: David Turnley; S. 43 u.: Gideon Mendel for Action Aid; S. 54 o.: Parth Sanyal/Reuters; S. 117 u.: Stephane Cardinale); **dfd Deutscher Fotodienst**, Berlin (S. 68); **Dreamstime**, Brentwood, USA (S. 21 u.: Monkey Business Images; S. 38: Peterbetts; S. 49 C: Sunil Lal, E: Leaf; S. 55 o.: David Watts Jr.; S. 103 re.: Shootzpics); **Mary Evans Picture Library**, Blackheath, UK (S. 20 o. + M.: Illustrated London News Ltd); **fotolia**, New York, USA (S. 17 C: Warren Rosenberg; S. 41 re.: Cécile Cousin Bertheau); Courtesy **Gautrain Rapid Rail Link**, Johannesburg, Südafrika (S. 112); **Getty Images**, München (S. 15: Pierre Verdy/AFP; S. 34 o.: John Macdougall/AFP; S. 42 o.: Strdel/AFP, u.: Manan Vatsyayana/AFP; S. 50: Fox Photos/Hulton Archive; S. 54 u.: Indranil Mukherjee/AFP; S. 81: Greg Campbell/Stringer; S. 83: Alexander Nemenov; S. 105 M.: Kevin Winter; S. 117 o.: Evan Agostini); Courtesy **Gina Gallant**, Prince George, Kanada (S. 82); **David Haggerton**, Newcastle upon Tyne, UK (S. 113); **IPNSTOCK** (S. 58: Clay McLachlan/IPN); **iStockphoto** (S. 9: Duncan Walker; S. 22 u.: Jayesh Bhagat; S. 23 o.: Toa Payoh; S. 27 *Delani*: asiseeit; S. 35 u.: Steven Allan; S. 37 o.: Heiko Bennewitz; S. 39: Kelly Cline; S. 40 li.: x-drew, re.: Suzan Charnock; S. 49 D: Elena Elisseeva, F + H: Linda & Colin McKie; S. 52 *Kala*: Silvia Jansen, *Dinkar*: Robert Churchill, S. 52 *Uttam + Neela* + S. 53 *Lalit* + S. 55 M. + S. 56 o.: VikramRaghuvanshi; S. 53 *Ela* + S. 106 o.: TheFinalMiracle; S. 67 B: Crystal Chatham; S. 72 u.: Corepics; S. 74 o.: Erlend Kvalsvik, u.: Joseph Luoman; S. 75 o.: domin_domin, M.: Tobias Helbig; S. 78 o.: Andreas Sandberg; S. 86 u.: Jeremy Mayes; S. 97: Aldo Murillo; S. 103 M.li.: Georg Hanf; S. 111 u.re.: Daniel Cooper; S. 116 M.li.: Dmitriy Shironosov; S. 124 *doughnut*: Pierangelo Rendina; S. 134 *sofa*: Stephanie Phillips; S. 135 *hoodie*: Gary Alvis; S. 137 *footprint*: DNY59; S. 139 *bee*: Gabor Izso; S. 140 *harp*: Floortje); **letsgetalife.co.uk** (S. 108); **Lushpix/Unlisted Images Inc.** (S. 87); **Pacemaker Press International**, Belfast (S. 10 u.); **Photolibrary**, London (S. 8 Bild 3: Stockbyte; S. 10 o. + S. 17 D: The Irish Image Collection; S. 34 u.re.: John Snelling; S. 49 B: Joy Skipper; S. 55 u.: Mark Hannaford / John Warburton-Lee Photography; S. 77 li.: Mark Henley); **Picture - Alliance**, Frankfurt/M. (S. 24 o.re.: dpa; S. 26 o. + S. 28 o.: dpa – Bildarchiv; S. 31 + S. 87: dpa – Report); **Radio Diaries**, New York, USA (S. 33 M.: Melikhaya Mpumela, S. 33 u.: Sue Johnson); **Georg Raspe**, Düsseldorf (S. 122/126 u. + 130 M. + 138 *clouds*); **Hannah Raspe**, Düsseldorf (S. 138 *big wheel*); **Ingrid Raspe**, Düsseldorf (S. 125 *halfpenny*; S. 133 *motorway*; S. 138 *concrete*); **Shutterstock Inc**. New York (S. 6-7 Hintergrund: Jerome Scholler; S. 7 o.: Patricia Hofmeester, M.: PhotoSky 4t com, u.: Sam DCruz; S. 8-9 Hintergrund: Carly Rose Hennigan; S. 8 Bild 4: Eoghan McNally, Bild 6: RexRover, Bild 7: Mr.XuTaKuPu; S. 11 o.: Miroslav Tolimir, M.: Monkey Business Images, u.: Cindy Haggerty; S. 17 o. A: Lance Bellers; S. 17 u. A: Marek Slusarczyk, E: Eoghan McNally, F: Thierry Maffeis; S. 24-25 Hintergrund: Burcu Arat Sup; S. 24 Bild 3: Sportsphotographer.eu, Bild 4: ShutterVision; S. 25 *flag*: Dusan Po; S. 28 M.li.: photobar, M.re.: Ecoimages; S. 40-41 Hintergrund + S. 107 M.: Dana Ward; S. 43 o.: Studio 1One; S. 46 re.: Paul Prescott; S. 49 G: Monkey Business Images; S. 51: PhotoBarmaley; S. 60-61 Hintergrund: sabri deniz kizil; S. 67 A: Ilker Canikligil; S. 73: Lydia Kruger ; S. 74-75 M.: syba; S. 103 M.: Granata1111; S. 111 M.: Brian A Jackson; S. 114: Emin Kuliyev; S. 127 *penguins*: Jan Martin Will); Courtesy **Titanic Quarter Ltd.**, Belfast (S. 8 Bild 1); **Ullstein Bild**, Berlin (S. 17 o. B: AISA; S. 29 Bild 1: Reuters; S. 66: KPA)

u.= unten, o. = oben, re. = rechts, li. = links, M. = Mitte

Cover Lonely Planet Images, London, UK

TEXTQUELLEN

S. 25 Tortendiagramm: Statistics South Africa;
S. 25 Balkendiagramme: The Good News (www.sagoodnews.co.za)
S. 56-59: Excerpt from „Nightmare" by Meenal Dave. From: *Katha: Short Stories by Indian Women* by Urvashi Butalia (editor). London: Telegram Books, 2008
S. 61 Balkendiagramme: UNICEF, Child poverty in perspective: An overview of child well-being in rich countries, *Innocenti Report Card 7*, 2007, UNICEF Innocenti Research Centre, Florence.
S. 64-65: Excerpt from *About a boy* by Nick Hornby. London: Penguin Books Ltd, 2000

LIEDQUELLEN

S. 81: "Big Yellow Taxi", K. + T.: Joni Mitchell, Copyright: Crazy Crow Music, Sony/ATV Music Publishing (Germany) GmbH, Berlin